Infrastructure as Code
Managing Servers in the Cloud

Kief Morris

Beijing · Boston · Farnham · Sebastopol · Tokyo

Infrastructure as Code

by Kief Morris

Printed in the United States of America.

Published by O'Reilly Media, Inc., 1005 Gravenstein Highway North, Sebastopol, CA 95472.

O'Reilly books may be purchased for educational, business, or sales promotional use. Online editions are also available for most titles (*http://safaribooksonline.com*). For more information, contact our corporate/institutional sales department: 800-998-9938 or *corporate@oreilly.com*.

Editor: Brian Anderson
Production Editor: Kristen Brown
Copyeditor: Amanda Kersey
Proofreader: Jasmine Kwityn

Indexer: Judy McConville
Interior Designer: David Futato
Cover Designer: Karen Montgomery
Illustrator: Rong Tang and Rebecca Demarest

June 2016:   First Edition

Revision History for the First Edition
2016-06-07:   First Release

See *http://oreilly.com/catalog/errata.csp?isbn=9781491924358* for release details.

978-1-491-92435-8

[LSI]

Table of Contents

Part I. Foundations

Part II. Patterns

Preface

Infrastructure and software development teams are increasingly building and managing infrastructure using automated tools that have been described as "infrastructure as code." These tools expect users to define their servers, networking, and other elements of an infrastructure in files modeled after software source code. The tools then compile and interpret these files to decide what action to take.

This class of tool has grown naturally with the DevOps movement.[1] The DevOps movement is mainly about culture and collaboration between software developers and software operations people. Tooling that manages infrastructure based on a software development paradigm has helped bring these communities together.

Managing infrastructure as code is very different from classic infrastructure management. I've met many teams who have struggled to work out how to make this shift. But ideas, patterns, and practices for using these tools effectively have been scattered across conference talks, blog posts, and articles. I've been waiting for someone to write a book to pull these ideas together into a single place. I haven't seen any sign of this, so finally took matters into my own hands. You're now reading the results of this effort!

How I Learned to Stop Worrying and to Love the Cloud

I set up my first server, a dialup BBS,[2] in 1992. This led to Unix system administration and then to building and running hosted software systems (before we called it SaaS, aka "Software as a Service") for various companies, from startups to enterprises.

---

[1] Andrew Clay Shafer and Patrick Debois triggered the DevOps movement with a talk at the Agile 2008 conference (*http://www.jedi.be/presentations/agile-infrastructure-agile-2008.pdf*). The movement grew, mainly driven by the series of DevOpsDays (*http://www.devopsdays.org/*) conferences organized by Debois.

[2] A BBS is a bulletin board system (*https://en.wikipedia.org/wiki/Bulletin_board_system*).

I've been on a journey to infrastructure as code the entire time, before I'd ever heard the term.

Things came to a head with virtualization. The story of my stumbling adoption of virtualization and the cloud may be familiar, and it illustrates the role that infrastructure as code has to play in modern IT operations.

My First Virtual Server Farm

I was thrilled when my team got the budget to buy a pair of beefy HP rack servers and licenses for VMware ESX Server back in 2007.

We had in our office's server racks around 20 1U and 2U servers named after fruits (Linux servers) and berries (Windows database servers) running test environments for our development teams. Stretching these servers to test various releases, branches, and high-priority, proof-of-concept applications was a way of life. Network services like DNS, file servers, and email were crammed onto servers running multiple application instances, web servers, and database servers.

So we were sure these new virtual servers would change our lives. We could cleanly split each of these services onto its own virtual machine (VM), and the ESX hypervisor software would help us to squeeze the most out of the multicore server machines and gobs of RAM we'd allocated. We could easily duplicate servers to create new environments and archive those servers that weren't needed onto disk, confident they could be restored in the future if needed.

Those servers did change our lives. But although many of our old problems went away, we discovered new ones, and we had to learn completely different ways of thinking about our infrastructure.

Virtualization made creating and managing servers much easier. The flip side of this was that we ended up creating far more servers than we could have imagined. The product and marketing people were delighted that we could give them a new environment to demo things in well under a day, rather than need them to find money in the budget and then wait a few weeks for us to order and set up hardware servers.

The Sorcerer's Apprentice

A year later, we were running well over 100 VMs and counting. We were well underway with virtualizing our production servers and experimenting with Amazon's new cloud hosting service. The benefits virtualization had brought to the business people meant we had money for more ESX servers and for shiny SAN devices to feed the surprising appetite our infrastructure had for storage.

But we found ourselves a bit like Mickey Mouse in "The Sorcerer's Apprentice" from *Fantasia*. We spawned virtual servers, then more, then even more. They overwhelmed us. When something broke, we tracked down the VM and fixed whatever was wrong with it, but we couldn't keep track of what changes we'd made where.

> Well, a perfect hit!
> See how he is split!
> Now there's hope for me,
> and I can breathe free!
>
> Woe is me! Both pieces
> come to life anew,
> now, to do my bidding
> I have servants two!
> Help me, O great powers!
> Please, I'm begging you!
>
> > —Excerpted from Brigitte Dubiel's translation of "Der Zauberlehrling" ("The Sorcerer's Apprentice") by Johann Wolfgang von Goethe

As new updates to operating systems, web servers, app servers, database servers, JVMs, and various other software packages came out, we would struggle to install them across all of our systems. We would apply them successfully to some servers, but on others the upgrades broke things, and we didn't have time to stomp out every incompatibility. Over time, we ended up with many combinations of versions of things strewn across hundreds of servers.

We had been using configuration automation software even before we virtualized, which should have helped with these issues. I had used CFEngine in previous companies, and when I started this team, I tried a new tool called Puppet. Later, when spiking out ideas for an AWS infrastructure, my colleague Andrew introduced Chef. All of these tools were useful, but particularly in the early days, they didn't get us out of the quagmire of wildly different servers.

The problem was that, although Puppet (and Chef and the others) should have been set up and left running unattended across all of our servers, we couldn't trust it. Our servers were just too different. We would write manifests to configure and manage a particular application server. But when we ran it against another, theoretically similar app server, we found that different versions of Java, application software, and OS components would cause the Puppet run to fail, or worse, break the application server.

So we ended up using Puppet ad hoc. We could safely run it against new VMs, although we might need to make some tweaks after it ran. We would write manifests for a specific task and then run them against servers one at a time, carefully checking the result and making fixes as needed.

So configuration automation was a useful aid, somewhat better than shell scripts, but the way we used it didn't save us from our sprawl of inconsistent servers.

Cloud from Scratch

Things changed when we began moving things onto the cloud. The technology itself wasn't what improved things; we could have done the same thing with our own VMware servers. But because we were starting fresh, we adopted new ways of managing servers based on what we had learned with our virtualized farm and on what we were reading and hearing from IT Ops teams at companies like Flickr, Etsy, and Netflix. We baked these new ideas into the way we managed services as we migrated them onto the cloud.

The key idea of our new approach was that every server could be automatically rebuilt from scratch, and our configuration tooling would run continuously, not ad hoc. Every server added into our new infrastructure would fall under this approach. If automation broke on some edge case, we would either change the automation to handle it, or else fix the design of the service so it was no longer an edge case.

The new regime wasn't painless. We had to learn new habits, and we had to find ways of coping with the challenges of a highly automated infrastructure. As the members of the team moved on to other organizations and got involved with communities such as DevOpsDays, we learned and grew. Over time, we reached the point where we were habitually working with automated infrastructures with hundreds of servers, with much less effort and headache than we had been in our "Sorcerer's Apprentice" days.

Joining ThoughtWorks was an eye-opener for me. The development teams I worked with were passionate about using XP engineering practices like test-driven development (*http://martinfowler.com/bliki/TestDrivenDevelopment.html*) (TDD), continuous integration (*http://www.martinfowler.com/articles/continuousIntegration.html*) (CI) and continuous delivery (*http://martinfowler.com/books/continuousDelivery.html*) (CD). Because I had already learned to manage infrastructure scripts and configuration files in source control systems, it was natural to apply these rigorous development and testing approaches to them.

Working with ThoughtWorks has also brought me into contact with many IT operations teams, most of whom are using virtualization, cloud, and automation tools to handle a variety of challenges. Working with them to share and learn new ideas and techniques has been a fantastic experience.

Why I'm Writing This Book

I've run across many teams who are in the same place I was a few years ago: people who are using cloud, virtualization, and automation tools but haven't got it all running as smoothly as they know they could.

Much of the challenge is time. Day-to-day life for system administrators is coping with a never-ending flow of critical work. Fighting fires, fixing problems, and setting up new business-critical projects doesn't leave much time to work on the fundamental improvements that will make the routine work easier.

My hope is that this book provides a practical vision for how to manage IT infrastructure, with techniques and patterns that teams can try and use. I will avoid the details of configuring and using specific tools so that the content will be useful for working with different tools, including ones that may not exist yet. Meanwhile, I will use examples from existing tools to illustrate points I make.

The infrastructure-as-code approach is essential for managing cloud infrastructure of any real scale or complexity, but it's not exclusive to organizations using public cloud providers. The techniques and practices in this book have proven effective in virtualized environments and even for bare-metal servers that aren't virtualized.

Infrastructure as Code is one of the cornerstones of DevOps. It is the "A" in "CAMS" (*http://itrevolution.com/devops-culture-part-1/*): culture, automation, measurement, and sharing.

Who This Book Is For

This book is for people who work with IT infrastructure, particularly at the level of managing servers and collections of servers. You may be a system administrator, infrastructure engineer, team lead, architect, or a manager with technical interest. You might also be a software developer who wants to build and use infrastructure.

I'm assuming you have some exposure to virtualization or IaaS (Infrastructure as a Service) cloud, so you know how to create a server, and the concepts of configuring operating systems. You've probably at least played with configuration automation software like Ansible, Chef, or Puppet.

While this book may introduce some readers to infrastructure as code, I hope it will also be interesting to people who work this way already and a vehicle through which to share ideas and start conversations about how to do it even better.

What Tools Are Covered

This book doesn't offer instructions in using specific scripting languages or tools. There are code examples from specific tools, but these are intended to illustrate concepts and approaches, rather than to provide instruction. This book should be helpful to you regardless of whether you use Chef on OpenStack, Puppet on AWS, Ansible on bare metal, or a completely different stack.

The specific tools that I do mention are ones which I'm aware of, and which seem to have a certain amount of traction in the field. But this is a constantly changing landscape, and there are plenty of other relevant tools.

The tools I use in examples tend to be ones with which I am familiar enough to write examples that demonstrate the point I'm trying to make. For example, I use Terraform for examples of infrastructure definitions because it has a nice, clean syntax, and I've used it on multiple projects. Many of my examples use Amazon's AWS cloud platform because it is likely to be the most familiar to readers.

How to Read This Book

Read Chapter 1, or at least skim it, to understand the terms this book uses and the principles this book advocates. You can then use this to decide which parts of the book to focus on.

If you're new to this kind of automation, cloud, and infrastructure orchestration tooling, then you'll want to focus on Part I, and then move on to Part II. Get comfortable with those topics before proceeding to Part III.

If you've been using the types of automation tools described here, but don't feel like you're using them the way they're intended after reading Chapter 1, then you may want to skip or skim the rest of Part I. Focus on Part II, which describes ways of using dynamic and automated infrastructure that align with the principles outlined in Chapter 1.

If you're comfortable with the dynamic infrastructure and automation approaches described in Chapter 1, then you may want to skim Parts I and II and focus on Part III, which gets more deeply into the infrastructure management regime: architectural approaches as well as team workflow.

Conventions Used in This Book

The following typographical conventions are used in this book:

Italic
> Indicates new terms, URLs, email addresses, filenames, and file extensions.

`Constant width`
> Used for program listings, as well as within paragraphs to refer to program elements such as variable or function names, databases, data types, environment variables, statements, and keywords.

`Constant width bold`
> Shows commands or other text that should be typed literally by the user.

Constant width italic

> Shows text that should be replaced with user-supplied values or by values determined by context.

This element signifies a tip or suggestion.

This element signifies a general note.

This element indicates a warning or caution.

Safari® Books Online

 *Safari Books Online* is an on-demand digital library that delivers expert content in both book and video form from the world's leading authors in technology and business.

Technology professionals, software developers, web designers, and business and creative professionals use Safari Books Online as their primary resource for research, problem solving, learning, and certification training.

Safari Books Online offers a range of plans and pricing for enterprise, government, education, and individuals.

Members have access to thousands of books, training videos, and prepublication manuscripts in one fully searchable database from publishers like O'Reilly Media, Prentice Hall Professional, Addison-Wesley Professional, Microsoft Press, Sams, Que, Peachpit Press, Focal Press, Cisco Press, John Wiley & Sons, Syngress, Morgan Kaufmann, IBM Redbooks, Packt, Adobe Press, FT Press, Apress, Manning, New Riders, McGraw-Hill, Jones & Bartlett, Course Technology, and hundreds more. For more information about Safari Books Online, please visit us online.

How to Contact Us

Please address comments and questions concerning this book to the publisher:

O'Reilly Media, Inc.
1005 Gravenstein Highway North
Sebastopol, CA 95472
800-998-9938 (in the United States or Canada)
707-829-0515 (international or local)
707-829-0104 (fax)

We have a web page for this book, where we list errata, examples, and any additional information. You can access this page at *http://bit.ly/infrastructureAsCode_1e*.

To comment or ask technical questions about this book, send email to *bookquestions@oreilly.com*.

For more information about our books, courses, conferences, and news, see our website at *http://www.oreilly.com*.

Find us on Facebook: *http://facebook.com/oreilly*

Follow us on Twitter: *http://twitter.com/oreillymedia*

Watch us on YouTube: *http://www.youtube.com/oreillymedia*

Acknowledgments

When I started working on this book, I assumed the result would be a product that was entirely my own. But in the end, it's just the opposite: this book is the product of the ideas, thoughts, opinions, and experiences of far more people than I could have imagined. I have probably mangled, oversimplified, and misrepresented this input. But this book would not exist as it is without these contributions.

The people I worked with on the University of Tennessee's computer science lab staff taught me my Unix chops and inducted me into the culture. Chad Mynhier was particularly responsible for hooking me into the Unix world. He explained why I could no longer cd into my own home area after I had experimented with the chmod command.

Working with a series of companies, including Syzygy, Vizyon, Cellectivity, and the Map of Medicine, gave me the arena to develop my understanding and to learn how to apply infrastructure automation to real-world business and user problems. I owe much to the many good people of those organizations. I'll specifically call out Jonathan Waywell and Ketan Patel for their unending support and encouragement,

Andrew Fulcher for quickly learning what I had to teach and then teaching me even more, and Nat Billington for his inspiration.

This book would truly never have happened without my current home, Thought-Works. I've learned much about the ideas in this book and how to think about and explain them to other people, thanks to more than five years of exposure to a dizzying number of organizations of various sizes, sectors, and technologies. The endless curiosity of my colleagues, past and present, and their heartfelt drive to improve our industry and the experiences of people in it, continually challenges me.

Generous support and encouragement from ThoughtWorks as an organization has been vital for this book, especially as my energy flagged with the finish line coming into view. Chris Murphy, Dave Elliman, Maneesh Subherwal, and Suzi Edwards-Alexander are a few among many who have made this more than a personal project for me.

An incomplete list of past and present ThoughtWorks colleagues who have gone out of their way to contribute suggestions, feedback, and other support include: Abigail Bangser, Ashok Subramanian, Barry O'Reilly, Ben Butler-Cole, Chris Bird (DevOops!), Chris Ford, David Farley, Gurpreet Luthra, Inny So, Jason Yip, Jim Gumbley, Kesha Stickland, Marco Abis, Nassos Antoniou, Paul Hammant, Peter Gillard-Moss, Peter Staples, Philip Potter, Rafael Gomes, Sam Newman, Simon Brunning, Tom Duckering, Venu Murthy, and Vijay Raghavan Aravamudhan.

Martin Fowler has given me tremendous encouragement and practical support in writing this book. He gave me far more time than I could have asked, thoroughly reviewing the manuscript several times. Martin gave me detailed, useful feedback and advice based on his considerable experience of organizing and conveying technical concepts. He has been a true champion of this book.

My colleague Rong Tang created the images for this book. She was extremely patient with my muddled explanations of what I wanted. Any failings of clarity or consistency is down to me, but the great look is a credit to her.

The folks behind the long-dormant Infrastructures.org (*http://www.infrastructures.org/index.shtml*) exposed me to the ideas of Infrastructure as Code before the term existed.[3]

I owe a great debt to the people of the DevOpsDays community, who are collectively responsible for bringing the ideas of DevOps and Infrastructure as Code to prominence. Regardless of who actually coined the term "Infrastructure as Code," people like Adam Jacob, Andrew Clay-Shafer, John Allspaw, John Willis, Luke Kaines, Mark

---

3 Sadly, as of early 2016, Infrastructures.org hasn't been updated since 2007.

Burgess, and of course, Patrick Debois ("The Godfather of DevOps") have given me inspiration and many great ideas.

A number of other people have given me feedback and advice on earlier drafts of this book, including Axel Fontaine, Jon Cowie, Jose Maria San Jose Juarez, Marcos Hermida, and Matt Jones. I also want to thank Kent Spillner, although I don't recall why. Ovine and dairy. Putney Bridge.

Last, but the furthest from least, everlasting love to Ozlem and Erel, who endured my obsession with this book.

## PART I

Foundations

## CHAPTER 1

Challenges and Principles

The new generation of infrastructure management technologies promises to transform the way we manage IT infrastructure. But many organizations today aren't seeing any dramatic differences, and some are finding that these tools only make life messier. As we'll see, infrastructure as code is an approach that provides principles, practices, and patterns for using these technologies effectively.

Why Infrastructure as Code?

Virtualization, cloud, containers, server automation, and software-defined networking should simplify IT operations work. It should take less time and effort to provision, configure, update, and maintain services. Problems should be quickly detected and resolved, and systems should all be consistently configured and up to date. IT staff should spend less time on routine drudgery, having time to rapidly make changes and improvements to help their organizations meet the ever-changing needs of the modern world.

But even with the latest and best new tools and platforms, IT operations teams still find that they can't keep up with their daily workload. They don't have the time to fix longstanding problems with their systems, much less revamp them to make the best use of new tools. In fact, cloud and automation often makes things worse. The ease of provisioning new infrastructure leads to an ever-growing portfolio of systems, and it takes an ever-increasing amount of time just to keep everything from collapsing.

Adopting cloud and automation tools immediately lowers barriers for making changes to infrastructure. But managing changes in a way that improves consistency and reliability doesn't come out of the box with the software. It takes people to think through how they will use the tools and put in place the systems, processes, and habits to use them effectively.

Some IT organizations respond to this challenge by applying the same types of processes, structures, and governance that they used to manage infrastructure and software before cloud and automation became commonplace. But the principles that applied in a time when it took days or weeks to provision a new server struggle to cope now that it takes minutes or seconds.

Legacy change management processes are commonly ignored, bypassed, or overruled by people who need to get things done.[1] Organizations that are more successful in enforcing these processes are increasingly seeing themselves outrun by more technically nimble competitors.

Legacy change management approaches struggle to cope with the pace of change offered by cloud and automation. But there is still a need to cope with the ever-growing, continuously changing landscape of systems created by cloud and automation tools. This is where infrastructure as code[2] comes in.

The Iron Age and the Cloud Age

In the "iron age" of IT, systems were directly bound to physical hardware. Provisioning and maintaining infrastructure was manual work, forcing humans to spend their time pointing, clicking, and typing to keep the gears turning. Because changes involved so much work, change management processes emphasized careful up-front consideration, design, and review work. This made sense because getting it wrong was expensive.

In the "cloud age" of IT, systems have been decoupled from the physical hardware. Routine provisioning and maintenance can be delegated to software systems, freeing the humans from drudgery. Changes can be made in minutes, if not seconds. Change management can exploit this speed, providing better reliability along with faster time to market.

---

1 "Shadow IT" is when people bypass formal IT governance to bring in their own devices, buy and install unapproved software, or adopt cloud-hosted services. This is typically a sign that internal IT is not able to keep up with the needs of the organization it serves.

2 The phrase "infrastructure as code" doesn't have a clear origin or author. While writing this book, I followed a chain of people who have influenced thinking around the concept, each of whom said it wasn't them, but offered suggestions. This chain had a number of loops. The earliest reference I could find was from the Velocity conference in 2009, in a talk by Andrew Clay-Shafer and Adam Jacob. John Willis may be the first to document the phrase, in an article about the conference (*http://itknowledgeexchange.techtarget.com/cloud-computing/infrastructure-as-code/*). Luke Kaines has admitted that he may have been involved, the closest anyone has come to accepting credit.

What Is Infrastructure as Code?

Infrastructure as code is an approach to infrastructure automation based on practices from software development. It emphasizes consistent, repeatable routines for provisioning and changing systems and their configuration. Changes are made to definitions and then rolled out to systems through unattended processes that include thorough validation.

The premise is that modern tooling can treat infrastructure as if it were software and data. This allows people to apply software development tools such as version control systems (VCS), automated testing libraries, and deployment orchestration to manage infrastructure. It also opens the door to exploit development practices such as test-driven development (TDD), continuous integration (CI), and continuous delivery (CD).

Infrastructure as code has been proven in the most demanding environments. For companies like Amazon, Netflix, Google, Facebook, and Etsy, IT systems are not just business critical; they *are* the business. There is no tolerance for downtime. Amazon's systems handle hundreds of millions of dollars in transactions every day. So it's no surprise that organizations like these are pioneering new practices for large scale, highly reliable IT infrastructure.

This book aims to explain how to take advantage of the cloud-era, infrastructure-as-code approaches to IT infrastructure management. This chapter explores the pitfalls that organizations often fall into when adopting the new generation of infrastructure technology. It describes the core principles and key practices of infrastructure as code that are used to avoid these pitfalls.

Goals of Infrastructure as Code

The types of outcomes that many teams and organizations look to achieve through infrastructure as code include:

- IT infrastructure supports and enables change, rather than being an obstacle or a constraint.
- Changes to the system are routine, without drama or stress for users or IT staff.
- IT staff spends their time on valuable things that engage their abilities, not on routine, repetitive tasks.
- Users are able to define, provision, and manage the resources they need, without needing IT staff to do it for them.
- Teams are able to easily and quickly recover from failures, rather than assuming failure can be completely prevented.

- Improvements are made continuously, rather than done through expensive and risky "big bang" projects.
- Solutions to problems are proven through implementing, testing, and measuring them, rather than by discussing them in meetings and documents.

Infrastructure as Code Is Not Just for the Cloud

Infrastructure as code has come into its own with cloud, because it's difficult to manage servers in the cloud well without it. But the principles and practices of infrastructure as code can be applied to infrastructure whether it runs on cloud, virtualized systems, or even directly on physical hardware.

I use the phrase "dynamic infrastructure" to refer to the ability to create and destroy servers programmatically; Chapter 2 is dedicated to this topic. Cloud does this naturally, and virtualization platforms can be configured to do the same. But even hardware can be automatically provisioned so that it can be used in a fully dynamic fashion. This is sometimes referred to as "bare-metal cloud."

It is possible to use many of the concepts of infrastructure as code with static infrastructure. Servers that have been manually provisioned can be configured and updated using server configuration tools. However, the ability to effortlessly destroy and rebuild servers is essential for many of the more advanced practices described in this book.

Challenges with Dynamic Infrastructure

This section looks at some of the problems teams often see when they adopt dynamic infrastructure and automated configuration tools. These are the problems that infrastructure as code addresses, so understanding them lays the groundwork for the principles and concepts that follow.

Server Sprawl

Cloud and virtualization can make it trivial to provision new servers from a pool of resources. This can lead to the number of servers growing faster than the ability of the team to manage them as well as they would like.

When this happens, teams struggle to keep servers patched and up to date, leaving systems vulnerable to known exploits. When problems are discovered, fixes may not be rolled out to all of the systems that could be affected by them. Differences in versions and configurations across servers mean that software and scripts that work on some machines don't work on others.

This leads to inconsistency across the servers, called *configuration drift*.

Configuration Drift

Even when servers are initially created and configured consistently, differences can creep in over time:

- Someone makes a fix to one of the Oracle servers to fix a specific user's problem, and now it's different from the other Oracle servers.

- A new version of JIRA needs a newer version of Java, but there's not enough time to test all of the other Java-based applications so that everything can be upgraded.

- Three different people install IIS on three different web servers over the course of a few months, and each person configures it differently.

- One JBoss server gets more traffic than the others and starts struggling, so someone tunes it, and now its configuration is different from the other JBoss servers.

Being different isn't bad. The heavily loaded JBoss server probably should be tuned differently from ones with lower levels of traffic. But variations should be captured and managed in a way that makes it easy to reproduce and to rebuild servers and services.

Unmanaged variation between servers leads to snowflake servers and automation fear.

Snowflake Servers

A snowflake server is different from any other server on your network. It's special in ways that can't be replicated.

Years ago I ran servers for a company that built web applications for clients, most of which were monstrous collections of Perl CGI. (Don't judge us, this was the dot-com era, and everyone was doing it.) We started out using Perl 5.6, but at some point the best libraries moved to Perl 5.8 and couldn't be used on 5.6. Eventually almost all of our newer applications were built with 5.8 as well, but there was one particularly important client application that simply wouldn't run on 5.8.

It was actually worse than this. The application worked fine when we upgraded our shared staging server to 5.8, but crashed when we upgraded the staging environment. Don't ask why we upgraded production to 5.8 without discovering the problem with staging, but that's how we ended up. We had one special server that could run the application with Perl 5.8, but no other server would.

We ran this way for a shamefully long time, keeping Perl 5.6 on the staging server and crossing our fingers whenever we deployed to production. We were terrified to touch anything on the production server, afraid to disturb whatever magic made it the only server that could run the client's application.

This situation led us to discover Infrastructures.Org (*http://www.infrastructures.org/index.shtml*), a site that introduced me to ideas that were a precursor to infrastructure as code. We made sure that all of our servers were built in a repeatable way, installing the operating system with the Fully Automated Installation (FAI) tool (*http://bit.ly/1spUXvl*), configuring the server with CFEngine, and checking everything into our CVS version control system (*http://www.nongnu.org/cvs/*).

As embarrassing as this story is, most IT operations teams have similar stories of special servers that couldn't be touched, much less reproduced. It's not always a mysterious fragility; sometimes there is an important software package that runs on an entirely different OS than everything else in the infrastructure. I recall an accounting package that needed to run on AIX, and a PBX system running on a Windows NT 3.51 server specially installed by a long-forgotten contractor.

Once again, being different isn't bad. The problem is when the team that owns the server doesn't understand how and why it's different, and wouldn't be able to rebuild it. An operations team should be able to confidently and quickly rebuild any server in their infrastructure. If any server doesn't meet this requirement, constructing a new, reproducible process that can build a server to take its place should be a leading priority for the team.

Fragile Infrastructure

A fragile infrastructure is easily disrupted and not easily fixed. This is the snowflake server problem expanded to an entire portfolio of systems.

The solution is to migrate everything in the infrastructure to a reliable, reproducible infrastructure, one step at a time. The *Visible Ops Handbook*[3] outlines an approach for bringing stability and predictability to a difficult infrastructure.

Don't touch that server. Don't point at it. Don't even look at it.

There is the possibly apocryphal story of the data center with a server that nobody had the login details for, and nobody was certain what the server did. Someone took the bull by the horns and unplugged the server from the network. The network failed completely, the cable was plugged back in, and nobody ever touched the server again.

---

3 First published in 2005, the *Visible Ops Handbook* (*http://www.amazon.com/Visible-Ops-Handbook-Implementing-Practical-ebook/dp/B002BWQBEE*) by Gene Kim, George Spafford, and Kevin Behr (IT Process Institute, Inc.) was written before DevOps, virtualization, and automated configuration became mainstream, but it's easy to see how infrastructure as code can be used within the framework described by the authors.

Automation Fear

At an Open Space session (*http://en.wikipedia.org/wiki/Open_Space_Technology*) on configuration automation at a DevOpsDays conference (*http://www.devopsdays.org/*), I asked the group how many of them were using automation tools like Puppet or Chef. The majority of hands went up. I asked how many were running these tools unattended, on an automatic schedule. Most of the hands went down.

Many people have the same problem I had in my early days of using automation tools. I used automation selectively—for example, to help build new servers, or to make a specific configuration change. I tweaked the configuration each time I ran it, to suit the particular task I was doing.

I was afraid to turn my back on my automation tools, because I lacked confidence in what they would do.

I lacked confidence in my automation because my servers were not consistent.

My servers were not consistent because I wasn't running automation frequently and consistently.

This is the automation fear spiral, as shown in Figure 1-1, and infrastructure teams need to break this spiral to use automation successfully. The most effective way to break the spiral is to face your fears. Pick a set of servers, tweak the configuration definitions so that you know they work, and schedule them to run unattended, at least once an hour. Then pick another set of servers and repeat the process, and so on until all of your servers are continuously updated.

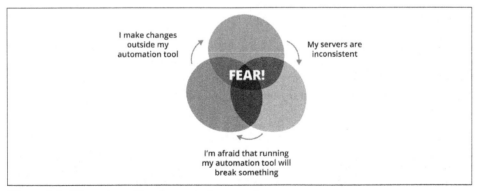

Figure 1-1. The automation fear spiral

Good monitoring and effective automated testing regimes as described in Part III of this book will help build confidence that configuration can be reliably applied and problems caught quickly.

Erosion

In an ideal world, you would never need to touch an automated infrastructure once you've built it, other than to support something new or fix things that break. Sadly, the forces of entropy mean that even without a new requirement, infrastructure decays over time. The folks at Heroku call this *erosion* (*https://devcenter.heroku.com/articles/erosion-resistance*). Erosion is the idea that problems will creep into a running system over time.

The Heroku folks give these examples of forces that can erode a system over time:

- Operating system upgrades, kernel patches, and infrastructure software (e.g., Apache, MySQL, SSH, OpenSSL) updates to fix security vulnerabilities
- The server's disk filling up with logfiles
- One or more of the application's processes crashing or getting stuck, requiring someone to log in and restart them
- Failure of the underlying hardware causing one or more entire servers to go down, taking the application with it

Principles of Infrastructure as Code

This section describes principles that can help teams overcome the challenges described earlier in this chapter.

Systems Can Be Easily Reproduced

It should be possible to effortlessly and reliably rebuild any element of an infrastructure. Effortlessly means that there is no need to make any significant decisions about how to rebuild the thing. Decisions about which software and versions to install on a server, how to choose a hostname, and so on should be captured in the scripts and tooling that provision it.

The ability to effortlessly build and rebuild any part of the infrastructure is powerful. It removes much of the risk, and fear, when making changes. Failures can be handled quickly and with confidence. New services and environments can be provisioned with little effort.

Approaches for reproducibly provisioning servers and other infrastructure elements are discussed in Part II of this book.

Systems Are Disposable

One of the benefits of dynamic infrastructure is that resources can be easily created, destroyed, replaced, resized, and moved. In order to take advantage of this, systems should be designed to assume that the infrastructure will always be changing. Software should continue running even when servers disappear, appear, and when they are resized.

The ability to handle changes gracefully makes it easier to make improvements and fixes to running infrastructure. It also makes services more tolerant to failure. This becomes especially important when sharing large-scale cloud infrastructure, where the reliability of the underlying hardware can't be guaranteed.

Cattle, Not Pets

A popular expression is to "treat your servers like cattle, not pets."[4] I miss the days of having themes for server names and carefully selecting names for each new server I provisioned. But I don't miss having to manually tweak and massage every server in our estate.

A fundamental difference between the iron age and cloud age is the move from unreliable software, which depends on the hardware to be very reliable, to software that runs reliably on unreliable hardware.[5] See Chapter 14 for more on how embracing disposable infrastructure can be used to improve service continuity.

The Case of the Disappearing File Server

The idea that servers aren't permanent things can take time to sink in. On one team, we set up an automated infrastructure using VMware and Chef, and got into the habit of casually deleting and replacing VMs. A developer, needing a web server to host files for teammates to download, installed a web server onto a server in the development environment and put the files there. He was surprised when his web server and its files disappeared a few days later.

---

4 CloudConnect CTO Randy Bias attributed this expression to former Microsoft employee Bill Baker, from his presentation "Architectures for Open and Scalable Clouds" (*http://www.slideshare.net/randybias/architectures-for-open-and-scalable-clouds*). I first heard it in Gavin McCance's presentation "CERN Data Centre Evolution" (*http://www.slideshare.net/gmccance/cern-data-centre-evolution*). Both of these presentations are excellent.

5 Sam Johnson described this view of the reliability of hardware and software in his article, "Simplifying Cloud: Reliability" (*http://samj.net/2012/03/08/simplifying-cloud-reliability/*).

After a bit of confusion, the developer added the configuration for his file repository to the Chef configuration, taking advantage of tooling we had to persist data to a SAN. The team ended up with a highly reliable, automatically configured file sharing service.

To borrow a cliche, the disappearing server is a feature, not a bug. The old world where people installed ad hoc tools and tweaks in random places leads straight to the old world of snowflakes and untouchable fragile infrastructure. Although it was uncomfortable at first, the developer learned how to use infrastructure as code to build services—a file repository in this case—that are reproducible and reliable.

Systems Are Consistent

Given two infrastructure elements providing a similar service—for example, two application servers in a cluster—the servers should be nearly identical. Their system software and configuration should be the same, except for those bits of configuration that differentiate them, like their IP addresses.

Letting inconsistencies slip into an infrastructure keeps you from being able to trust your automation. If one file server has an 80 GB partition, while another has 100 GB, and a third has 200 GB, then you can't rely on an action to work the same on all of them. This encourages doing special things for servers that don't quite match, which leads to unreliable automation.

Teams that implement the reproducibility principle can easily build multiple identical infrastructure elements. If one of these elements needs to be changed (e.g., one of the file servers needs a larger disk partition), there are two ways that keep consistency. One is to change the definition so that all file servers are built with a large enough partition to meet the need. The other is to add a new class, or role, so that there is now an "xl-file-server" with a larger disk than the standard file server. Either type of server can be built repeatedly and consistently.

Being able to build and rebuild consistent infrastructure helps with configuration drift. But clearly, changes that happen after servers are created need to be dealt with. Ensuring consistency for existing infrastructure is the topic of Chapter 8.

Processes Are Repeatable

Building on the reproducibility principle, any action you carry out on your infrastructure should be repeatable. This is an obvious benefit of using scripts and configuration management tools rather than making changes manually, but it can be hard to stick to doing things this way, especially for experienced system administrators.

For example, if I'm faced with what seems like a one-off task like partitioning a hard drive, I find it easier to just log in and do it, rather than to write and test a script. I can look at the system disk, consider what the server I'm working on needs, and use my experience and knowledge to decide how big to make each partition, what filesystem to use, and so on.

The problem is that later on, someone else on my team might partition a disk on another machine and make slightly different decisions. Maybe I made an 80 GB /var partition using ext3 on one file server, but Priya made /var 100 GB on another file server in the cluster, and used xfs. We're failing the consistency principle, which will eventually undermine the ability to automate things.

Effective infrastructure teams have a strong scripting culture. If a task can be scripted, script it. If a task is hard to script, drill down and see if there's a technique or tool that can help, or whether the problem the task is addressing can be handled in a different way.

Design Is Always Changing

With iron-age IT, making a change to an existing system is difficult and expensive. So limiting the need to make changes to the system once it's built makes sense. This leads to the need for comprehensive initial designs that take various possible requirements and situations into account.

Because it's impossible to accurately predict how a system will be used in practice, and how its requirements will change over time, this approach naturally creates overly complex systems. Ironically, this complexity makes it more difficult to change and improve the system, which makes it less likely to cope well in the long run.

With cloud-age dynamic infrastructure, making a change to an existing system can be easy and cheap. However, this assumes everything is designed to facilitate change. Software and infrastructure must be designed as simply as possible to meet current requirements. Change management must be able to deliver changes safely and quickly.

The most important measure to ensure that a system can be changed safely and quickly is to make changes frequently. This forces everyone involved to learn good habits for managing changes, to develop efficient, streamlined processes, and to implement tooling that supports doing so.

Practices

The previous section outlined high-level principles. This section describes some of the general practices of infrastructure as code.

Use Definition Files

The cornerstone practice of infrastructure as code is the use of definition files. A definition specifies infrastructure elements and how they should be configured. The definition file is used as input for a tool that carries out the work to provision and/or configure instances of those elements. Example 1-1 is an example of a definition file for a database server node.

The infrastructure element could be a server; a part of a server, such as a user account; network configuration, such as a load balancer rule; or many other things. Different tools have different terms for this: for example, playbooks (Ansible), recipes (Chef), or manifests (Puppet). The term "configuration definition file" is used in this book as a generic term for these.

Example 1-1. Example of a definition file using a DSL

```
server: dbnode
  base_image: centos72
  chef_role: dbnode
  network_segment: prod_db
  allowed_inbound:
    from_segment: prod_app
    port: 1521
  allowed_inbound:
    from_segment: admin
    port: 22
```

Definition files are managed as text files. They may use a standard format such as JSON, YAML, or XML. Or they may define their own domain-specific language (DSL).[6]

Keeping specifications and configurations in text files makes them more accessible than storing them in a tool's internal configuration database. The files can also be treated like software source code, bringing a wide ecosystem of development tools to bear.

Self-Documented Systems and Processes

IT teams commonly struggle to keep their documentation relevant, useful, and accurate. Someone might write up a comprehensive document for a new process, but it's

---

6 As defined by Martin Fowler and Rebecca Parsons in *Domain-Specific Languages* (*http://martinfowler.com/books/dsl.html*) (Addison-Wesley Professional), "DSLs are small languages, focused on a particular aspect of a software system. You can't build a whole program with a DSL, but you often use multiple DSLs in a system mainly written in a general-purpose language." Their book is a good reference on domain-specific languages, although it's written more for people thinking about implementing one than for people using them.

rare for such documents to be kept up to date as changes and improvements are made to the way things are done. And documents still often leave gaps. Different people find their own shortcuts and improvements. Some people write their own personal scripts to make parts of the process easier.

So although documentation is often seen as a way to enforce consistency, standards, and even legal compliance, in practice it's a fictionalized version of what really happens.

With infrastructure as code, the steps to carry out a process are captured in the scripts, definition files, and tools that actually implement the process. Only a minimum of added documentation is needed to get people started. The documentation that does exist should be kept close to the code it documents, to make sure it's close to hand and mind when people make changes.

Automatically Generating Documentation

On one project, my colleague Tom Duckering found that the team responsible for deploying software to production insisted on doing it manually. Tom had implemented an automated deployment using Apache Ant, but the production team wanted written documentation for a manual process.

So Tom wrote a custom Ant task that printed out each step of the automated deployment process. This way, a document was generated with the exact steps, down to the command lines to type. His team's continuous integration server generated this document for every build, so they could deliver a document that was accurate and up to date. Any changes to the deployment script were automatically included in the document without any extra effort.

Version All the Things

The version control system (VCS) is a core part of infrastructure that is managed as code. The VCS is the source of truth for the desired state of infrastructure. Changes to infrastructure are driven by changes committed to the VCS.

Reasons why VCS is essential for infrastructure management include:

Traceability
> VCS provides a history of changes that have been made, who made them, and ideally, context about why. This is invaluable when debugging problems.

Rollback
> When a change breaks something—and especially when multiple changes break something—it's useful to be able to restore things to exactly how they were before.

Correlation

When scripts, configuration, artifacts, and everything across the board are in version control and correlated by tags or version numbers, it can be useful for tracing and fixing more complex problems.

Visibility

Everyone can see when changes are committed to a version control system, which helps situational awareness for the team. Someone may notice that a change has missed something important. If an incident happens, people are aware of recent commits that may have triggered it.

Actionability

VCSs can automatically trigger actions when a change is committed. This is a key to enabling continuous integration and continuous delivery pipelines.

Chapter 4 explains how VCS works with configuration management tools, and Chapter 10 discusses approaches to managing your infrastructure code and definitions.

Continuously Test Systems and Processes

Effective automated testing is one of the most important practices that infrastructure teams can borrow from software development. Automated testing is a core practice of high-performing development teams. They implement tests along with their code and run them continuously, typically dozens of times a day as they make incremental changes to their codebase.

It's difficult to write automated tests for an existing, legacy system. A system's design needs to be decoupled and structured in a way that facilitates independently testing components. Writing tests while implementing the system tends to drive clean, simple design, with loosely coupled components.

Running tests continuously during development gives fast feedback on changes. Fast feedback gives people the confidence to make changes quickly and more often. This is especially powerful with automated infrastructure, because a small change can do a lot of damage very quickly (aka DevOops, as described in "DevOops" on page 228). Good testing practices are the key to eliminating automation fear.

Chapter 11 explores practices and techniques for implementing testing as part of the system, and particularly how this can be done effectively for infrastructure.

Small Changes Rather Than Batches

When I first got involved in developing IT systems, my instinct was to implement a complete piece of work before putting it live. It made sense to wait until it was "done" before spending the time and effort on testing it, cleaning it up, and generally making it "production ready." The work involved in finishing it up tended to take a lot of time and effort, so why do the work before it's really needed?

However, over time I've learned to the value of small changes. Even for a big piece of work, it's useful to find incremental changes that can be made, tested, and pushed into use, one by one. There are a lot of good reasons to prefer small, incremental changes over big batches:

- It's easier, and less work, to test a small change and make sure it's solid.
- If something goes wrong with a small change, it's easier to find the cause than if something goes wrong with a big batch of changes.
- It's faster to fix or reverse a small change.
- One small problem can delay everything in a large batch of changes from going ahead, even when most of the other changes in the batch are fine.
- Getting fixes and improvements out the door is motivating. Having large batches of unfinished work piling up, going stale, is demotivating.

As with many good working practices, once you get the habit, it's hard to *not* do the right thing. You get much better at releasing changes. These days, I get uncomfortable if I've spent more than an hour working on something without pushing it out.

Keep Services Available Continuously

It's important that a service is always able to handle requests, in spite of what might be happening to the infrastructure. If a server disappears, other servers should already be running, and new ones quickly started, so that service is not interrupted. This is nothing new in IT, although virtualization and automation can make it easier.

Data management, broadly defined, can be trickier. Service data can be kept intact in spite of what happens to the servers hosting it through replication and other approaches that have been around for decades. When designing a cloud-based system, it's important to widen the definition of data that needs to be persisted, usually including things like application configuration, logfiles, and more.

The chapter on continuity (Chapter 14) goes into techniques for keeping service and data continuously available.

Antifragility: Beyond "Robust"

Robust infrastructure is a typical goal in IT, meaning systems will hold up well to shocks such as failures, load spikes, and attacks. However, infrastructure as code lends itself to taking infrastructure beyond robust, becoming antifragile.

Nicholas Taleb coined the term "antifragile" with his book of the same title (*http://www.amazon.com/Antifragile-Things-that-Gain-Disorder/dp/0141038225*), to describe systems that actually grow stronger when stressed. Taleb's book is not IT-specific—his main focus is on financial systems—but his ideas are relevant to IT architecture.

The effect of physical stress on the human body is an example of antifragility in action. Exercise puts stress on muscles and bones, essentially damaging them, causing them to become stronger. Protecting the body by avoiding physical stress and exercise actually weakens it, making it more likely to fail in the face of extreme stress.

Similarly, protecting an IT system by minimizing the number of changes made to it will not make it more robust. Teams that are constantly changing and improving their systems are much more ready to handle disasters and incidents.

The key to an antifragile IT infrastructure is making sure that the default response to incidents is improvement. When something goes wrong, the priority is not simply to fix it, but to improve the ability of the system to cope with similar incidents in the future.

The Secret Ingredient of Antifragile IT Systems

People are the part of the system that can cope with unexpected situations and modify the other elements of the system to handle similar situations better the next time around. This means the people running the system need to understand it quite well and be able to continuously modify it.

This doesn't fit the idea of automation as a way to run things without humans. Someday it might be possible to buy a standard corporate IT infrastructure off the shelf and run it as a black box, without needing to look inside, but this isn't possible today. IT technology and approaches are constantly evolving, and even in nontechnology businesses, the most successful companies are the ones continuously changing and improving their IT.

The key to continuously improving an IT system is the people who build and run it. So the secret to designing a system that can adapt as needs change is to design it around the people.[7]

---

7 Brian L. Troutwin gave a talk at DevOpsDays Ghent in 2014 titled "Automation, with Humans in Mind" (*http://www.slideshare.net/BrianTroutwine1/automation-with-humans-in-mind-making-complex-systems-predictable-reliable-and-humane*). He gave an example from NASA of how humans were able to modify the systems on the Apollo 13 spaceflight to cope with disaster. He also gave many details of how the humans at the Chernobyl nuclear power plant were prevented from interfering with the automated systems there, which kept them from taking steps to stop or contain disaster.

Conclusion

The hallmark of an infrastructure team's effectiveness is how well it handles changing requirements. Highly effective teams can handle changes and new requirements easily, breaking down requirements into small pieces and piping them through in a rapid stream of low-risk, low-impact changes.

Some signals that a team is doing well:

- Every element of the infrastructure can be rebuilt quickly, with little effort.
- All systems are kept patched, consistent, and up to date.
- Standard service requests, including provisioning standard servers and environments, can be fulfilled within minutes, with no involvement from infrastructure team members. SLAs are unnecessary.
- Maintenance windows are rarely, if ever, needed. Changes take place during working hours, including software deployments and other high-risk activities.
- The team tracks mean time to recover (MTTR) and focuses on ways to improve this. Although mean time between failure (MTBF) may also be tracked, the team does not rely on avoiding failures.[8]
- Team members feel their work is adding measurable value to the organization.

What's Next?

The next four chapters focus on the tooling involved in infrastructure as code. Readers who are already familiar with these tools may choose to skim or skip these chapters and go straight to Part II, which describes infrastructure-as-code patterns for using the tools.

I have grouped tools into four chapters. As with any model for categorizing things, this division of tools is not absolute. Many tools will cross these boundaries or have a fuzzy relationship to these definitions. This grouping is a convenience, to make it easier to discuss the many tools involved in running a dynamic infrastructure:

Dynamic infrastructure platforms
Used to provide and manage basic infrastructure resources, particularly compute (servers), storage, and networking. These include public and private cloud infrastructure services, virtualization, and automated configure of physical devices. This is the topic of Chapter 2.

---

8 See John Allspaw's seminal blog post, "MTTR is more important than MTBF (for most types of F)" (*http://www.kitchensoap.com/2010/11/07/mttr-mtbf-for-most-types-of-f/*).

Infrastructure definition tools

Used to manage the allocation and configuration servers, storage, and networking resources. These tools provision and configure infrastructure at a high level. This is the subject of Chapter 3.

Server configuration tools

These tools deal with the details of servers themselves. This includes software packages, user accounts, and various types of configuration. This group, which is typified by specific tools including CFEngine, Puppet, Chef, and Ansible, are what many people think of first when discussing infrastructure automation and infrastructure as code. These tools are discussed in Chapter 4.

Infrastructure services

Tools and services that help to manage infrastructure and application services. Topics such as monitoring, distributed process management, and software deployment are the subject of Chapter 5.

## CHAPTER 2

Dynamic Infrastructure Platforms

This chapter describes different types of dynamic infrastructure platforms, which provide the foundation for provisioning and managing core infrastructure resources. The goal is to understand the typical capabilities and service models available, and the requirements a platform must provide to effectively support infrastructure as code.

What Is a Dynamic Infrastructure Platform?

A dynamic infrastructure platform is a system that provides computing resources, particularly servers, storage, and networking, in a way that they can be programmatically allocated and managed.

Table 2-1 lists several types of dynamic infrastructure platforms with examples. The best-known examples are public IaaS (Infrastructure as a Service) cloud services like AWS, and private IaaS products like OpenStack. But infrastructure can also be managed dynamically using virtualization systems such as VMware vSphere, which don't meet the definition of cloud. (I'll define *cloud* a bit later in this chapter.) And some organizations automate the provisioning and management of bare-metal physical hardware, using tools such as Cobbler or Foreman.

Table 2-1. Examples of dynamic infrastructure platforms

Type of Platform	Providers or Products
Public IaaS cloud	AWS, Azure, Digital Ocean, GCE, and Rackspace Cloud
Community IaaS cloud	Cloud services shared between governmental departments
Private IaaS cloud	CloudStack, OpenStack, and VMware vCloud
Bare-metal cloud	Cobbler, FAI, and Foreman

It doesn't matter whether a dynamic infrastructure platform is cloud, virtualization, or bare metal. What is important is that scripts and tools can use it to automatically create and destroy elements of infrastructure, report on their status, and manage metadata.

Different types of platforms, and considerations for choosing between them, is discussed later in this chapter.

Implementing Your Dynamic Infrastructure Platform

While public infrastructure clouds like AWS are the best-known examples of dynamic infrastructure platforms, many organizations implement their own, private infrastructure clouds. This book focuses on building infrastructure on top of an existing platform, and so sidesteps the question of how to build your own infrastructure platform. That said, this chapter should help to understand the requirements needed from a platform in order to support infrastructure as code.

Requirements for a Dynamic Infrastructure Platform

Infrastructure as code is about treating infrastructure as a software system, which means the dynamic infrastructure platform needs to have certain characteristics. The platform needs to be:

- Programmable
- On-demand
- Self-service

The next few sections will discuss each of these characteristics in detail.

Characteristics of a Cloud, According to NIST

The US National Institute of Standards and Technology (NIST) has published an excellent definition of cloud computing (*http://www.nist.gov/itl/cloud/*). It lists five essential characteristics of cloud:

- On-demand self-service (provisioning)
- Broad network access (available over the network using "standard mechanisms")
- Resource pooling (multitenancy)
- Rapid elasticity (elements can be added and removed quickly, even automatically)

- Measured service (you can meter your usage of resources)

The definition of a dynamic infrastructure platform is broader than cloud. Resource pooling isn't a requirement for infrastructure as code, which in turn means that metering may not be necessary.

Programmable

The dynamic infrastructure platform must be programmable. A user interface is handy, and most virtualization products and cloud providers have one. But scripts, software, and tools must be able to interact with the platform, and this requires a programming API.

Even when using off-the-shelf tools, most teams end up writing at least some custom scripts and tools. So the infrastructure platform's API must have good support for scripting languages that the team is comfortable using.

Most infrastructure platforms expose their management functionality through a network API, with REST-based APIs (*http://en.wikipedia.org/wiki/Representational_state_transfer*) being the most popular due to their ease of use and flexibility (Figure 2-1).

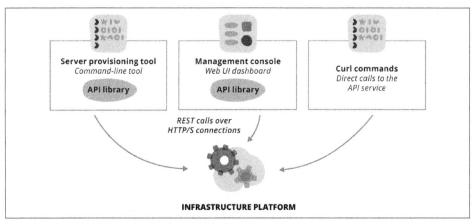

Figure 2-1. Infrastructure platform API clients

Programming and scripting against a REST API is fairly straightforward, but it can be helpful to use a language-specific library that wraps the details of the API, providing classes and structures to represent the infrastructure elements and operations on them. The developers of dynamic infrastructure platforms usually offer an SDK in at least a few languages, and there are a number of open source projects that provide comprehensive APIs for multiple platforms, such as the Ruby Fog (*http://fog.io*) and Python Boto (*http://boto3.readthedocs.org/*) libraries.

Example of a script using an SDK for a dynamic infrastructure platform

Example 2-1 uses Amazon's Ruby SDK (*http://aws.amazon.com/sdk-for-ruby/*) (version 2) to create an EC2 instance.

The script first uses the API to create a client object. This object opens an authenticated session with AWS. It handles authentication transparently, reading AWS API keys from environment variables that will have been set before the script is run.

The run_instances API call specifies the AMI to use to create the new instance, and the size of the instance to create, as well as how many instances to start.

The script then calls describe_instances, which lists all of the EC2 instances this account has in the region. It prints the ID for each instance along with its state.

Example 2-1. Simple Ruby script that uses the AWS SDK

```ruby
require 'aws-sdk'

@client = Aws::EC2::Client.new(:region => 'eu-west-1')

@client.run_instances({
  image_id: 'ami-903686e7',
  instance_type: "t1.micro",
  min_count: 1,
  max_count: 1
})

@client.describe_instances()[:reservations].each { |reservation|
  reservation[:instances].each { |instance|
    puts "Instance #{instance.instance_id} is #{instance.state.name}"
  }
}
```

On-Demand

It is essential for infrastructure as code that the dynamic infrastructure platform allows resources to be created and destroyed immediately.

This should be obvious, but it's not always the case. Some managed hosting providers, and internal IT departments, offer services they describe as cloud, but which require raising requests for staff to actually carry out the activities. For an organization to use infrastructure as code, its hosting platform must be able to fulfill provisioning requests within minutes, if not seconds.

Billing and budgeting also need to be structured to support on-demand, incremental charging. Traditional budgeting is based on long-term commitments of months or years. Dynamic infrastructure should not require long-term commitments, with hourly billing periods at most.

An organization may make a long-term commitment to buy or lease a fixed pool of hardware. But provisioning virtual instances from that pool should not involve additional costs, especially not long-term ones.

Self-Service

Self-service adds a bit more onto the on-demand requirement for the infrastructure platform. Not only should infrastructure users be able to have resources quickly, they must have the ability to tailor and customize those resources to their requirements.

This is in contrast with the more traditional approach, where a central team (or group of teams) designs solutions for teams that need infrastructure. Even a common request such as a new web server may involve a detailed request form, design and specification documents, and implementation plan.

This is like buying a box of LEGO bricks, but having the shop staff decide how to assemble them for you. It prevents the requesting team from taking ownership of the infrastructure they use and learning how to to shape it to their own needs and improve it over time.

With the advent of cloud, some central infrastructure teams are offering self-service resources, but from a very narrow menu. For example, teams may be able to provision one of three types of servers: a web server, application server, or database server, each with a specific build of software and no ability to customize it.

This is like only being able to buy a preassembled LEGO toy that has been glued together. This doesn't help a team that needs to customize a solution, such as optimizing the web server software for their application. Teams who need a new type of solution, such as running software on a different application server, may be completely out of luck.

Infrastructure as code assumes, and requires, that teams use scripts and tools to automatically specify and provision resources, and make changes to them. This empowers the teams using the infrastructure to tailor and evolve it to their own needs.

Infrastructure as code offers alternatives to forcing centralized teams to act as gatekeepers. The ability for infrastructure users to easily and routinely modify their infrastructure means they can fix their mistakes quickly. And the use of automated testing and staging of changes, as discussed throughout this book, mitigates the risk of disruption to other services.

Infrastructure Resources Provided by the Platform

Infrastructure management has many moving parts. There are three key building blocks provided by a dynamic infrastructure platform: compute, storage, and networking (Figure 2-2).

Most platforms offer a larger list of services than just these three, but nearly all of the other services are just variations of these services (e.g., different types of storage) or things that combine and run on top of them. Examples include server image management (storage to support compute), load balancing (networking, possibly using compute instances), messaging (networking and compute), and authentication (an application running on compute instances). Even a serverless compute service like Kinesis (*https://aws.amazon.com/kinesis/*) is implemented by running jobs on a normal compute resource.

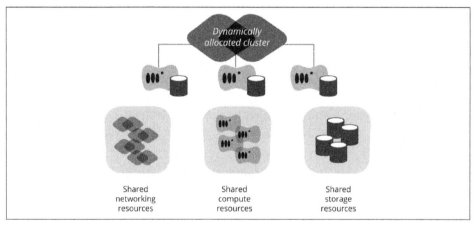

Figure 2-2. Core resources provided by a dynamic infrastructure platform

Compute Resources

Compute resources are server instances. Any dynamic infrastructure platform will have ways to create and destroy virtual servers (VMs), as well as a host of services and features to make server management easier and more powerful.

Systems and processes to build, configure, and manage servers take the bulk of most infrastructure teams' time and attention, so much of the material in this book focuses on doing this.

Storage Resources

Virtualized infrastructure consumes incredible amounts of storage—dynamically creating servers gobbles up disk space at an alarming rate. The infrastructure platform needs to allocate disk space to servers, snapshots, and templates. It also needs to make storage available for applications and services running on the servers.

A cloud platform should manage disk space allocation for server resources transparently; this is an implementation detail for the platform, but the person or process that creates a server shouldn't need to worry about where it's stored. Virtualization platforms may not provide storage transparently, so scripts that provision servers may need to find a storage pool with enough space and assign it to the new instance.

Even when space is transparently allocated for servers, there will be limits. These may be hard limits, based on how much physical disk space your organization has attached to your private cloud. Otherwise you may have budgetary limits, especially with public clouds, which will deliver astronomical disk capacity as long as your credit card holds out.

So it's important for infrastructure teams to manage their use of disk space. At a minimum, usage and costs should be made visible through a dashboard (a good use of information radiators, which are discussed in "What Is An Information Radiator?" on page 88), so that people know when to go through and cull things that are no longer needed. Automatic cleanup scripts for old templates and snapshots will be even more helpful.

Beyond the storage needs for the compute resources, a dynamic infrastructure platform should provide storage for services and applications that run on it. Most cloud platforms have two classes of storage as a service: block storage and object storage.

Block storage

A block storage volume can be mounted on a server instance as if it were a local disk. Examples of block storage services provided by cloud platforms include AWS EBS, OpenStack Cinder, and GCE persistent disk.

Server instances normally have a root volume, which is what the server boots and runs from. But additional persistent volumes can also be mounted and unmounted from a server. These live beyond the lifespan of a particular server, making it especially useful for managing persistent data and for continuity strategies, as discussed in Chapter 14.

A block volume appears to be a local disk drive, but it's important to understand what lies underneath this abstraction. These volumes are usually allocated from network storage, so they may have issues with latency. The best approach is to research the implementation, run tests that emulate your use cases, and tune how you configure and use storage to get the appropriate performance.

Object storage

Many cloud platforms offer an object storage service, where files can be stored and accessed from different parts of the infrastructure, and even made available publicly. Amazon's S3, Google Cloud Storage, Rackspace Cloud Files, and OpenStack Swift are all examples.

Object storage is usually designed for longer-term storage, with higher reliability than block storage, less cost, but potentially higher latency. It's useful for storing artifacts that need to be accessed from multiple servers, as opposed to a block storage volume which is only available to the server that mounts it.

Networked filesystems

Infrastructure teams often find the need to share storage more directly between server instances. One way to do this is using file sharing network protocols like NFS or SMB/CIFS. A server instance can mount local or block storage and make it available for other servers to mount and use. These file server technologies have long been used in pre-virtualized environments, but care should be taken before jumping into implementing them on a virtualized or cloud-based infrastructure.

Sharing a filesystem over a network when the "local" filesystem is itself mounted over the network may be adding unnecessary overhead and complications. Using a traditional network filesystem on cloud servers also creates extra administrative complexity and overhead. These file server technologies don't necessarily cope well with file server nodes that are routinely added and removed, which makes continuity challenging.

Distributed and/or clustered file service tools such as GlusterFS, HDFS, or Ceph are designed in a way that can make them more suitable for use in a dynamic infrastructure. They ensure data availability across multiple server nodes and can usually handle nodes being added and removed more gracefully. However, don't make assumptions about how well this will work; be sure to test not only for performance and latency, but also for the impact of changes to the cluster and for failure scenarios.

Before leaping into the specific technologies and tools to use, think through the use cases. I've seen at least one team implement a complex and fragile glusterfs cluster simply to achieve fault tolerance—to make sure the data from a server would be available for a failover server to pick up if the first server fails. It is generally simpler and more reliable to make direct use of services built into the platform, such as block storage replication.

Network Resources

A dynamic infrastructure platform needs to manage connectivity between its own elements, and with external networks. Networking routes, load balancing pools, and firewall rules need to be updated as servers are added and removed from the infrastructure.

Most virtualized and cloud infrastructure platforms provide dynamic, virtualized networking to handle connectivity. However, these platforms are normally installed and run as part of a larger estate with its own networking infrastructure. In order for the dynamic infrastructure elements to work seamlessly with everything else, they need to integrate with the surrounding network.

In many cases, it's possible to configure the surrounding network in a fairly static way so that it passes traffic through to the infrastructure platform. This can work well enough when the outer network is kept simple. The more complex logic for things like security, routing, and load balancing are handled by the dynamic platform. The goal is to avoid needing to make manual changes to networking infrastructure in order to support changes to the dynamic infrastructure.

However, it's also possible to automate the configuration of the surrounding networking so that it can handle dynamic infrastructure changes easily. This brings all of the benefits of infrastructure as code to the networking estate, including repeatability, continuous testing, and consistency.

Networking vendors are improving their support for software-defined networking (SDN) (*http://en.wikipedia.org/wiki/Software-defined_networking*). Devices may not directly integrate with the virtualization or cloud platform. But infrastructure definition tools (discussed in Chapter 3) can be used to orchestrate across the different platforms, making changes to networking definitions to match changes made to compute resources.

Automating Network Device Configuration

Although vendors are beginning to support software-defined networking, there are still many networking devices in use that are not easy to automatically configure. Many networking teams are used to carrying out configuration changes manually, using a command-line interface. This has some obvious drawbacks:

- It's easy to make a mistake, potentially causing outages.
- It isn't easy to ensure configuration is consistent across devices.
- Reproducing configuration relies on backups, which may not be easily portable across devices.
- Even routine changes need to be made by someone with strong knowledge of the particular device.

Teams adopting infrastructure as code look for ways to automate device configuration to get around these issues. The first step is to understand the different ways the particular device can be configured, and then options can be considered to manage this automatically.

Most network devices have an option to import a configuration file, often using TFTP. In this case, the configuration file can be checked into an VCS and automatically applied to devices by a CI or CD server. The techniques described for server configuration definitions in Chapter 4 can be applied.

A more sophisticated approach is to dynamically generate the configuration file before uploading it. This allows networking to be automatically defined with the rest of the infrastructure—for example, setting firewall rules and load balancing configuration for devices as they are added.

With any approach, having test devices where configuration can be automatically applied and tested for correctness is essential. This allows the use of a change management pipeline (as discussed in Chapter 12). Sometimes a particular device is too expensive for a team to afford test instances. Any team in this situation should evaluate their priorities and less expensive options. A responsible team must ensure that any critical part of its infrastructure can be routinely tested.

Types of Dynamic Infrastructure Platforms

The options for platforms to build a dynamic infrastructure are growing and changing as more vendors and startups jump into the game. The following sections cover categories that may be useful as a starting point to think about the approach that's right for your organization. These are loosely based on the definitions of cloud deployment models in the NIST cloud definition mentioned earlier in this chapter.

Public IaaS Cloud

A public cloud is built and run by a vendor as a standard service. The computing resources are shared with the vendor's other customers, and you only pay for what you use. Examples include Amazon AWS, Microsoft Azure, Digital Ocean, Google GCE, and Rackspace Cloud.

Community IaaS Cloud

A community cloud is built and run for a limited group of customers (e.g., a cloud for government agencies). The cloud may be tailored to meet requirements peculiar to this group, such as following certain security standards. It may also limit exposure —for example, guaranteeing that no customer data is stored or transferred over systems or hardware shared with customers outside the community.

Depending on the commercial model, the vendor running the community cloud may be paid for the total capacity available, no matter how much is actually used. Otherwise, each customer may pay only for what it uses, leaving the vendor responsible for unused capacity.

Private IaaS Cloud

A private cloud is built and run for multiple consumers inside a single organization (e.g., departments or teams within a company). A vendor may build it, run, or even host it for the organization, but the resources are not shared with other organizations. The company will typically pay for the total capacity available, even if not all of it is used, although the company might have internal charges or capacity limits for departments based on their use and budgets.

As with all clouds, a private IaaS cloud allows consumers to automatically provision resources on demand in a self-service model, and they can be created and destroyed automatically. Some organizations set up virtualized infrastructure without these characteristics and call it a private cloud, but this is really hand-cranked virtualization, as explained in the next section.

Examples of IaaS cloud products include CloudStack, OpenStack, and VMware vCloud.

Types of Clouds: IaaS, PaaS, and SaaS

IaaS, PaaS, and SaaS are terms that are used to understand the different service models for cloud. Each of these is a cloud in the sense that it allows multiple users to share computing resources, but their users tend to be very different.

The NIST cloud definition has very clear and useful definitions of these three service models. Here is how I describe them:

Software as a Service (SaaS)
> An application shared between end users. This may be user-facing, such as web-hosted email, but there are actually a number of SaaS products aimed at infrastructure teams, including monitoring and even configuration management servers.

Platform as a Service (PaaS)
> A shared platform for application developers to build, test, and host their software. It abstracts the underlying infrastructure, so developers don't need to worry about things like how many servers to allocate for their application or database cluster: it just happens. Many IaaS cloud vendors offer services that are essentially elements of a PaaS (e.g., managed databases like Amazon RDS).

Infrastructure as a Service (IaaS)
> A shared hardware infrastructure that system administrators can use to build virtual infrastructure for services.

Antipattern: Hand-Cranked Cloud

Hand-cranked virtual infrastructure uses virtualization tools to manage hardware resources, but doesn't provide them to users dynamically or with a self-service model. I've seen organizations do this with expensive virtualization software, and even cloud-capable software like VMware vCloud. They keep the old, centralized model, requiring users to file tickets to request a server. An IT person creates each server, working under an SLA that gives them a few days to do the work, and then returns the login details to the user.

No matter how impressive and expensive the software used is, if the service model is neither dynamic nor self-service, it won't support infrastructure as code.

Hybrid and Mixed Cloud Options

Hybrid cloud is simply where parts of the infrastructure runs in a private cloud, and parts run in a public cloud. Although not strictly hybrid cloud, it's very common to have some services running on cloud infrastructure, integrated with other services running in a more traditionally managed infrastructure.

There are several reasons for this mixed infrastructure situation:

- Regulatory or other security requirements may require some data to be kept in a more restricted environment.

- Some services may have more variable capacity needs, which makes public cloud hosting compelling, while others may be fairly static and so don't have as much need to run in a public cloud.

- It may not make sense to invest in migrating some existing services out of traditional infrastructure. This is especially true when an organization is still fairly early in adopting public cloud. But in many cases, there may be a limited number of services that will never be suitable for moving to public cloud.

Bare-Metal Clouds

With virtualized infrastructure, multiple servers can run on a single physical server and be shuffled between servers as needed. This helps to maximize the utilization of available hardware. But there are still many reasons to run an OS directly on server hardware rather than in a VM. Fortunately, even in these cases, infrastructure as code can still be applied.

There are many reasons why running directly on hardware may be the best choice for a given application or service. Virtualization adds performance overhead, because it inserts extra software layers between the application and the hardware resources it uses.

Processes on one VM can impact the performance of other VMs running on the same host. For example, a VM running a database carrying out an intensive operation could monopolize I/O, creating issues for other VMs. This type of contention is especially bad for applications that need to guarantee consistent performance.

Even the abstractions themselves can cause issues. Software written to assume a mounted disk is truly local may suffer when the disk is actually mounted over the network from a SAN.

Of course, even when processes can run happily in a VM, the host systems themselves need to be well managed. Infrastructure as code practices can help ensure that the hypervisors and management services of the infrastructure platform are kept consistent, easily rebuilt, well tested, and updated, as with other elements of the infrastructure.

In these cases, the team needs an automated, dynamic infrastructure platform that works at the level of hardware. It needs to have the same capabilities looked at earlier in this chapter. This includes being able to provision and allocate compute resource, storage, and networking. It should be programmable, dynamic, and support a self-service model so that these activities can be scripted.

Some tools that can be used to implement a dynamic infrastructure platform with bare-metal servers include Cobbler (*http://cobbler.github.io/*), FAI - Fully Automatic Installation (*http://fai-project.org/*), Foreman (*http://theforeman.org/*), and Crowbar (*http://opencrowbar.github.io/*). These tools can take advantage of the PXE specification Preboot Execution Environment (*https://en.wikipedia.org/wiki/Preboot_Execu tion_Environment*) to boot a basic OS image downloaded from the network, which then runs an installer to download and boot an OS installer image. The installer image will run a script, perhaps with something like Kickstart (*http://www.linux-mag.com/id/6747/*), to configure the OS, and then potentially run a configuration management tool like Chef or Puppet.

Often, triggering a server to use PXE to boot a network image requires pressing a function key while the server starts. This could be tricky to do unattended. However, many hardware vendors have lights-out management (LOM (*http://en.wikipedia.org/wiki/Out-of-band_management*)) functionality that makes it possible to do this remotely, and even automatically.

Many cases that lead to bare-metal infrastructure—for example, high performance database servers—are driven by the need to use storage directly attached to the server, which removes the need for sophisticated dynamic storage management. In other cases, storage area networks (SANs) and related technologies and products can be used to provision and allocate storage. There are a growing number of sophisticated storage virtualization products that may be of interest as well.

Managing the configuration of hardware network devices to support a dynamic infrastructure is a particular challenge. For example, you may need to add and remove servers from a load balancer if they are created and destroyed automatically in response to demand. Network devices tend to be difficult to automatically configure, although many are able to load configuration files over the network—for example, from a TFTP server.

Teams can and do build tooling to automatically build, test, and load configuration files to hardware network devices. Fortunately, as mentioned earlier, the growing *software-defined networking (SDN)* movement is leading vendors to make this easier for their customers, and even create cross-vendor standards for doing it.

Deciding on a Dynamic Infrastructure Platform

Having looked at the characteristics a dynamic infrastructure platform needs to support infrastructure as code, and different types of platforms, let's explore some of the key considerations when choosing a platform.

Public or Private?

Proposing to move an organization's IT infrastructure to a public cloud provider raises the following concerns.

Security and data protection

The number one concern with moving to public cloud is usually security. Unlike normal dedicated hosting providers, a cloud provider hosts your organization's data and computing resources on physical hardware, networks, and storage devices alongside those of their other customers. Some of these other customers may be your competitors, and others may be criminals looking to exploit weaknesses to access confidential data or to damage your organization.

But many organizations use public cloud successfully and securely, including massive commercial operations handling sensitive financial transactions and customer data. Examples include Amazon's own ecommerce operations, Suncorp,[1] and Tesco.[2] Keeping data on dedicated hardware, and even in dedicated data centers, does not guarantee security. There are a number of examples of high-profile companies that have lost thousands of customer credit card numbers from private data centers, and far more that haven't been revealed to the public.

As always, whether using public cloud, external vendor, or internal IT, there is no substitute for good security strategy and implementation. Your team should thoroughly consider the security concerns and threat models for your services. They can

---

[1] "AWS Case Study: Suncorp" (*https://aws.amazon.com/solutions/case-studies/suncorp/*); see also "Pssst, Amazon Cloud Is Not Really New to Banks" (*http://fortune.com/2016/02/25/yes-banks-do-use-aws/*).

[2] "How Tesco Bank has adopted AWS cloud as 'business as usual' in eight months" (*http://www.computerworl duk.com/cloud-computing/how-tesco-bank-has-adopted-aws-cloud-as-business-as-usual-in-eight-months-3629767/*)

then apply this understanding to the different options for hosting and work out the best approach. In many cases, a hybrid or mixed infrastructure approach may be appropriate to isolate certain classes of data and operations.

Legal constraints on hosting locations

Some organizations have constraints around where their data and systems can be hosted. Systems contracted by governmental organizations may be required to be hosted in the same country, or might be forbidden to be hosted in certain others. Privacy laws in some jurisdictions don't allow user data to be transferred to countries with less strict protections on its use.

For example, it is illegal (as of this writing) for systems running in Europe to store user data on computers running in countries such as the United States that don't have strong personal privacy laws (*https://ico.org.uk/for-organisations/guide-to-data-protection/principle-8-international/*). When I've worked with European companies using AWS, we had to take care to only store data in the EU regions.

Your organization should understand what constraints apply. If you do have these constraints, you need to be aware of where your cloud service providers host your systems and data, and be sure they have sufficient guarantees to adhere to these. This is true not only of IaaS cloud providers, but also of services you use for things like monitoring, email, and log aggregation.

Requirements for variable capacity

Be clear on your organization's need for capacity, and how this is affected by having dedicated infrastructure versus using a vendor's shared pool. An important benefit of using a public cloud is that you can adjust your capacity quickly, and only pay for what you need as you use it.

This is useful for services with variable usage levels. It's very common for services to have daily and weekly cycles with significant differences between their peaks and low periods. A business application may be heavily used during working hours, but very little during the evening and weekends. Entertainment applications often have the reverse pattern. Retail services, especially in Western countries, need considerably more capacity in the periods leading up to the annual holidays than they do for the rest of the year.

Another case for using shared resources are a rapidly growing service, such as a new product. These often grow in spurts, as features and marketing bring new users in waves. Paying for fixed capacity that you may or may not need is a risk for a new business or product, so being able to rapidly add capacity only when it's proven to be needed is hugely useful.

While the public cloud model is perfectly adapted to handle variable capacity and rapid growth, some vendors providing dedicated infrastructure may also be able to meet these requirements. A vendor that has a large inventory of hardware, or a highly efficient supply chain, may be able to guarantee very short turnaround times for adding dedicated hardware capacity to your infrastructure. They may also be willing to offer short-term periods—for example, adding hardware for a few days or weeks for a particular event.

Total costs of building your own cloud

The sunk cost of existing infrastructure, data centers, and knowledge is a common but questionable driver for self-hosting. Moving to the cloud and potentially scrapping existing investment feels wasteful. But this is an example of the sunk cost fallacy. Sticking with hardware you already own will force you to continue investing in it, which may well be more expensive than moving to an alternative in the medium term.

A common mistake in comparing hosting costs is to only count the price of the hardware. Managing physical infrastructure takes skills and time, not to mention management focus. Before taking the decision to build or keep your own hardware and related infrastructure, make sure you're being realistic about the total costs.

Commodity or differentiator

There are many aspects of IT that seem cheap to outsource, but have a high risk of compromising the organization's ability to respond quickly and effectively. Hosting, particularly at the hardware level, is not one of these. Infrastructure provisioning has become a commodity, to the point where it can be offered as a standardized, interchangeable, automated service with a programmable interface.

Very few organizations today can turn the ability to select which model hard drive to install in their servers into a competitive advantage. Not many can build up enough competency in data center operations that they can do it cheaply or more responsively than Google, Amazon, or Microsoft.

This isn't to say there are no organizations that can build competitive offerings using innovations or specializations in the data center. But be realistic about whether or not you're one of them.

Managed Cloud and Virtualization Vendors

Public cloud vendors provide a "hands-off," one-size fits-all service. Smaller and specialist cloud vendors may offer more customized services, including better support and consultancy services, or services specialized for smaller target markets. Some vendors will even build and manage private clouds for you in data centers of your

---

choosing. This can be particularly appealing when going into countries where the major public cloud vendors don't yet offer data centers, such as China (as of the publication of this book).

Unfortunately, many IT service providers are quick to put the "cloud" label on service offerings that aren't suitable for customers who are looking to manage their own software infrastructure on a dynamic infrastructure. As described earlier in this chapter, your dynamic infrastructure platform needs to be programmable, dynamic, and self-service.

Watch out for pricing models and contracts that assume the number of virtual machines will be static. The process to provision a machine should not need a change request, raising a ticket, or any human involvement. The cost for a VM should not be fixed for a long period; an hour is pretty normal in the cloud market.

Cloud Portability

When planning a move to a cloud-based infrastructure, one requirement that often comes up is avoiding lock-in to a single cloud vendor. Some toolsets and products offer to make portability between cloud platforms easier. However, care is needed to avoid spending significant time and money on this requirement only to find later on that migrating to a different cloud vendor is still complex, costly, and risky.

It's important to be realistic about what can be achieved in terms of portability. Typical drivers for this requirement are to manage the risk of needing to change cloud vendors at a future point, and to keep the option of making such a change viable by keeping the cost and risk of a potential migration low. In these cases, it's not necessary to guarantee migration will involve zero effort.

The only way to guarantee leaving a cloud vendor will be nearly painless is to build an infrastructure across multiple vendors from the start. All services should be routinely running on more than one cloud vendor, all changes applied and used across the clouds, and all data replicated. Having the services actually in use, as opposed to deployed in cold standby, guarantees their operability. This strategy has the added advantage of offering tolerance to failures within a single cloud vendor.

Running across multiple clouds eliminates the risk of migration and lock-in, while adding significantly to the upfront and ongoing cost and time of implementing and operating the infrastructure.

Techniques for portability

If systems are run on a single cloud, there are some techniques that make it easier to migrate later.

One technique is to avoid using vendor-specific functionality. This has the drawback of missing out on useful features and services that may save time and cost in building and running systems. It may be enough to keep track of those vendor-provided services that are used by the infrastructure, and noting that migration would require either finding a vendor that offers comparable services, or else building custom implementations to replace them.

Once systems are successfully running and in use on the first cloud, the organization can make priority calls about refactoring systems to reduce dependence on the vendor over time.

This highlights another key strategy for making a future vendor migration easier, which is to have the capability to refactor infrastructure and services easily and confidently. This, of course, is what this book intends to help with. By ensuring that changes to an infrastructure are made using fast and rigorous automated testing processes, a team can confidently refactor it for use on a different cloud platform.

The point is that building the capability to make changes to infrastructure in response to changing requirements—including the requirement to change vendors of parts of the infrastructure—is more powerful and realistic than attempting to build an infrastructure that won't need to be changed in the future, even as unknown requirements emerge.

There are some tools and technologies that may help with portability. Some vendors offer tools or services for automating infrastructure that handle the details of cloud-specific integration for you. This means your infrastructure can run on any cloud supported by the vendor. The pitfall, of course, is that you may lock yourself into the portability tool vendor.

Containerization may be useful to reduce cloud-vendor lock-in. Packaging applications removes application-specific configuration and files from the underlying servers, which makes them easier to run in new hosting environments. But a heavily containerized infrastructure needs tooling and services to manage and orchestrate the containers, so teams going this route will need to consider how that can be ported across clouds. Container orchestration is discussed in more detail in "Container Orchestration Tools" on page 92.

A final potential strategy to avoid lock-in is to use a cloud vendor whose service is run on a nonproprietary platform. In other words, if a cloud is built using standard virtualization software that is also used by other, competing cloud vendors, migration is likely to be easier than moving from a vendor with a proprietary platform.

Mechanical Sympathy with the Cloud and Virtualization

Martin Thompson has borrowed the term *mechanical sympathy* from Formula One driver Jackie Stewart and brought it to IT.[3] A successful driver like Stewart has an innate understanding of how his car works, so he can get the most out of it and avoid failures. For an IT professional, the deeper and stronger your understanding of how the system works down the stack and into the hardware, the more proficient you'll be at getting the most from it.

The history of software has involved layering one abstraction over another. Operating systems, programming languages, and now virtualization have each helped people to be more productive by simplifying the way they interact with computer systems. You don't need to worry about which CPU register to store a particular value in, you don't need to think about how to allocate heap to different objects to avoid overlapping them, and you don't care which hardware server a particular virtual machine is running on.

Except when you do.

Hardware still lurks beneath the abstractions, and understanding what happens behind the facade of APIs and virtual CPU units is useful (Figure 2-3). It can help you to build systems that gracefully handle hardware failures, avoid hidden performance bottlenecks, and exploit potential sympathies—tweaks that make the software align with the underlying systems to work more reliably and effectively than naively written software would.

For example, the Netflix team knew that a percentage of AWS instances, when provisioned, will perform much worse than the average instance, whether because of hardware issues or simply because they happen to be sharing hardware with someone else's poorly behaving systems. So they wrote their provisioning scripts to immediately test the performance of each new instance. If it doesn't meet their standards, the script destroys the instance and tries again with a new instance.

Understanding the typical memory and CPU capacity of the hardware servers used by your platform can help to size your VMs to get the most out of them. Some teams choose their AWS instance size to maximize their chances of getting a hardware server entirely to themselves, even when they don't need the full capacity.

---

3 See Martin's blog post "Why Mechanical Sympathy" (*http://mechanical-sympathy.blogspot.co.uk/2011/07/ why-mechanical-sympathy.html*).

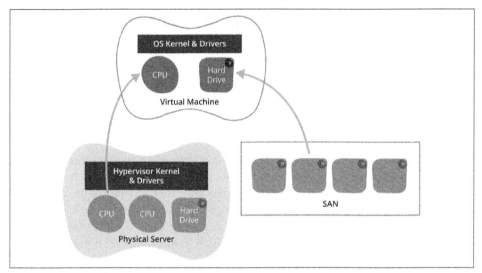

Figure 2-3. Abstractions with virtualization

Understanding storage options and networking is useful to ensure that disk reads and writes don't become a bottleneck. It's not a simple matter of choosing the fastest type of storage option available; selecting high performance local SSD drives may have implications for portability, cost, and even availability of resources.

This extends up and down the stack. Software and infrastructure should be architected, designed, and implemented with an understanding of the true architecture of the hardware, networking, storage, and the dynamic infrastructure platform.

An infrastructure team should seek out and read through every whitepaper, article, conference talk, and blog post they can find about the platform they're using. Bring in experts from your vendor to review your systems, from high-level architecture down to implementation details. Be sure to ask questions about how your designs and implementation will work with their physical infrastructure.

If you're using virtualization infrastructure managed by your own organization, then there's no excuse not to collaborate. Make sure your software and infrastructure are designed holistically, and continuously measured and modified to get the best performance and reliability possible.

Conclusion

With a dynamic infrastructure platform in place, the next step is to select and implement tools to define and manage the resources provided by the platform. This is the topic of the next chapter.

## CHAPTER 3

Infrastructure Definition Tools

The previous chapter described virtualization and cloud platforms that provide dynamic infrastructure resources, including compute, networking, and storage. This chapter discusses tools that teams can use to manage those resources following the principles of infrastructure as code.

An infrastructure definition tool, such Cloud Formation, Terraform, or OpenStack Heat, allows people to specify what infrastructure resources they want to allocate and how they should be configured. The tool then uses the dynamic infrastructure platform to implement the specification.

Of course, people can simply use the platform's user interface to create and manage resources. There are also third-party products that provide a graphical user interface (GUI) to interactively manage virtual and cloud infrastructure. But to gain the benefits of infrastructure as code, infrastructure needs to be managed in a way that is repeatable, testable, reusable, and self-documenting.

The first half of this chapter will offer guidelines for selecting and using tools to support this way of working. These guidelines are not specific to infrastructure definition tools; they also apply to server configuration tools and other infrastructure services.

The second half of this chapter is specifically about infrastructure definition files and tools. It gives examples of types and ways of defining infrastructure resources. It also looks at the use of configuration registries to support infrastructure configuration.

 Patterns for Defining Infrastructure

Chapter 9 builds on the understanding of infrastructure definition tools from this chapter. That chapter will delve into different architectural design patterns for infrastructure.

Choosing Tools for Infrastructure as Code

Infrastructure as code approaches automation with the challenges, principles, and practices described in Chapter 1 in mind. But many tools and products on the market aren't designed according to these principles. Although it can be possible to make these tools fit with infrastructure as code, it's much easier to use tools that are aligned to work this way.

The following sections discuss a few requirements for tools to work well with infrastructure as code. These apply to all infrastructure management tools, from the infrastructure automation platform, to infrastructure definition tools described in this chapter, as well as server configuration tools and services described in later chapters.

Requirement: Scriptable Interface

Tools that treat APIs and command-line tools as a first-class interface are easier to script than those that treat a GUI or web-based UI as the most important way of interacting with it.

Many infrastructure management tools are sold on the basis of a slick graphical interface. The idea is that dragging and dropping objects and selecting items from catalogs simplifies the job of infrastructure management. There's even the promise that less skilled people can manage infrastructure using these tools.

Giving infrastructure users the ability to provision and manage their own infrastructure is valuable. It can free infrastructure team members to focus on work that needs their deeper skills. However, in order for self-service tooling to work effectively, it must be possible for technical people to get under the hood of the tools.

The automobile industry is fairly mature, being over 100 years old. But you still wouldn't buy a car with the hood welded shut. Even if you don't know a spark plug from a gasket, you want to know a mechanic can get it and fix things. You don't want to send your car back to the factory to get the oil changed.

Command-line tools, programmable APIs, and open source code are how teams get under the hood of their infrastructure. This is necessary not only to tweak and fix things, but also to integrate different tools and services.

Requirement: Unattended Mode for Command-Line Tools

A command-line interface (CLI) tool should be easy to script. This means it should be designed to be run within an unattended shell or batch script:

- It should be able to take input from other tools and the scripting language—for example, through standard input, environment variables, and command-line parameters.

- Output should be easily usable by other other tools and the scripting language. It helps if output is structured so that it can be parsed, rather than embedded in text.

- It should not require input to be manually typed on the console, even passwords. There should be scriptable alternatives for accepting licenses, providing credentials, or otherwise authorizing the tool.

A tool that stops for interactive input, such as accepting license terms or prompting for a manually entered password, is a tool not designed for automation. Tools should take arguments or configuration parameters that let them run without prompting for input.

The common Unix command-line tools are the exemplar of good CLI design. Rather than a single tool that does everything, they are a collection of small tools, each of which does one thing well (`grep` includes or excludes lines, `sed` alters the content of lines, `sort` sorts them, etc.). These simple tools can be chained together in pipelines to carry out complex tasks.

 For tools that run as services, a good programmable API is essential. The guidelines for APIs for dynamic infrastructure platforms, discussed in "Programmable" on page 23, apply here.

Requirement: Support for Unattended Execution

Most system administrators start out writing scripts to help them with common tasks. Writing a script that can be run on a new server to install and configure a web server ticks many of the boxes for infrastructure is code. The processes is repeatable, consistent, and transparent.

But often, people write scripts that require manual steps. For example, a web server script might need a sysadmin to copy it to a new server and start it. They might need to edit the script to specify host names and IP addresses for the particular server.

Scripts that need this kind of manual attention don't free team members to focus on other things.[1] Tasks that can be reliably carried out without any human involvement are building blocks for a truly automated infrastructure. Scripts that can be triggered

---

[1] In *The Practice of Cloud System Administration* (*http://www.amazon.com/The-Practice-Cloud-System-Administration/dp/032194318X*) (Addison-Wesley Professional), Limoncelli, Chalup, and Hogan talk about tool building versus automation. Tool building is writing a script or tools to make a manual task easier. Automation is eliminating the need for a human to carry out the task. They make the comparison to an auto factory worker using a high-powered paint sprayer to paint car doors, versus having an unattended robotic painting system.

and run by other scripts and tools can then be automatically tested with no effort. They can also be used as part of automated scaling and recovery routines.

Ad Hoc Scripts Lead to the Automation Fear Spiral

I visited a systems team at a financial services company. The team had been using Puppet for nearly a year, writing manifests and checking them into source control. But they only applied the manifests when they had a specific change to make. They would tweak the manifests to implement the specific change they wanted, and to specify which machines they would apply to. More often than not, Puppet would run with errors or even fail on at least some of the machines.

The team decided it was time to move beyond treating Puppet as a scripting tool, and learn how to run it continuously. They sent people to a Puppet course, and began migrating their servers into a continuously synchronized regime. A year later, they had far more confidence in their automation and were exploring ways to increase their use of automated testing to gain even more confidence.

These are some characteristics of scripts and tasks that help to support reliable unattended execution:

Idempotent

> It should be possible to execute the same script or task multiple times without bad effects.

Pre-checks

> A task should validate its starting conditions are correct, and fail with a visible and useful error if not, leaving things in a usable state.

Post-checks

> A task should check that it has succeeded in making the changes. This isn't just a matter of checking return codes on commands, but proving that the end result is there. For example, checking that a virtual host has been added to a web server could involve making an HTTP request to the web server.

Visible failure

> When a task fails to execute correctly, it should be visible to the team. This may involve an information radiator and/or integration with monitoring services (covered in "What Is An Information Radiator?" on page 88 and "Alerting: Tell Me When Something Is Wrong" on page 87).

Parameterized

> Tasks should be applicable to multiple operations of a similar type. For example, a single script can be used to configure multiple virtual hosts, even ones with different characteristics. The script will need a way to find the parameters for a par-

ticular virtual host, and some conditional logic or templating to configure it for the specific situation.

Implementing this takes discipline for the infrastructure team. Be ruthless about finding manual tasks that can be automated. Use good coding practices to ensure scripts are robust. And strip out tasks that are difficult to automate, even if it means replacing major pieces of the infrastructure with ones that offer better support for unattended automation.

Idempotency

In order to allow a tool to repeatedly run unattended, it needs to be idempotent. This means that the result of running the tool should be the same no matter how many times it's run. Idempotent scripts and tools can be set to run continuously (for example, at a fixed time interval), which helps to prevent configuration drift and improve confidence in automation.

Here's an example of a shell script that is not idempotent:

```
echo "spock:*:1010:1010:Spock:/home/spock:/bin/sh" \
    >> /etc/passwd
```

Running this script once may have the result you want: the user *spock* is added to the */etc/passwd* file. But running it multiple times will end up with many duplicate entries for the user.

A good domain-specific language (DSL) for server configuration works by having you define the state you want something to be in, and then doing whatever is needed to bring it into that state. This should happen without side effects from being applied to the same server many times. The following Puppet snippet is an example of this:

```
user { "spock":
  ensure => present,
  gid    => "science",
  home   => "/home/spock",
  shell  => "/bin/sh"
}
```

This definition can be applied to a server many times.

Requirement: Externalized Configuration

Some infrastructure management tools are designed to store configuration data internally, in a "black box" fashion. The only way to access and edit the configuration is through the tool's interfaces. The alternative is storing configuration externally, in files that can be read and edited using common text editing tools.

The black box configuration pattern is intended to simplify management. The tool can offer a helpful interface to users, only presenting valid options. But the externalized configuration pattern tends to be more flexible, especially when used as part of an ecosystem of similar infrastructure tooling.

Lessons from Software Source Code

The externalized configuration pattern mirrors the way software source code works. There are some development environments that keep the source code hidden away, such as Visual Basic for Applications. But the dominant model is keeping programming source code in external files.

An integrated development environment (IDE) can provide an excellent user experience for managing and editing externalized source files while still keeping the source available to other tools and systems outside the IDE. This gives development teams, and even individual developers in a team, the freedom to choose the tools they prefer.

Some IDEs have support for server configuration definitions like Chef recipes and Puppet manifests. This may not be as mature as support for general-purpose programming languages like Java and C#, but it's possible that the increasing popularity of infrastructure automation will bring better IDE support over time.

Externalized configuration for a server, environment, network rule, or any other infrastructure element simplifies repeatability. It makes it easy to:

- Consistently provision many instances of the element type
- Create accurate test instances of the element
- Quickly rebuild a lost or broken instance of the element

Systems configured by clicking in a GUI inevitably become inconsistent. Applying configuration from a definition file ensures that every system is built the same way, every time.

A team's ability to work with configuration that's managed internally by a tool is limited to interactions that the tool supports. Configuration externalized as text files, on the other hand, can be accessed and manipulated by any off-the-shelf tool. You can edit them with whatever text editor you prefer, manipulate them with common command-line tools, and write your own scripts to manage them.

The ability to use this vast ecosystem of text file–friendly tools to bear on infrastructure configuration gives a team far more control than it can have with a proprietary tool.

Using a standard VCS tool

The most important off-the-shelf tool that can be used with externalized configuration is a VCS. This supports the benefits of "Version All the Things" on page 15: traceability of changes, ability to roll back changes that go wrong, correlation between changes to different parts of the infrastructure, visibility to everyone in the team, and the actionability to trigger automated tests and pipelines.

Some black box automation tools embed their own VCS functionality. But because this isn't the core function of these tools, they're normally not nearly as full featured as a standalone VCS. Externalized configuration allows teams to select the VCS with the features they need, and to swap it out later if they find a better one.

The Basics of Using a VCS

Modern software development teams use a VCS without even thinking about it. For many system administration teams, however, it's not a natural part of their workflow.

The VCS acts as the hub of infrastructure as code. Anything that can be done to infrastructure is captured in scripts, configuration files, and definition files checked into version control. When someone wants to make a change, they can check the files out of the VCS, make the changes by editing the files, and then commit the new file versions back into the VCS.

Committing a change into the VCS makes it available to be applied to infrastructure. If the team uses a change management pipeline (as described in Chapter 12), the change is automatically applied to test environments and tested. The changes are progressed through a series of test stages, and are only made available for use in important environments after passing all of them.

The VCS is a single source of truth. If two different team members check out files and work on changes to the infrastructure, they could make incompatible changes. For example, I might add configuration for an application server while Jim is making a firewall rule change that happens to block access to my server. If we each apply our change directly to the infrastructure, we have no visibility of what the other is doing. We may reapply our changes to try to force what we want, but we'll keep undoing each other's work.

But if we each need to commit our change in order for it to be applied, then we will quickly understand how our changes have conflicted. The current state of the files in the VCS are an accurate representation of what's being applied to our infrastructure.

If we use continuous integration to automatically apply our changes to test infrastructure every time we commit, then we'll be notified as soon as someone makes a change that breaks something. And if we have good habits of pulling the latest changes before we commit our own changes, then the second person to commit will discover (before they commit) that someone has changed something that may affect their own work.

Workflows for infrastructure teams are discussed in more detail in Chapter 13.

Configuration Definition Files

"Configuration definition file" is a generic term for the tool-specific files used to drive infrastructure automation tools. Most tools seem to have their own names: playbooks, cookbooks, manifests, templates, and so on. A configuration definition could be any one of these, or even a configuration file or script.

System administrators have been using scripts to automate infrastructure management tasks for decades. General-purpose scripting languages like Bash, Perl, Powershell, Ruby, and Python are still an essential part of an infrastructure team's toolkit.

But the newer generation of infrastructure tools provide their own DSLs (domain-specific languages, as mentioned earlier), which are specialized for a particular purpose. Server configuration tools like CFEngine, Puppet, and Chef have languages that are focused on what goes onto a server. Infrastructure definition tools like Cloud Formation, Heat, and Terraform have languages that are tailored for specifying high-level infrastructure elements and relationships. Packer has a language specifically for defining how to build server images.

Example 3-1 defines a user account. A server configuration tool will read this definition and ensure that it exists on the relevant server, and that is has the specified attributes.

Example 3-1. Configuration definition for a user account

```
user "spock"
  state active
  gid   "science"
  home  "/home/spock"
  shell "/bin/sh"
```

Defining the user account in a definition file has several advantages over writing a script to explicitly create the account.

One advantage is clarity. The definition is easy to understand, as it only contains the key information for the user account, rather than embedding it within scripting logic. This makes it easier to understand and easier to find errors.

Another advantage is that the logic for applying each type of change is separated and reusable. Most configuration tools have an extensive library of definition types for things like managing user accounts, software packages, files and directories, and many other things. These are written to be comprehensive, so that out of the box they do the right thing across different operating systems, distributions, and versions. They tend to have options for handling the various systems an infrastructure team may use—for example, different authentication systems for users, network filesystem mounts, and DNS.

This prebuilt logic saves infrastructure teams from the work of writing fairly standard logic themselves and tends to be well written and well tested. Even if the off-the-shelf definition types available from a tool aren't enough, almost all of these tools allow teams to write their own custom definitions and implementations.

Reusability with Configuration Definitions

The ability to reuse a configuration definition across elements and environments is essential for a consistent infrastructure and repeatable processes. Rather than having three different definition files for the QA, staging, and production environments, the same definition file should be used for all three. Any reasonable DSL for infrastructure configuration should have a way to use parameters.

Example 3-2 takes parameters for which size of VM to create, which AMI image to use to create the server, and the name of the environment the web server will run in.

Example 3-2. Parameterized environment definition

```
aws_instance: web_server
  name: web-${var.environment}
  ami: ${var.web_server_ami}
  instance_type: ${var.instance_type}
```

There may be different methods to pass parameters into the infrastructure tool when it applies this definition. It could take command-line arguments, environment variables, or read the parameters from a file or configuration registry service (as described later in this chapter).

Parameters should be set in a consistent, repeatable way, rather than being entered manually on a command line. When using a change management pipeline, the pipeline orchestration tool (e.g., a CI or CD server like Jenkins or GoCD) can be used to set parameters for each stage of the pipeline. Alternatively, parameters may be managed in a configuration registry.

Working with Infrastructure Definition Tools

Now that we've covered general guidelines for infrastructure as code tools, we can dig more deeply into the specifics. Sometimes called infrastructure orchestration tools, these tools are used to define, implement, and update IT infrastructure architecture. The infrastructure is specified in configuration definition files. The tool uses these definitions to provision, modify, or remove elements of the infrastructure so that it matches the specification. It does this by integrating with the dynamic infrastructure platform's APIs (as discussed in the previous chapter).

Examples of infrastructure definition tools that work this way include AWS Cloud Formation (*https://aws.amazon.com/cloudformation/*), HashiCorp Terraform (*https://terraform.io/*), OpenStack Heat (*https://wiki.openstack.org/wiki/Heat*), and Chef Provisioning (*https://github.com/chef/chef-provisioning*).[2]

Many teams use procedural scripts to provision infrastructure, especially those who started working this way before more standard tools emerged. These can be shell or batch scripts that call CLI tools to interact with the infrastructure platform—for example, AWS CLI (*https://aws.amazon.com/cli/*) for AWS. Or they might be written in a general-purpose language with a library to use the infrastructure platform API. These could be Ruby scripts using the Fog library (*http://fog.io*), Python scripts with the Boto (*http://boto3.readthedocs.org*) library, or Golang scripts with the AWS SDK for Go (*http://aws.amazon.com/sdk-for-go*) or Google Cloud library (*https://godoc.org/google.golang.org/cloud*).

---

2 As with many of the tools described in this book, infrastructure definition tools are evolving quickly, so the list of tools is likely to change by the time you read this.

Definition of "Provisioning"

"Provisioning" is a term that can be used to mean somewhat different things. In this book, provisioning is used to mean making an infrastructure element such as a server or network device ready for use. Depending on what is being provisioned, this can involve:

- Assigning resources to the element
- Instantiating the element
- Installing software onto the element
- Configuring the element
- Registering the element with infrastructure services

At the end of the provisioning process, the element is fully ready for use.

"Provisioning" is sometimes used to refer to a more narrow part of this process. For instance, Terraform and Vagrant both use it to define the callout to a server configuration tool like Chef or Puppet to configure a server after it has been created.

Provisioning Infrastructure with Procedural Scripts

On one team, we wrote our own command-line tool in Ruby to standardize our server provisioning process on Rackspace Cloud. We called the tool "spin," as in, "spin up a server." The script took a few command-line arguments so that it could be used to create a few different types of servers in different environments. An early version of the script shown in Example 3-3 would be run like this to create an application server in our QA environment:

```
# spin qa app
```

Our spin script included the logic for defining what a server of type "appserver" should be: what size, what starting image to use, and so on. It also used "qa" to select details about the environment the server should be added into. Whenever we needed to change the specification for a particular server type or environment, we would edit the script to make the change, and all new servers would consistently be created according to the new specification.

Example 3-3. Script to provision a server based on type and environment

```
#!/usr/bin/env ruby

require 'aws-sdk'
require 'yaml'

usage = 'spin <qa|stage|prod> <web|app|db>'
```

```ruby
abort("Wrong number of arguments. Usage: #{usage}") unless ARGV.size == 2
environment = ARGV[0]
server_type = ARGV[1]

#
# Set subnet_id based on the environment defined on the command line.
# The options are hardcoded in this script.
subnet_id = case environment
when 'qa'
  'subnet-12345678'
when 'stage'
  'subnet-abcdabcd'
when 'prod'
  'subnet-a1b2c3d4'
else
  abort("Unknown environment '#{environment}'. Usage: #{usage}")
end

#
# Set the AMI image ID based on the server type specified on the command line.
# Again, the options are hardcoded here.
image_id = case server_type
when 'web'
  'ami-87654321'
when 'app'
  'ami-dcbadcba'
when 'db'
  'ami-4d3c2b1a'
else
  abort("Unknown server type '#{server_type}'. Usage: #{usage}")
end

#
# Use the AWS Ruby API to create the new server
ec2 = Aws::EC2::Client.new(region: 'eu-west-1')
resp = ec2.run_instances(
  image_id: image_id,
  min_count: 1,
  max_count: 1,
  key_name: 'my-key',
  instance_type: 't2.micro',
  subnet_id: subnet_id
)

#
# Print the server details returned by the API
puts resp.data[:instances].first.to_yaml
```

This met our requirement for a repeatable, transparent process. The decisions of how to create the server—how much RAM to allocate, what OS to install, and what subnet to assign it to—were all captured in a transparent way, rather than needing us to decide each time we created a new server. The "spin" command was simple enough to use in scripts and tools that trigger actions, such as our CI server, so it worked well as part of automated processes.

Over time, we moved the information about the server types and environments into configuration files, called *servers.yml* and *environments.yml*, respectively. This meant we needed to change the script itself less often. We only needed to make sure it was installed on the workstations or servers that needed to run it. Our focus was then on putting the right things into the configuration file, and treating those as artifacts to track, test, and promote.

Interestingly, by changing our scripts to make use of configuration files like *servers.yml* and *environments.yml*, we were moving toward declarative definitions.

Defining Infrastructure Declaratively

Splitting definitions into their own files encourages moving away from needing to think about provisioning procedurally, such as "first do X, then do Y." Instead, definition files can be declarative, such as "should be Z."

Procedural languages are useful for tasks where it's important to understand how something should be done. Declarative definitions are useful when it's more important to understand what you want. The logic of how it is done becomes the responsibility of the tool that reads the definition and applies it.

Declarative definitions are nicely suited to infrastructure configuration. You can specify how you would like things to be: the packages that should be installed, user accounts that should be defined, and files that should exist. The tool then makes the system match your specification.

You don't need to worry about the state of the system before the tool runs. The file may not exist. Or maybe it exists, but has a different owner or permissions. The tool includes all of the logic to figure out what changes need to be made, and what to leave alone.

So declarative definitions lend themselves to running idempotently. You can safely apply your definitions over and over again, without thinking about it too much. If something is changed to a system outside of the tool, applying the definition will bring it back into line, eliminating sources of configuration drift. When you need to make a change, you simply modify the definition, and then let the tooling work out what to do.

Example 3-4 shows a declarative Terraform configuration file that could be used instead of my earlier procedural spin script to create web servers. The definition uses a variable named environment to set the subnet for the servers.

Example 3-4. Terraform configuration file

```
variable "environment" {
  type = "string"
}

variable "subnets" {
  type = "map"

  default = {
    qa = "subnet-12345678"
    stage = "subnet-abcdabcd"
    prod = "subnet-a1b2c3d4"
  }
}

resource "aws_instance" "web" {
  instance_type = "t2.micro"
  ami = "ami-87654321"
  subnet_id = "${lookup(var.subnets, var.environment)}"
}
```

The difference between this definition and the spin script is what happens when you run it multiple times with the same arguments. If you run the spin script five times specifying the same environment and the web server role, it will create five identical web servers. If you apply the Terraform definition five times, it will only create one web server.

Using Infrastructure Definition Tools

Most infrastructure definition tools use a command-line tool to apply a configuration definition. For example, if the example Terraform definition was saved to a file called *web_server.tf*, the command-line tool to create or update it would be run using a command like this:

```
# terraform apply -var environment=qa web_server.tf
```

Infrastructure team members can run the tool from their local workstations or laptops, but it's better to have it run unattended. Running the tool interactively is handy for testing changes to the infrastructure, by applying it to a personal sandbox instance of the infrastructure. But the definition file should then be committed to the VCS, and a CI or CD server agent should automatically apply and test the updated configuration to relevant environments. See Chapter 12 for more details on this.

Configuring Servers

An infrastructure definition tool will create servers but isn't responsible for what's on the server itself. So the definition tool declares that there are two web servers, but

---

does not install the web server software or configuration files onto them. The next chapter covers tools and approaches for configuring servers.[3]

But the infrastructure definition tool often needs to pass configuration information to a server configuration tool when creating a server. For example, it may specify the server's role so the configuration tool installs the relevant software and configuration. It may pass network configuration details such as DNS server addresses.

Example 3-5 runs Chef on the newly created web server. The `run_list` argument specifies the Chef role to apply, which Chef uses to run a certain set of cookbooks. The `attributes_json` argument passes configuration parameters to Chef in the JSON format that it prefers. In this case, it is passing an array with two IP addresses for the DNS servers. One of the Chef cookbooks that is run will presumably use these parameters to build the server's */etc/resolv.conf* file.

Example 3-5. Passing configuration to Chef from Terraform

```
resource "aws_instance" "web" {
  instance_type = "t2.micro"
  ami = "ami-87654321"

  provisioner "chef"  {
    run_list = [ "role::web_server" ]
    attributes_json = {
      "dns_servers": [
        "192.168.100.2",
        "192.168.101.2"
      ]
    }
  }
}
```

Another way to provide configuration information to servers is through a configuration registry.

Configuration Registries

A configuration registry is a directory of information about the elements of an infrastructure. It provides a means for scripts, tools, applications, and services to find the information they need in order to manage and integrate with infrastructure. This is particularly useful with dynamic infrastructure because this information changes continuously as elements are added and removed.

---

3 In practice, some tools, such as Ansible, can fill the role of defining infrastructure and also define the contents of the server. But in this book, I'm describing these responsibilities separately.

For example, the registry could hold a list of the application servers in a load balanced pool. The infrastructure definition tool would add new servers to the registry when it creates them and remove them when the servers are destroyed. One tool might use this information to ensure the VIP configuration in the load balancer is up to date. Another might keep the monitoring server configuration up to date with the list of these servers.

There are different ways to implement a configuration registry. For simpler infrastructures, the configuration definition files used by the definition tool may be enough. When the tool is run, it has all of the information it needs within the configuration definitions. However, this doesn't scale very well. As the number of things managed by the definition files grows, having to apply them all at once can become a bottleneck for making changes.

There are many configuration registry products. Some examples include Zookeeper (*https://zookeeper.apache.org/*), Consul (*https://www.consul.io/*), and etcd (*https://github.com/coreos/etcd*). Many server configuration tool vendors provide their own configuration registry—for example, Chef Server, PuppetDB, and Ansible Tower. These products are designed to integrate easily with the configuration tool itself, and often with other elements such as a dashboard.

In order to work well with a dynamic infrastructure, the configuration registry service must support programmatically adding, updating, and removing entries from the registry.

Lightweight Configuration Registries

Rather than using a configuration registry server, many teams implement a lightweight configuration registry using files stored in a central, shared location, such as an object store like an AWS S3 bucket or a VCS. The files can then be made available using off-the-shelf static web hosting tools.

A variation of this is packaging configuration settings into system packages, such as a *.deb* or *.rpm* file, and pushing them to an internal APT or YUM repository. The settings can then be pulled to local servers using the normal package management tools.

These lightweight approaches for implementing a configuration registry take advantage of mature, off-the-shelf tooling, such as web servers and package management repositories. These are simple to manage, fault tolerant, and easy to scale. Registry files can be versioned in a VCS and then distributed, cached, and promoted following infrastructure as code practices. There may be some complexity in handling frequent updates from large infrastructures, but these can often be managed by splitting or sharding registry files.

Pitfall: Tight Coupling with the Configuration Registry

A heavily used registry can become a source of tight coupling and/or brittleness. It can be unclear which scripts and services depend on a given entry in the registry. Changing the format of an entry, or removing ones that no longer seem necessary, can cause unexpected breakages. This in turn leads to hesitation to make changes to the registry, until it grows into a fragile, overly complicated mess.

For example, I once had a provisioning script add entries for web servers to the registry under the key `/environments/${environment}/web-servers/${servername}`. This was used by another script that configured load balancers to add and remove web servers from a VIP so that it matched the entries under this key. Later on, I changed these scripts to use a key under an entry for each server, like: `/servers/${servername}/environment=${environment}` and `/servers/${servername}/pool=web-servers`. I changed the load balancer configuration script to use this structure, and I changed the provisioning script to put an entry there, no longer creating the original key.

What I hadn't known was that a colleague had written a script to automatically update monitoring checks for web servers, using the original key structure. After I made my change, because the old registry keys no longer existed, the web server monitoring checks were automatically removed. None of us noticed the problem at first, as the monitoring checks simply disappeared. It was over a week later that someone noticed the missing checks, and it took nearly a day to investigate to figure out what had happened.

Good design and communication can help to avoid this kind of problem. Automated testing can help as well. Some variation of consumer-driven contract (CDC) testing (as described in "Practice: Run Consumer-Driven Contract (CDC) Tests" on page 255) could have helped here. People who write scripts that make use of the registry could write simple tests that raise an alert when registry structures and formats they rely on have changed.

Is a Configuration Registry a CMDB?

The concept of a configuration management database (CMDB) pre-dates the rise of automated, dynamic infrastructure. A CMDB is a database of IT assets, referred to as configuration items (CI), and relationships between those assets. It is many ways similar to a configuration registry: they're both databases listing the stuff in an infrastructure.

But a CMDB and a configuration registry are used to address two different core problems. Although they handle overlapping concerns, they do it in very different ways. For these reasons, it's worth discussing them as separate things.

A configuration registry is designed to allow automation tools to share data about things in the infrastructure so that they can dynamically modify their configuration based on the current state of things. It needs a programmable API, and the infrastructure team should use it in a way that guarantees it is always an accurate representation of the state of the infrastructure.

CMDBs were originally created to track IT assets. What hardware, devices, and software licenses do you own, where are they used, and what are they used for? In my distant youth, I built a CMDB with a spreadsheet and later moved it into a Microsoft Access database. We managed the data by hand, and this was fine because it was the iron age, when everything was built by hand, and things didn't change very often.

So these are the two different directions that configuration registries and CMDBs come from: sharing data to support automation, and recording information about assets.

But in practice, CMDB products, especially those sold by commercial vendors, do more than just track assets. They can also discover and track details about the software and configuration of things in an infrastructure, to make sure that everything is consistent and up to date. They even use automation to do this.

An advanced CMDB can continuously scan your network, discover new and unknown devices, and automatically add them to its database. It can log into servers or have agents installed on them, so it can inventory everything on every server. It will flag issues like software that needs to be patched, user accounts that should not be installed, and out-of-date configuration files.

So a CMDB aims to address the same concerns as infrastructure as code, and they even use automation to do it. However, their approach is fundamentally different.

The CMDB Audit and Fix Antipattern

The CMDB approach to ensuring infrastructure is consistent and compliant is reactive. It emphasizes reporting which elements of the infrastructure have been incorrectly or inconsistently configured so that they can be corrected. This assumes infrastructure will be routinely misconfigured, which is common with manually driven processes.

The problem is that resolving these inconsistencies adds a constant stream of work for the team. Every time a server is created or changed, new work items are added to fix them. This is obviously wasteful and tedious.

The Infrastructure-as-Code Approach to CMDB

The infrastructure-as-code approach is to ensure that all servers are provisioned consistently to start with. Team members should not be making ad hoc decisions when they provision a new server, or when they change an existing server. Everything should be driven through the automation. If a server needs to be built differently, then the automation should be changed to capture the difference.

This doesn't address 100% of the concerns addressed by a CMDB, although it does simplify what a CMDB needs to do. Here are some guidelines for handling CMDB concerns when managing an infrastructure as code:

- Make sure everything is built by automation and so is recorded correctly and accurately.

- If you need to track assets, consider using a separate database for this and have your automation update it. This should be kept very simple.

- Your automation should accurately record and report your use of commercial software licenses in the configuration registry. A process can report on license usage, and alert when you are out of compliance, or when you have too many unused licenses.

- Use scanning to find and report on things that were not built and configured by your automation. Then either remove them (if they don't belong) or else add them to the automation and rebuild them correctly.

For example, you can have scripts that use your infrastructure provider API to list all resources (all servers, storage, network configurations, etc.) and compare this with your configuration registry. This will catch errors in your configuration (e.g., things not being added correctly to the registry), as well as things being done outside the proper channels.

Conclusion

Defining infrastructure as code is the basis for managing infrastructure so that changes can be made routinely, safely, and reliably.

This chapter has discussed the types of tools to manage high-level infrastructure according to the principles and practices of infrastructure as code. Later, Chapter 9 will build on the concepts described in this chapter to suggest patterns and techniques for designing and organizing infrastructure at a high level, using the types of tools described in this chapter. But the next chapter will continue exploring tooling, moving down to tools for configuring servers.

## CHAPTER 4

Server Configuration Tools

Using scripts and automation to create, provision, and update servers is not especially new, but a new generation of tools has emerged over the past decade or so. CFEngine, Puppet, Chef, Ansible, and others define this category of tooling. Virtualization and cloud has driven the popularity of these tools by making it easy to create large numbers of new server instances which then need to be configured and updated.

Containerization tools such as Docker have emerged even more recently as a method for packaging, distributing, and running applications and processes. Containers bundle elements of the operating system with the application, which has implications for the way that servers are provisioned and updated.

As mentioned in the previous chapter, not all tools are designed to treat infrastructure as code. The guidelines from that chapter for selecting tools apply equally well to server configuration tools; they should be scriptable, run unattended, and use externalized configuration.

This chapter describes how server automation tools designed for infrastructure as code work. This includes different approaches that tools can take and different approaches that teams can use to implement these tools for their own infrastructure.

 Patterns for Managing Servers

Several of the chapters in Part II build on the material covered in this chapter. Chapter 6 discusses general patterns and approaches for provisioning servers, Chapter 7 explores ways of managing server templates in more depth, and then Chapter 8 discusses patterns for managing changes to servers.

Goals for Automated Server Management

Using infrastructure as code to manage server configuration should result in the following:

- A new server can be completely provisioned[1] on demand, without waiting more than a few minutes.

- A new server can be completely provisioned without human involvement—for example, in response to events.

- When a server configuration change is defined, it is applied to servers without human involvement.

- Each change is applied to all the servers it is relevant to, and is reflected in all new servers provisioned after the change has been made.

- The processes for provisioning and for applying changes to servers are repeatable, consistent, self-documented, and transparent.

- It is easy and safe to make changes to the processes used to provision servers and change their configuration.

- Automated tests are run every time a change is made to a server configuration definition, and to any process involved in provisioning and modifying servers.

- Changes to configuration, and changes to the processes that carry out tasks on an infrastructure, are versioned and applied to different environments, in order to support controlled testing and staged release strategies.

Tools for Different Server Management Functions

In order to understand server management tooling, it can be helpful to think about the lifecycle of a server as having several phases (shown in Figure 4-1).

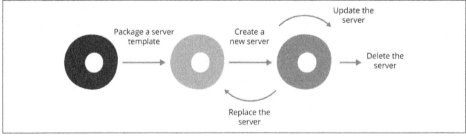

Figure 4-1. A server's lifecycle

---

1 See Definition of "Provisioning" in Chapter 3 for clarity on how I use the term in this book.

This lifecycle will be the basis for discussing different server management patterns, starting in Chapter 6.

This section will explore the tools involved in this lifecycle. There are several functions, some of which apply to more than one lifecycle phase. The functions discussed in this section are creating servers, configuring servers, packaging templates, and running commands on servers.

Tools for Creating Servers

A new server is created by the dynamic infrastructure platform using an infrastructure definition tool, as described in the previous chapter. The server is created from a server template, which is a base image of some kind. This might be in a VM image format specific to the infrastructure platform (e.g., an AWS AMI image or VMware VM template), or it could be an OS installation disk image from a vendor (e.g., an ISO image of the Red Hat installation DVD). Most infrastructure platforms allow servers to be created interactively with a UI, as in Figure 4-2. But any important server should be created automatically.

Figure 4-2. AWS web console for creating a new server

There are many use cases where new servers are created:

- A member of the infrastructure team needs to build a new server of a standard type—for example, adding a new file server to a cluster. They change an infrastructure definition file to specify the new server.

- A user wants to set up a new instance of a standard application—for example, a bug-tracking application. They use a self-service portal, which builds an application server with the bug-tracking software installed.

- A web server VM crashes because of a hardware issue. The monitoring service detects the failure and triggers the creation of a new VM to replace it.

- User traffic grows beyond the capacity of the existing application server pool, so the infrastructure platform's autoscaling functionality creates new application servers and adds them to the pool to meet the demand.

- A developer commits a change to the software they are working on. The CI software (e.g., Jenkins or GoCD) automatically provisions an application server in a test environment with the new build of the software so it can run an automated test suite against it.

Tools for Configuring Servers

Ansible, CFEngine, Chef, Puppet, and Saltstack are examples of tools specifically designed for configuring servers with an infrastructure-as-code approach. They use externalized configuration definition files, with a DSL designed for server configuration. The tool reads the definitions from these files and applies the relevant configuration to a server.

Many server configuration tools use an agent installed on each server. The agent runs periodically, pulling the latest definitions from a central repository and applying them to the server. This is how both Chef and Puppet are designed to work in their default use case.[2]

Other tools use a push model, where a central server triggers updates to managed servers. Ansible uses this model by default, using SSH keys to connect to server and run commands.[3] This has the advantage of not requiring managed servers to have configuration agents installed on them, but arguably sacrifices security. Chapter 8 discusses these models in more detail.

---

2 It is perfectly possible to use Chef or Puppet in a pull model, for example, by having a central server run an ssh command to connect to servers and run the client command-line tool.

3 Although Ansible's main use case is the push model, it can also be run in a pull model, as described in a blog post by Jan-Piet Mens (*http://jpmens.net/2012/07/14/ansible-pull-instead-of-push/*).

Security Trade-Offs with Automated Server Configuration Models

A centralized system that controls how all of your servers are configured creates a wonderful opportunity for evil-doers. Push-based configuration opens ports on your servers, which an attacker can potentially use to connect. An attacker might impersonate the configuration master and feed the target server configuration definitions that will open the server up for malicious use. It could even allow an attacker to execute arbitrary commands. Cryptographic keys are normally used to prevent this, but this requires robust key management.

A pull model simplifies security, but of course there are still opportunities for evil. The attack vector in this case is wherever the client pulls its configuration definitions from. If an attacker can compromise the repository of definitions, then they can gain complete control of the managed servers.

In any case, the VCS used to store scripts and definitions is a critical part of your infrastructure's attack surface, and so must be part of your security strategy. The same is true if you use a CI or CD server to implement a change management pipeline, as described in Chapter 12.

Security concerns with infrastructure as code are discussed in more detail in "Security" on page 298.

Server configuration products have wider toolchains beyond basic server configuration. Most have repository servers to manage configuration definitions—for example, Chef Server, Puppetmaster, and Ansible Tower. These may have additional functionality, providing configuration registries, CMDBs, and dashboards. Chapter 5 discusses broader infrastructure orchestration services of this type.

Arguably, choosing a vendor that provides an all-in-one ecosystem of tools simplifies things for an infrastructure team. However, it's useful if elements of the ecosystem can be swapped out for different tools so the team can choose the best pieces that fit their needs.

Tools for Packaging Server Templates

In many cases, new servers can be built using off-the-shelf server template images. Infrastructure platforms, such as IaaS clouds, often provide template images for common operating systems. Many also offer libraries of templates built by vendors and third parties, who may provide images that have been preinstalled and configured for particular purposes, such as application servers.

But many infrastructure teams find it useful to build their own server templates. They can pre-configure them with their team's preferred tools, software, and configuration.

Packaging common elements onto a template makes it faster to provision new servers. Some teams take this further by creating server templates for particular roles such as web servers and application servers. Chapter 7 discusses trade-offs and patterns around baking server elements into templates versus adding them when creating servers ("Provisioning Servers Using Templates" on page 118).

One of the key trade-offs is that, as more elements are managed by packaging them into server templates, the templates need to be updated more often. This then requires more sophisticated processes and tooling to build and manage templates.

Unikernel Server Templates

A server template is normally built by starting a server with an existing template or OS image, customizing its contents, then storing it as a server image. However, a Unikernel (*https://en.wikipedia.org/wiki/Unikernel*) is an OS image that is custom-compiled with the application it will run. The image only includes the parts of the OS kernel needed for the application, so is small and fast. This image is run directly as a VM or container (see later in this chapter) but has a single address space.

Netflix pioneered approaches for building server templates with everything pre-packaged. They open sourced the tool they created for building AMI templates an AWS, Aminator (*https://github.com/Netflix/aminator*).[4]

Aminator is fairly specific to Netflix's needs, limited to building CentOS/Red Hat servers for the AWS cloud. But HashiCorp has released the open source Packer (*http://packer.io*) tool, which supports a variety of operating systems as well as different cloud and virtualization platforms. Packer defines server templates using a file format that is designed following the principles of infrastructure as code.

Different patterns and practices for building server templates using these kinds of tools are covered in detail in Chapter 7.

Tools for Running Commands on Servers

Tools for running commands remotely across multiple machines can be helpful for teams managing many servers. Remote command execution tools like MCollective,

---

4 Netflix described their approach to using AMI templates in this blog post (*http://techblog.netflix.com/2013/03/ami-creation-with-aminator.html*).

Fabric, and Capistrano can be used for ad hoc tasks such as investigating and fixing problems, or they can be scripted to automate routine activities. Example 4-1 shows an example of an MCollective command.

Some people refer to this kind of tool as "SSH-in-a-loop." Many of them do use SSH to connect to target machines, so this isn't completely inaccurate. But they typically have more advanced features as well, to make it easier to script them, to define groupings of servers to run commands on, or to integrate with other tools.

Although it is useful to be able to run ad hoc commands interactively across servers, this should only be done for exceptional situations. Manually running a remote command tool to make changes to servers isn't reproducible, so isn't a good practice for infrastructure as code.

Example 4-1. Sample MCollective command

```
$ mco service httpd restart -S "environment=staging and /apache/"
```

If people find themselves routinely using interactive tools, they should consider how to automate the tasks they're using them for. The ideal is to put it into a configuration definition if appropriate. Tasks that don't make sense to run unattended can be scripted in the language offered by the team's preferred remote command tool.

The danger of using scripting languages with these tools is that over time they can grow into a complicated mess. Their scripting languages are designed for fairly small scripts and lack features to help manage larger codebases in a clean way, such as reusable, shareable modules. Server configuration tools are designed to support larger codebases, so they are more appropriate.

General Scripting Languages

The usefulness of specialized tools for server configuration doesn't mean there's no role for general-purpose scripting languages. Every infrastructure team I've known needs to write custom scripts. There are always ad hoc tasks that need a bit of logic, like a script that scrapes information from different servers to find out which ones need a particular patch. There are little tools and utilities to make life easier, as well as plug-ins and extensions to standard tools.

It's important for an infrastructure team to build up and continuously improve their skills with scripting. Learn new languages, learn better techniques, learn new libraries and frameworks. Not only does this help you make tools for yourselves, it also enables you to dig into the code of open source tools to understand how they work, fix bugs, and make improvements you can contribute to improve the tools for everyone.

Many teams tend to focus on a particular language, even standardizing on one for building tools. There's a balance to keep with this. On the one hand, it's good to build

---

up deep expertise in a language, and to ensure that everyone on the team can understand, maintain, and improve in-house tools and scripts.

But on the other hand, broadening your expertise means you have more options to apply to a given problem: one language may be better at working with text and data, and another may have a more powerful library for working with your cloud vendor API. A more polyglot[5] team is able to work more deeply with a wider variety of tools.

I prefer to maintain a balance, having one or two "go-to" languages, but being open to experiment with new ones.

I like the way John Allspaw of Etsy put it in an interview (*http://bit.ly/1spVZaN*), "We want to prefer a small number of well-known tools." Although Allspaw is specifically talking about databases at that point of the interview, he is describing the Etsy team's approach to diversity versus standardization of tools and technologies.

The pitfall is having tools written in a variety of languages that nobody really understands well. When these underpin core services in the infrastructure, they become snowflake scripts that people are afraid to touch, in which case it's time to rewrite them in one of the team's core languages.

It should go without saying by now that all of the scripts, tools, utilities, and libraries the team develops should be managed in a version control system.

Using Configuration from a Central Registry

Chapter 3 described using a configuration registry to manage information about different elements of an infrastructure. Server configuration definitions can read values from a configuration registry in order to set parameters (as described in "Reusability with Configuration Definitions" on page 49).

For example, a team running VMs in several data centers may want to configure monitoring agent software on each VM to connect to a monitoring server running in the same data center. The team is running Chef, so they add these attributes to the Chef server as shown in Example 4-2.

Example 4-2. Using Chef server attributes as configuration registration entries

```
default['monitoring']['servers']['sydney'] = 'monitoring.au.myco'
default['monitoring']['servers']['dublin'] = 'monitoring.eu.myco'
```

When a new VM is created, it is given a registry field called *data_center*, which is set to *dublin* or *sydney*.

---

5 Neal Ford coined the term "polyglot programming." See this interview (*http://oreil.ly/1A6lWsO*) with Neal for more about it.

When the chef-client runs on a VM, it runs the recipe in Example 4-3 to configure the monitoring agent.

Example 4-3. Using configuration registry entries in a Chef recipe

```
my_datacenter = node['data_center']
template '/etc/monitoring/agent.conf' do
  owner 'root'
  group 'root'
  mode 0644
  variables(
    :monitoring_server => node['monitoring']['servers'][my_datacenter]
  )
end
```

The Chef recipe retrieves values from the Chef server configuration registry with the `node['attribute_name']` syntax. In this case, after putting the name of the data center into the variable `my_datacenter`, that variable is then used to retrieve the monitoring server's IP address for that data center. This address is then passed to the template (not shown here) used to create the monitoring agent configuration file.

Server Change Management Models

Dynamic infrastructure and containerization are leading people to experiment with different approaches for server change management. There are several different models for managing changes to servers, some traditional, some new and controversial. These models are the basis for Part II of this book, particularly Chapter 8, which digs into specific patterns and practices.

Ad Hoc Change Management

Ad hoc change management makes changes to servers only when a specific change is needed. This was the traditional approach before the automated server configuration tools became mainstream, and is still the most commonly used approach. It is vulnerable to configuration drift, snowflakes, and all of the evils described in Chapter 1.

Configuration Synchronization

Configuration synchronization repeatedly applies configuration definitions to servers, for example, by running a Puppet or Chef agent on an hourly schedule. This ensures that any changes to parts of the system managed by these definitions are kept in line. Configuration synchronization is the mainstream approach for infrastructure as code, and most server configuration tools are designed with this approach in mind.

The main limitation of this approach is that many areas of a server are left unmanaged, leaving them vulnerable to configuration drift.

Immutable Infrastructure

Immutable infrastructure makes configuration changes by completely replacing servers. Changes are made by building new server templates, and then rebuilding relevant servers using those templates. This increases predictability, as there is little variance between servers as tested, and servers in production. It requires sophistication in server template management.

Containerized Services

Containerized services works by packaging applications and services in lightweight containers (as popularized by Docker). This reduces coupling between server configuration and the things that run on the servers. So host servers tend to be very simple, with a lower rate of change. One of the other change management models still needs to be applied to these hosts, but their implementation becomes much simpler and easier to maintain. Most effort and attention goes into packaging, testing, distributing, and orchestrating the services and applications, but this follows something similar to the immutable infrastructure model, which again is simpler than managing the configuration of full-blown virtual machines and servers.

Containers

Containerization systems such as Docker (*http://docker.io*), Rocket (*https://coreos.com/blog/rocket/*), Warden (*https://docs.cloudfoundry.org/concepts/architecture/warden.html*), and Windows Containers (*https://msdn.microsoft.com/en-us/virtualization/windowscontainers/about/about_overview*) have emerged as an alternative way to install and run applications on servers. A container system is used to define and package a runtime environment for a process into a container image. It can then distribute, create, and run instances of that image. A container uses operating system features to isolate the processes, networking, and filesystem of the container, so it appears to be its own, self-contained server environment.

The value of a containerization system is that it provides a standard format for container images and tools for building, distributing, and running those images. Before Docker, teams could isolate running processes using the same operating system features, but Docker and similar tools make the process much simpler.

The benefits of containerization include:

- Decoupling the runtime requirements of specific applications from the host server that the container runs on
- Repeatably create consistent runtime environments by having a container image that can be distributed and run on any host server that supports the runtime

- Defining containers as code (e.g.,in a Dockerfile) that can be managed in a VCS, used to trigger automated testing, and generally having all of the characteristics for infrastructure as code

---

Not All Containers Are Docker

Docker has popularized the concept of lightweight containers and stolen the lion's share of attention. However, there are several other container implementations available as of early 2016. These include:

- CoreOS rkt (*https://coreos.com/rkt/*)

- CloudFoundry Warden (*https://docs.cloudfoundry.org/concepts/architecture/warden.html*) from Pivotal

- Virtuozzo OpenVZ (*https://openvz.org/Main_Page*) from Odin

- lmctfy (*https://github.com/google/lmctfy*) from Google, which has been discontinued and merged into libcontainer, which is used by Docker[6]

- Bonneville (*http://blogs.vmware.com/cloudnative/introducing-project-bonneville/*) from VMware

---

The benefits of decoupling runtime requirements from the host system are particularly powerful for infrastructure management. It creates a clean separation of concerns between infrastructure and applications. The host system only needs to have the container runtime software installed, and then it can run nearly any container image.[7] Applications, services, and jobs are packaged into containers along with all of their dependencies, as shown in Figure 4-3. These dependencies can include operating system packages, language runtimes, libraries, and system files. Different containers may have different, even conflicting dependencies, but still run on the same host without issues. Changes to the dependencies can be made without any changes to the host system.

---

6 The pace of change in containerization is currently quite fast. In the course of writing this book, I've had to expand coverage from a couple of paragraphs, to a section, and made it one of the main models for managing server configuration. Many of the details I've described will have changed by the time you read this. But hopefully the general concepts, particularly how containers relate to infrastructure-as-code principles and practices, will still be relevant.

7 There is actually some dependency between the host and container. In particular, container instances use the Linux kernel of the host system, so a given image could potentially behave differently, or even fail, when run on different versions of the kernel.

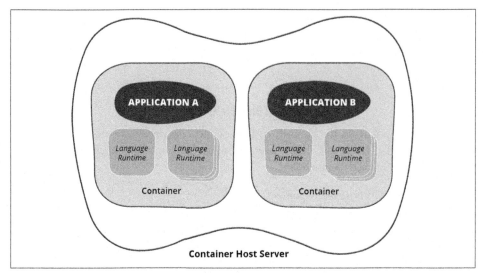

Figure 4-3. Isolating packages and libraries in containers

Managing Ruby Applications with and without Containers

For example, suppose a team runs many Ruby applications. Without containers, the server they run on might need to have multiple versions of the Ruby runtime installed. If one application requires an upgrade, the upgrade needs to be rolled out to any server where the application needs to run.

This could impact other Ruby applications. Those other applications might start running with the newer Ruby version, but may have incompatibilities. Two applications that use the same version of Ruby might use different versions of a library that has been installed as a system gem (a Ruby shared library package). Although both versions of the gem can be installed, making sure each application uses the right version is tricky.

These issues are manageable, but it requires the people configuring the servers and applications to be aware of each requirement and potential conflict and do some work to make everything play nicely. And each new conflict tends to pop up and interrupt people from working on other tasks.

With Docker containers, each of these Ruby applications has its own Dockerfile, which specifies the Ruby version and which gems to bundle into the container image. These images can be deployed and run on a host system that doesn't need to have *any* version of Ruby installed. Each Ruby application has its own runtime environment and can be replaced and upgraded with different dependencies, regardless of the others applications running on the same host.

Example 4-4 is a Dockerfile that packages a Ruby Sinatra application.

Example 4-4. Dockerfile to create a Ruby Sinatra application

```
# Start with a CentOS docker image
FROM    centos:6.4

# Directory of the Sinatra app
ADD . /app

# Install Sinatra
RUN cd /app ; gem install sinatra

# Open the Sinatra port
EXPOSE  4567

# Run the app
CMD ["ruby", "/app/hi.rb"]
```

Are Containers Virtual Machines?

Containers are sometimes described as being a type of virtual machine. There are similarities, in that they give multiple processes running on a single host server the illusion that they are each running in their own, separate servers. But there are significant technical differences. The use case of a container is quite different from that of a virtual machine.

The differences between virtual machines and containers

A host server runs virtual machines using a hypervisor, such as VMware ESX or Xen (which underlies Amazon's EC2 service). A hypervisor is typically installed on the bare metal of the hardware host server, as the operating system. However, some virtualization packages can be installed on top of another operating system, especially those like VMware Workstation and VirtualBox, which are intended to run on desktops.

A hypervisor provides emulated hardware to a VM. Each VM can have different emulated hardware from the host server, and different hardware from one another. Consider a physical server running the Xen hypervisor, with two different VMs. One VM can have an emulated SCSI hard drive, 2 CPUs, and 8 GB of RAM. The other can be given an emulated IDE hard drive, 1 CPU, and 2 GB of RAM. Because the abstraction is at the hardware level, each VM can have a completely different OS installed; for example, you can install CentOS Linux on one, and Windows Server on the other, and run them side by side on the same physical server.

Figure 4-4 shows the relationship between virtual machines and containers. Containers are not virtual servers in this sense. They don't have emulated hardware, and they use the same operating system as their host server, actually running on the same kernel. The system uses operating system features to segregate processes, filesystems, and networking, giving a process running in a container the illusion that it is running on its own. But this is an illusion created by restricting what the process can see, not by emulating hardware resources.

Container instances share the operating system kernel of their host system, so they can't run a different OS. Containers can, however, run different distributions of the same OS—for example, CentOS Linux on one and Ubuntu Linux on another. This is because a Linux distribution is just a different set of files and processes. But these instances would still share the same Linux kernel.

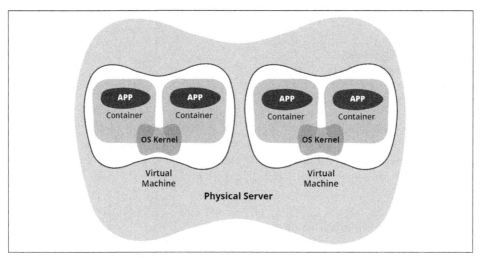

Figure 4-4. Containers and virtual machines

Sharing the OS kernel means a container has less overhead than a hardware virtual machine. A container image can be much smaller than a VM image, because it doesn't need to include the entire OS. It can start up in seconds, as it doesn't need to boot a kernel from scratch. And it consumes fewer system resources, because it doesn't need to run its own kernel. So a given host can run more container processes than full VMs.

Using Containers Rather than Virtual Machines

A naive approach to containers is to build them the same way that you would build a virtual machine image. Multiple processes, services, and agents could all be packaged into a single container and then run the same way you would run a VM. But this misses the sweet spot for containers.

The best way to think of a container is as a method to package a service, application, or job. It's an RPM on steroids, taking the application and adding in its dependencies, as well as providing a standard way for its host system to manage its runtime environment.

Rather than a single container running multiple processes, aim for multiple containers, each running one process. These processes then become independent, loosely coupled entities. This makes containers a nice match for microservice (*http://martin fowler.com/microservices/*) application architectures.[8]

A container built with this philosophy can start up extremely quickly. This is useful for long-running service processes, because it makes it easy to deploy, redeploy, migrate, and upgrade them routinely. But quick startup also makes containers well suited for processes run as jobs. A script can be packaged as a container image with everything it needs to run, and then executed on one or many machines in parallel.

Containers are the next step in the evolution of managing resources across an infrastructure efficiently. Virtualization was one step, allowing you to add and remove VMs to scale your capacity to your load on a timescale of minutes. Containers take this to the next level, allowing you to scale your capacity up and down on a timescale of seconds.[9]

Running Containers

Packaging and running a single application in a container is fairly simple. Using containers as a routine way to run applications, services, and jobs across multiple host servers is more complicated. Container orchestration systems automate the distribution and execution of containers across host systems (Chapter 5 touches on container orchestration in a bit more detail, in "Container Orchestration Tools" on page 92).

Containerization has the potential to create a clean separation between layers of infrastructure and the services and applications that run on it. Host servers that run containers can be kept very simple, without needing to be tailored to the requirements of specific applications, and without imposing constraints on the applications beyond those imposed by containerization and supporting services like logging and monitoring.

So the infrastructure that runs containers consists of generic container hosts. These can be stripped down to a bare minimum, including only the minimum toolsets to run containers, and potentially a few agents for monitoring and other administrative tasks. This simplifies management of these hosts, as they change less often and have fewer things that can break or need updating. It also reduces the surface area for security exploits.

---

8 See my colleague Sam Newman's book *Building Microservices* (*http://bit.ly/building-microservices*) (O'Reilly) for more on microservices.

9 The folks at force12 are doing interesting things with microscaling (*http://blog.force12.io/2015/10/ microscaling-in-box.html*).

Minimal OS Distributions

Container-savvy vendors are offering stripped down OS distributions for running container hosts, such as Red Hat Atomic (*http://red.ht/1r2GUKY/*), CoreOS (*http://bit.ly/25ASYpJ*), Microsoft Nano (*http://bit.ly/1TXII2d*), RancherOS (*http://bit.ly/1TXIwzP*), Ubuntu Snappy (*http://bit.ly/1Xgm09w*), and VMware Photon (*http://vmw.re/1Zd2Pe4*).

Note that these stripped-down OSes are not the same as the earlier mentioned Unikernel. A stripped-down OS combines a full OS kernel with a stripped-down distribution of preinstalled packages and services. A Unikernel actually strips down the OS kernel itself, building one up from a set of libraries and including the application in the kernel's memory space.

Some teams run container hosts as virtual machines on a hypervisor, which is in turn installed on hardware. Others take the next step and remove the hypervisor layer entirely, running the host OS directly on hardware. Which of these approaches to use depends on the context.

Teams that already have hypervisor-based virtualization and infrastructure clouds, but don't have much bare-metal automation, will tend to run containers on VMs. This is especially appropriate when the team is still exploring and expanding their use of containers, and particularly when there are many services and applications running outside of containers. This is likely to be the case for many organizations for some time.

When containerization becomes more routine for an organization, and when significant parts of their services are containerized, teams will probably want to test how well running containers directly on hardware-based hosts. This is likely to become easier as virtualization and cloud platform vendors build support for running containers directly into their hypervisors.

Security and Containers

One concern that is inevitably raised when discussing containers is security. The isolation that containers provide can lead people to assume they offer more inherent security than they actually do. And the model that Docker provides for conveniently building customer containers on top of images from community libraries can open serious vulnerabilities if it isn't managed with care.[10]

---

10 The folks at Docker have published an article on container security (*https://docs.docker.com/articles/security/*) that offers a number of useful insights.

Container isolation and security

While containers isolate processes running on a host from one another, this isolation is not impossible to break. Different container implementations have different strengths and weaknesses. When using containers, a team should be sure to fully understand how the technology works, and where its vulnerabilities may lie.

Teams should be particularly cautious with untrusted code. Containers appear to offer a safe way to run arbitrary code from people outside the organization. For example, a company running hosted software might offer customers the ability to upload and run code on the hosted platform, as a plug-in or extension model. The assumption is that, because the customer's code runs in a container, an attacker won't be able to take advantage of this to gain access to other customers' data, or to the software company's systems.

However, this is a dangerous assumption. Organizations running potentially untrusted code should thoroughly analyze their technology stack and its potential vulnerabilities. Many companies that offer hosted containers actually keep each customer's containers isolated to their own physical servers (not just hypervisor-based virtual machines running the container host). As of late 2015, this is true of the hosted container services run by both Amazon and Google.

So teams should use stronger isolation between containers running untrusted code than the isolation provided by the containerization stack. They should also take measures to harden the host systems, all the way down to the metal. This is another good reason to strip down the host OS to only the minimum needed to run the containerization system. Platform services should ideally be partitioned onto different physical infrastructure from that used to run untrusted code.

Even organizations that don't run arbitrary code from outsiders should take appropriate care to ensure the segregation of code, rather than assuming containers provide fully protected runtime environments. This can make it more difficult for an attacker who compromises one part of the system from leveraging it to widen their access.

Container image provenance

Even when outsiders can't directly run code in containers on your infrastructure, they may be able to do so indirectly. It's common for insiders to download outside code and then package and run it. This is not unique to containers. As will be discussed in "Provenance of Packages" on page 299 in Chapter 14, it's common to automatically download and install system packages and language libraries from community repositories.

Docker and other containerization systems offer the ability to layer container images. Rather than having to take an OS installation image and build a complete container from scratch, you can use common images that have a basic OS install already. Other images offer prepackaged applications such as web servers, application servers, and monitoring agents. Many OS and application vendors are offering this as a distribution mechanism.

A container image for an OS distribution like CentOS, for example, may be maintained by people with deep knowledge of that OS. The maintainers can make sure the image is optimized, tuned, and hardened. They can also make sure updated images are always made available with the latest security patches. Ideally, these maintainers are able to invest more time and expertise in maintaining the CentOS image than the people on an infrastructure team that is supporting a variety of systems, servers, and software. Spreading this model out over the various pieces of software used by the infrastructure team means the team is able to leverage a great deal of industry expertise.

The risk is when there aren't sufficient guarantees of the provenance of container base images used in a team's infrastructure. An image published on a public repository may be maintained by responsible, honest experts, or it could have been put there by evil hackers or the NSA. Even if the maintainers are well intentioned, someone evil could have compromised their work, adding subtle back doors.

While community-provided container images aren't inherently less trustworthy than community-provided RPMs or RubyGems, their growing popularity emphasizes the need to manage all of these things carefully. Teams should ensure the provenance of each image used within the infrastructure is well known, trusted, and can be verified and traced. Containerization tool vendors are building mechanisms to automatically validate the provenance of images.[11] Teams should ensure that they understand how these mechanisms work and that they are being properly used.

Conclusion

The intention of this chapter was to understand several different high-level models for managing individual servers and how these models relate to the types of tooling available. Hopefully it will help you consider how your team could go about provisioning and configuring servers.

---

11 See "Introducing Docker Content Trust" (*https://blog.docker.com/2015/08/content-trust-docker-1-8/*).

However, before selecting specific tools, it would be a good idea to be familiar with the patterns in Part II of this book. Those chapters provide more detail on specific patterns and practices for provisioning servers, building server templates, and updating running servers.

The next chapter will look at the bigger picture of the infrastructure, exploring the types of tools that are needed to run the infrastructure as a whole.

## CHAPTER 5

General Infrastructure Services

The previous chapters described tools to provide, provision, and configure core infrastructure resources: compute, networking, and storage. These provide the basic building blocks for infrastructure as code. However, most infrastructures will need a variety of other supporting services and tools.

A comprehensive list of these services and tools would be ridiculously large and would probably go out of date before I could finish typing it. Some are needed for the infrastructure itself to function—for example, DNS and monitoring. Others, such as message queues and databases, are required for at least some applications.

The purpose of this chapter isn't to list or explain these services and tools. Instead, it is intended to explain how they should work in the context of a dynamic infrastructure managed as code. This is the subject of the first section of this chapter.

Four key services are then used to illustrate these considerations and because they are particularly valuable in this kind of environment. The services and tools addressed are monitoring, service discovery, distributed process management, and software deployment.

Considerations for Infrastructure Services and Tools

The goals for any service or system that is involved in managing infrastructure are the same as those described for the infrastructure platform, definition tool, and server configuration tool in previous chapters.

The principles of infrastructure as code for services can be summarized as:

- The service can be easily rebuilt or reproduced.
- The elements of the service are disposable.

- The infrastructure elements managed by the service are disposable.
- The infrastructure elements managed by the service are always changing.
- Instances of the service are configured consistently.
- Processes for managing and using the service are repeatable.
- Routine requests are fulfilled quickly, with little effort, preferably through self-service or automatically.
- Complex changes can be made easily and safely.

Some of the specific practices include:

- Use externalized definition files.
- Self-document systems and processes.
- Version all the things.
- Continuously test systems and processes.
- Make small changes rather than batches of them.
- Keep services available continuously.

The previous chapters warned against products that don't naturally support infrastructure as code. Unfortunately, many general infrastructure tools don't work well with dynamic infrastructure, or lend themselves to configuration as code.[1]

The issue is that most products for monitoring, software deployment, and other services have been around since before virtualization was mainstream, much less cloud. So they tend to be built around assumptions that aren't true with dynamic infrastructure.

Issues with legacy infrastructure management software products include:

- Doesn't automatically handle infrastructure elements being added and removed.
- Assumes the product will itself be installed on static servers.
- Requires manual configuration, often driven through a UI.
- Doesn't make it easy to replicate configuration, and changes to configuration, across different instances of the product.
- Difficult to automatically test changes to configuration.

---

[1] This often seems to be inversely related to the price tag of the tool. The more expensive tools tend to have been written in the pre-cloud days. Some of these vendors have struggled to adapt their tools to the new model of infrastructure management. I suspect most are aware of the need to change, but like many of their customers, find it difficult to rebuild established codebases and business models as quickly as they would like.

The following are criteria for selecting infrastructure service products. These build on criteria described in earlier chapters.

Prefer Tools with Externalized Configuration

As with server and infrastructure management tools, externalized definition files can be managed in a VCS, tested and progressed through a pipeline, and can be automatically replicated and rebuilt as needed.

A closed-box tool that can only be configured through a GUI, and possibly an API, risks becoming a snowflake service. A snowflake service that has been handcrafted over time is fragile: difficult to manage and easy to break.

Automating Black Box Configuration

Sometimes a black box tool's configuration can be exported and imported by unattended scripts. This might make it possible to integrate the tool with infrastructure as code, although it will be clumsy. It's certainly not recommended for a core infrastructure tool, but could be useful for a specialized tool that doesn't have a good alternative.

This model has some limitations. It's often difficult to merge changes from different dumps. This means different team members can't work on changes to different parts of the configuration at the same time. People must be careful about making changes to downstream instances of the tool, to avoid conflicts with work being done upstream.

Depending on the format of the configuration dump, it may not be very transparent in that it may not be easy to tell at a glance the differences between one version and the next.

Another way to approach black box configuration is by injecting configuration automatically. Ideally this would be done using an API provided by the tool. However, I have seen it done by automating interaction with the tool's UI—for example, using scripted tools to make HTTP requests and post forms. This tends to be brittle, however, because the UI might change. A properly supported API will keep backward compatibility and so is more reliable.

The configuration injection approach allows configuration to be defined in external files. These may simply be scripts, or could involve a configuration format or DSL. If a tool is configured by automated injection from external files, then this should be the only way configuration changes are made. Changes made through the UI are likely to cause conflicts and inconsistencies.

Prefer Tools That Assume Infrastructure Is Dynamic

Many older infrastructure management products struggle to cope gracefully with a dynamic infrastructure. They were designed in the iron age of infrastructure, when the set of servers was static. In the cloud age, servers are continuously added and removed, often by unattended processes. A tool that needs someone to point and click on a GUI interface every time a new server is added is a liability.

Here are some useful criteria for considering tooling for dynamic infrastructure:

- Ability to gracefully handle infrastructure elements being added and removed, including entire environments
- Support aggregating and viewing historical data across devices, including those that have been removed or replaced by different devices
- Ability to make changes automatically in response to events, without human intervention
- Exposes information about current state and configuration automatically

Many infrastructure services, such as monitoring, need to know the state of servers or other elements of the infrastructure. It should be possible to add, update, and remove infrastructure elements from these services automatically—for example, through a RESTful API.

Prefer Products with Cloud-Compatible Licensing

Licensing can make dynamic infrastructure difficult with some products. Some examples of licensing approaches that work poorly include:

- A manual process to register each new instance, agent, node, etc., for licensing. Clearly, this defeats automated provisioning. If a product's license does require registering infrastructure elements, there needs to be an automatable process for adding *and* removing them.
- Inflexible licensing periods. Some products require customers to buy a fixed set of licenses for a long period. For example, a monitoring tool may have licensing based on the maximum number of nodes that can be monitored. The licenses may need to be purchased on a monthly cycle. This forces the customer to pay for the maximum number of nodes they might use during a given month, even when they only run that number of nodes for a fraction of the time. This cloud-unfriendly pricing model discourages customers from taking advantage of the ability to scale capacity up and down with demand. Vendors pricing for cloud charge by the hour at most.
- Heavyweight purchasing process to increase capacity. This is closely related to the licensing period. When an organization is hit with an unexpected surge in

business, they shouldn't need to spend days or weeks to purchase the extra capacity they need to meet the demand. It's common for vendors to have limits in place to protect customers against accidentally over-provisioning, but it should be possible to raise these limits quickly.

Prefer Products That Support Loose Coupling

It is important to ensure that a change can be made to any part of the infrastructure without requiring widespread changes to other parts. Coupling between parts of the system increases the scope and risk of changes, which leads to making changes less often, and with more fear.

This can be as much about how the organization designs and implements their infrastructure and management services as about the products themselves. Have strong design principles to watch for and avoid implementations that cause teams using infrastructure from interfering with one another. It should be possible for teams to make changes to their own infrastructure without impacting other teams. It takes vigilance and good design to prevent tight coupling from becoming an issue. Pay attention to the signs that parts of your infrastructure are becoming a bottleneck for changes, and aggressively redesign them to reduce friction.

Sharing a Service Between Teams

A common challenge is deciding whether or not a single instance of a given service can be shared between teams using it. Examples of potentially shared services include monitoring, continuous integration (CI), bug tracking, DNS, and artifact repository. The key question is whether multiple teams can share a single instance of a given service without conflicts.

For example, one client of mine uses a popular CI server. Most of the configuration for the server is global across the instance. When one team changes a configuration setting, or installs a plug-in, their change affects all of the other teams using the same CI server. This has become a source of conflict, forcing everyone involved to spend time haggling over their conflicting requirements.

A central group took ownership of the shared CI server's configuration to prevent it from being destabilized. But development teams found that centralized control blocked them from using the CI server to meet their needs. Soon they begin bypassing the central CI team to set up their own CI servers.

On the other hand, the same organization has few problems sharing a VCS service and artifact repository between teams. These tools tend to have simpler use cases, and so it's easier for teams to configure them for their own needs without conflicting with other teams.

Security may also be an issue with shared services. The shared CI server at my client made people nervous because potentially sensitive information used by one team may be visible to other teams. For example, the organization's CI server needed to store database credentials and provide them to a service when automatically deploying it. Many organizations, such as financial institutions, need to limit access to credentials such as these, even inside the organization.

Service Instance Templates

For services that don't cleanly segregate configuration between teams, it's better for each team to have a dedicated instance. They can then tailor the instance's configuration to their own requirements without impacting other teams. Data, credentials, and access can be more effectively segregated.

But running multiple instances of a single service runs the risk of configuration drift for things that should be kept consistent. For example, all of the CI servers may need to integrate with a common authentication service. And version updates should be quickly rolled out to all instances when they become available.

Rather than running a single instance, a central team can provide elements that teams can use to easily build their own instances. This could take the form of a server template and a set of server configuration definitions. They could use Packer to build an AMI with the CI server preinstalled, with plug-ins configured to use the organization's LDAP server. The server could include Puppet modules to keep the system and CI server up to date.

Some questions to consider when deciding whether to share service instances, or support multiple instances:

- Do the customizations that teams need impact other teams using the service instance? If so, multiple instances may be best.

- Can one team's use of the service impact performance for other teams? If so, multiple instances can prevent problems.

- Does the service involve executing code provided by individual teams? Does it effectively isolate the execution environment for this code? (Remember that containers and even VMs don't offer bulletproof isolation between processes!)

- Will the service hold data or credentials that should not be available to all of its users? How strong are the controls to protect this data?

- Is there a compelling need for teams to share data or content between them? In this case, shared instances may be a better fit.

Monitoring: Alerting, Metrics, and Logging

Monitoring is a broad topic and sometimes means different things to different people. System checks send alerts to wake people up at night to fix problems. Dashboards show the current status of applications. Other dashboards show graphs of resource utilization and activity. Databases of events and historical metrics can be searched and analyzed.

The goal of monitoring is to make the right information visible to the people who need it, when they need it. This information can be drawn from various parts of the system, from the core infrastructure, to services, to applications, to business metrics.

Different people need different information in different combinations. And people need information presented in different ways at different times. When the platform is running out of compute resource, the infrastructure team needs to know right away. But they can review trends of compute usage every week or so. A product manager needs to know immediately if a particular product has run out of inventory because of a sudden spike in orders. But normally, a daily summary of purchases and revenues is useful.

Monitoring information comes in two types: state and events. State is concerned with the current situation, whereas an event records actions or changes.[2]

Alerting: Tell Me When Something Is Wrong

As mentioned in Chapter 1, the secret ingredient of an antifragile, self-healing infrastructure is people. Alerts let people know when their attention is needed to prevent or recover from a problem.

End-user service is what really matters, so checking that everything is working correctly from the user's point of view is essential. Active checks can log into a service and carry out key transactions or user journeys. These prove that the end-to-end systems are working correctly and giving the correct results to users.

Indirect monitoring alerts when behavior strays outside the normal boundaries. When business transactions drop by an unusual amount, something may have gone wrong. It could have been caused by a system failure, a critical external dependency like a content distribution network (CDN), or a content issue such as malformed product data.

---

2 My colleague Peter Gillard-Moss has written an article, "Monitor Don't Log" (*http://peter.gillardmoss.me.uk/blog/2013/05/28/monitor-dont-log/*), which has excellent advice on a state-driven approach to designing monitoring.

It's important to ensure that alerts are relevant. Many teams suffer from an endless stream of trivial alerts, which teaches them to ignore the alerting system. A noisy alerting system is useless.

Teams should consider the various types of state and events in their systems and identify actions needed for each. Information that suggests the service has stopped working for users, or is likely to stop working soon, should get someone out of bed immediately. These alerts should be very few, and very easy to recognize.

Some events need human attention but can wait until working hours. Other conditions might indicate a problem, but only need to be looked at if they become frequent. For these, consider recording the condition as a metric, making sure the metric is visible on a dashboard or information radiator. Set alerts to trigger when the metric goes outside of expected bounds.

For example, it is probably fine that the number of web servers in an autoscaling pool grows and shrinks throughout the day. But if it flaps wildly, there may be a problem, or at least it may need to be tuned.

What Is An Information Radiator?

An information radiator (*http://alistair.cockburn.us/Information+radiator*), or a communal dashboard (*http://martinfowler.com/bliki/CommunalDashboard.html*), is a highly visible display of information put up in a team space so everyone can easily see key status information. Agile software development teams use these to show the status of the build in the CI and CD pipeline. Operations teams show the status of services. Cross-functional product teams show both of these, plus indicators of key business metrics.

Information radiators will be ignored unless they show actionable information in a concise way. A useful rule of thumb is that the radiator should make it immediately obvious which of two courses of action to take: (a) carry on with routine work, or (b) shout, stop what you're doing, and take action. Loads of tiny line graphs showing memory usage and CPU utilization doesn't grab anyone's attention. A large block that goes red when the database is about to run out of memory does.

As with alerts, an information radiator that always shows red has no value. If a condition shown on the radiator isn't important enough to fix immediately, then remove it.

An alerting system needs to handle dynamic infrastructure correctly. Nobody wants to be woken up when servers in a cluster are automatically destroyed because usage levels have dropped. But people probably do want to know when a server fails because it ran out of memory.

They might not want to be woken up for this, if the automated recovery keeps everything working for end users. But it should be brought to someone's attention the next day so they can check for underlying issues.

Even when an event doesn't warrant an alert, it is useful to record metrics and make sure unusual fluctuations are made visible to the team. Organizations such as Netflix, with cloud-based estates numbering in hundreds of servers, find that a certain percentage of instances fail during the course of a day. Their infrastructure replaces them without any drama. But having a chart that shows the failures makes the team aware if the number becomes unusually high. For example, a series of failures may be a sign of problems in one of the cloud provider's data centers, in which case the team can shift their resources to other data centers until the problems are resolved.

Metrics: Collect and Analyze Data

Another side of monitoring is collecting data in a database. This kind of data can be analyzed interactively and automatically included in dashboards, schedule reports, and information radiators.

This is another area where dynamic infrastructure makes things tricky for legacy tools. Graphing memory usage on an application server may be useful. But when the application server is replaced several times a week, the data for one server is less useful on its own.

It's useful to aggregate the data for the different application servers that ran a given application instance, so that graphs and reports can give a continuous picture. This requires the monitoring tool to automatically tag these servers as being related.

For example, a graph of CPU utilization across a fluctuating pool of application servers, mapped against the count of the number of servers in the pool, shows how well auto-scaling managed load.

Some monitoring tools don't cope properly with servers that have been removed. They insist on treating the server as *critical*, cluttering dashboards with red status indicators. Removing the server from the monitoring system gives a cleaner picture of the current health but means the data is no longer available for analyzing historical trends. If you run into a monitoring tool that does this, insist the vendor update it for the modern era, or replace it.

Log Aggregation and Analysis

IT infrastructures are awash with log files. Networking devices, servers, and utilities generate logs. Applications write their own log files, and even network devices can log events to syslog servers. One of the side effects of server sprawl is that it can be hard to know where to look to dig into problems. Logfiles kept on a virtual server's filesystem are lost when the server fails or is automatically destroyed.

Centralized log aggregation is a popular solution for this. Servers and devices are configured to send logs to a central storage service, such as a syslog server or Logstash. Tools such as Elasticsearch and Kibana can be added to make it easy to search the aggregated logs, build dashboards based on the activity in them, and raise alerts when bad things appear in them.

While it's no doubt useful to make all of this data available for investigation, it's wise to think about which events need to be used for alerting and for making key metrics visible. Log files are often a messy combination of message strings that are (maybe) meaningful to humans, but difficult for machines to reliably parse, and dumps produced by machines that aren't necessarily meaningful to humans, and probably also not very easy for machines to parse (stack traces spring to mind). Again, these are useful to muck around in when troubleshooting an issue, but they're less useful if you want to reliably detect and report problems or status. Applications and systems should be written and configured to generate more structured messages for automated consumption.

Service Discovery

Applications and services running in an infrastructure often need to know how to find other applications and services. For example, a frontend web application may send requests to a backend service in order to process transactions for users.

This isn't too difficult in a static environment. Applications may use a known hostname for other services, perhaps kept in a configuration file that can be updated as needed.

But with a dynamic infrastructure where the locations of services and servers are fluid, a more responsive way of finding services is needed.

A few popular discovery mechanisms are listed in Table 5-1.

Table 5-1. Common service discovery mechanisms

Mechanism	How	Comments
Fixed IP addresses	Decide on fixed IP addresses for services—for example, the monitoring server is `192.168.1.5`.	Doesn't work with hosting platforms that assign addresses automatically. Complicates replacement of a server, especially with zero downtime replacement strategies (see "Zero-Downtime Changes" on page 282). Doesn't work with resource pools that can vary in size, such as a pool of web servers. Difficult to change, and not very flexible. Not recommended.
Hostfile entries	Use automated configuration to ensure servers have */etc/hosts* files (or equivalent) that map resource server names to their current IP addresses.	Ensuring hostfiles are updated automatically as services change is a complicated way to solve a problem that DNS solved long ago.

Mechanism	How	Comments
DNS	Use DDNS (Dynamic DNS, Domain Name System) servers to map service names to their current IP address.	On this plus side, it's a mature, well-supported solution to the problem. However, some organizations don't enable dynamic updates (the first "D" in "DDNS"), which is needed for a dynamically changing infrastructure. While DNS can support pools of resources, it doesn't give the level of control needed for advanced zero downtime replacement strategies. Doesn't support tagging or annotations that can be used to dynamically build configuration (e.g., to update the configuration for a load balancer with the current set of active web servers in a pool).
Configuration registry	Centralized registry for data about infrastructure elements and services (see "Configuration Registries" on page 55).	Not directly useful for network-level routing (e.g., what you would use DNS for), but it works well for dynamically generating configuration and generally supplying more detailed information about resources in the infrastructure.

Server-Side Service Discovery Pattern

With server-side service discovery, each service has a load balancer (or load balancer VIP) that directs requests to a pool of servers hosting the relevant service. As servers are provisioned, destroyed, or fail, the load balancer is automatically updated.

Client-Side Service Discovery Pattern

With client-side service discovery,[3] the current list of servers providing a service are kept in the service registry. The client is written to look these up in the service registry and decide which server to use for a given request.

The client-side discovery pattern adds more sophistication (arguably, complexity) to the client. A variation of this pattern is to run a load balancer for each client application. This way, the client application only needs to send requests to its load balancer, but the logic for discovering the current server application instances is separated.

Distributed Process Management

Services that scale by running multiple instances create the need to orchestrate those instances. A simplistic approach is to manually decide where to deploy and run processes. But this is essentially static, requiring effort to adjust capacity and to handle failures. This approach also doesn't cope well running on dynamic infrastructure.

---

3 Chris Richardson of NGINX wrote about these service discovery patterns in "Service Discovery in a Micro-services Architecture" (*https://www.nginx.com/blog/service-discovery-in-a-microservices-architecture/*).

Orchestrating Processes with Server Roles

One way to manage processes is through server roles. For example, a server with the role "web server" runs the web server process. When you need to scale up capacity, you start more servers with this role. When demand drops, you can scale down by destroying servers. Spinning up web servers in multiple data centers can provide continuity.

This is a straightforward way to orchestrate server processes and comes naturally when using a dynamic infrastructure platform. However, it can be heavyweight. Spinning up an entire server, even a virtual one, can take too long for services that need to run quickly or have short bursts of demand.

Orchestrating Processes with Containers

Containerization offers a different model for managing server processes. Processes are packaged so that they can be run on servers that haven't been specifically built for the purpose. A pool of generic container hosts can be available to run a variety of different containerized processes or jobs.

Assigning containerized processes to hosts is flexible and quick. The number of container hosts can be adjusted automatically based on the aggregated demand across many different types of services. However, this approach requires a scheduler to start and manage container instances.

Scheduling Short Jobs

Many services and infrastructure management tasks involve running short jobs, either on demand or on a schedule. Some services include capability to manage these jobs for themselves. For example, CI servers can distribute jobs across a set of servers running agent processes. Others rely on operating system schedulers such as Cron. However, Cron is not designed for distributed jobs. This is another feature that some container orchestration tools offer.

Container Orchestration Tools

Container orchestration tools have emerged following the rise of containerization systems like Docker. Most of these run agents on a pool of container hosts and are able to automatically select hosts to run new container instances, replace failed instances, and scale numbers of instances up and down. Some tools also handle service discovery, network routing, storage, scheduled jobs, and other capabilities.

As of early 2016, the landscape of available tools is still evolving. Different tools take different approaches and focus on different aspects of container management. Examples include Fleet, Docker Swarm, Kubernetes, Mesos, and Nomad. PaaS (Platform as a Service) products such as CloudFoundry, Deis, and OpenShift can be thought of as highly opinionated container orchestration tools.

Software Deployment

Most of the software installed on servers provisioned through infrastructure as code comes either from the OS image or is installed using the package management system. But deploying software developed in-house is often more complicated.

An element may need to be installed across multiple servers, database schemas may need to be modified, and networking rules may need to be updated. Processes may need to be stopped and restarted in a certain order to avoid corrupting data or losing transactions.

In the worst cases, these software deployment processes are too complicated to automate. There are a few reasons why this happens:

- The software has been manually deployed from its start. As a system grows over time without the use of automation, retrofitting automation is extremely difficult without significant refactoring or even rearchitecting.

- The installation process for different releases of the software involves doing different things. You might call these "snowflake releases." The need for comprehensive release notes is a symptom of snowflake releases.

- Releases don't happen very often. This encourages people to treat each release as a special occasion, rather than a routine event.

- Environments are not consistent, so deploying to each one is a custom effort. Deployment to an environment needs special knowledge of how to tweak the software, its configuration, and the environment's configuration to make everything mesh. This is a variation of the snowflake release.

Many teams successfully automate complex deployment processes. Remote command execution tools (as described in "Tools for Running Commands on Servers" on page 66) can be useful for this. However, the best approach is to design and implement software and infrastructure to simplify the deployment process.

Deployment Pipeline Software

Chapter 12 discusses automatically promoting application and infrastructure changes through a series of environments for testing. Most organizations have separate test and production environments. Many have a series of environments for testing stages, including things like operational acceptance testing (OAT), QA (for humans to carry out exploratory testing), system integration testing (SIT), user acceptance testing (UAT), staging, preproduction, and performance.

Continuous delivery (CD) software orchestrates the promotion of software and infra‐structure configuration artifacts through this series of environments. The series of promotions for a given artifact is called a pipeline, and each point in the pipeline is a stage. For a each stage, the CD tool triggers the software deployment, or pushes con‐figuration to make it available to the given environment. It may then trigger automa‐ted tests, failing the pipeline if the tests fail. Figure 5-1 shows an example of a GoCD pipeline run.

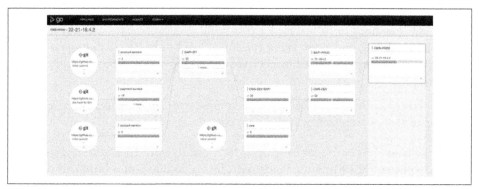

Figure 5-1. Example of a CD pipeline from GoCD

GoCD (*http://www.go.cd/*) is an open source continuous delivery tool developed by ThoughtWorks (disclosure: ThoughtWorks is my employer). Most continuous inte‐gration (CI) tools can also be used or extended to create release pipelines—for exam‐ple, Jenkins (*https://jenkins-ci.org/*), TeamCity (*https://www.jetbrains.com/teamcity/*), and Bamboo (*https://www.atlassian.com/software/bamboo*).

Packaging Software

The ideal way to deploy in-house software onto servers is to use the same processes and tooling that are used to install any other software. Packaging software into the native packaging format for the server—*.rpm* files, *.deb* files, Nuget packages, etc.—simplifies software deployment. These formats support pre- and post-installation scripting and versioning, and can be distributed with repository systems like APT and YUM.

Language and platform packaging formats like RubyGems and NodeJS NPMs can also be suitable, as long as they can handle everything needed to install and configure the software. This should include things like making sure the software is installed as a system process, creating directories, and using the correct user accounts and permis‐sions.

Other language packaging formats, like Java *.jar* and *.war* files, don't do these on their own, so they need other tooling. Some teams package these inside *.deb* or *.rpm* files, which can also include scripts to carry out installation activities. For example, an *.rpm* file can include an installation script that deploys a *.war* file into an application server.

When an application is built into a system package and made available from a repository, deployment is simply a part of the configuration definition for the server. The following Chef recipe snippet assumes that the version to be deployed has been set in the configuration registry. The team that this example comes from does this from their deployment pipeline. The deployment stage in the GoCD server runs a script that sets the version in the Chef server. This recipe then uses this to install the package from a YUM repository:

```
package "usermanager" do
  version node[:app][:version]
  action :install
end
```

Using packages this way can be challenging when orchestration is needed across servers. For example, installation may involve running a script to make changes to a database schema. This script could be run by the package installer. But if the package is installed on multiple servers in a pool, then the schema update may run multiple times, perhaps concurrently, which can have bad results. Database locking can help— the first script locks the database, and the others, finding it locked, skip the schema update.

Deploying Microservices

Microservice architecture[4] lends itself particularly well to safe, simple, and reliable software deployments in larger, more complex environments. The idea of microservices is to split the functionality of an application into independently deployable services that communicate with each other over the network. This can improve reusability and sharing if functionality is cleanly separated and interfaces are clearly defined.

Individual microservices should be small and simple to deploy. If they are implemented with loose coupling, changes to one microservice can be deployed without impacting other services that depend on it. However, a microservices application architecture requires sophisticated infrastructure management.[5] Organizations using microservices tend to have numerous deployable services, which are built and deployed frequently. Amazon's ecommerce site is implemented with over 200 micro-

---

4 For more on microservices, see Martin Fowler and James Lewis' series of posts (*http://martinfowler.com/articles/microservices.html*), and Sam Newman's excellent book *Building Microservices* (*http://bit.ly/building-microservices*) (O'Reilly). Disclosure/brag: these people are all my colleagues.

5 See "MicroservicePrerequisites" (*http://martinfowler.com/bliki/MicroservicePrerequisites.html*).

services.[6] They typically have dozens or hundreds of deployments to production per day.

Even smaller organizations with fewer than a dozen microservices will struggle to maintain and deploy these on a static, snowflake infrastructure. A microservices architecture not only needs dynamic environments with rigorously consistent configuration—it also needs to be able to roll out changes and improvements to servers easily and safely.

Conclusion

This chapter has given examples of some of the services and tools that may be needed to manage a dynamic infrastructure and how they can be implemented and used with infrastructure as code. There are of course many other services and capabilities that may be necessary for different teams and their infrastructures. Hopefully the examples here make it easy to think about how services you may need can fit into this approach.

Now that we've looked at the foundations and principles of infrastructure as code, Part II of this book will delve into more detailed patterns and practices for implementing it, including how to provision and maintain servers.

---

6 For more on Amazon's use of microservices, see the article "Amazon Architecture" (*http://highscalabil ity.com/amazon-architecture*) on HighScalability.com.

## PART II

Patterns

## CHAPTER 6

Patterns for Provisioning Servers

Part I of this book described the tooling involved in creating and configuring infrastructure elements. Now Part II will delve into patterns for using these tools.

There is more to an infrastructure than servers, but creating, configuring, and changing servers generally takes the most time and energy. So the bulk of Part II focuses on provisioning and updating servers. However, many of the patterns and approaches described for servers can also be applied to other infrastructure elements such as networking devices and storage, although they can often be simplified.

The Structure of Part II

There are separate chapters for provisioning servers, managing server template images, and managing changes to servers. The final chapter of Part II moves to the higher level, building on the patterns for server management to describe approaches to managing multiple infrastructure elements and environments.

As defined in Chapter 3, *provisioning* is the process of making an element, such as a server, ready to use. This involves assigning resources to the element, instantiating it, configuring it, and then registering it with infrastructure services such as monitoring and DNS. At the end of the provisioning process, the element is ready for use.

An effective provisioning process based on infrastructure as code has the following characteristics:

- Any existing infrastructure element can be effortlessly rebuilt on demand.
- A new element can be defined once, and then rolled out and replicated to multiple instances and environments.

- The definition of any element, and the process to provision it, is transparent and easily modified.

This chapter starts by outlining the lifecycle of a server, and then describes a model for thinking about the various pieces of a server that need to be provisioned. These are used as the basis for discussing different patterns for provisioning and configuration, and so are referred to not just in this chapter, but also in later chapters.

Server Provisioning

Typical provisioning tasks for a server include allocating hardware, creating the server instance, partitioning disks, loading an operating system, installing software, configuring the parts of the server, setting up networking, and registering the server with services that are needed to make it fully usable (e.g., DNS).

Server provisioning may be done at different points of a server's lifecycle. Most simply, they can all be done when creating each new physical server or virtual machine instance. But it may be more efficient to do some provisioning activities up front. For example, part of the provisioning can be saved onto a server template image, which can then be used to create multiple servers. Rather than installing the same software package on every new server as it is created, it can be installed one time. This makes it faster to create a new server and can help in keeping servers consistent.

Provisioning is not only done for a new server. Sometimes an existing server is re-provisioned, changing its role from one to another. Or a large server may be used for multiple roles and occasionally have a new role added. For example, many IT operations teams run multiple infrastructure services like DNS, DHCP, file servers, and mail servers together on shared servers, rather than having a dedicated server for each role. In this kind of environment, it's common to shift certain services between existing machines as needed to balance workloads.[1]

A Server's Life

The server lifecycle was touched on in Chapter 4. The patterns and practices for this chapter, and the ones following, are based around this lifecycle (shown in Figure 6-1).

---

1 Running multiple roles on a small number of servers was much more common in "the old days." Virtualization and automation have made it much easier to build and run services on dedicated servers. This in turn makes it easier to keep services segregated.

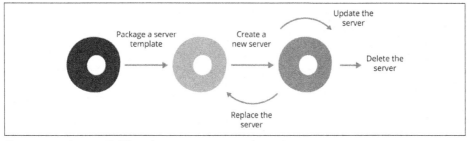

Figure 6-1. A server's lifecycle

Package a server template

As mentioned, it's often useful to create a server template image. This is a server image with common elements already provisioned that can be used to create multiple servers. Some infrastructure management platforms have direct support for templates, such as Amazon's AMIs and VMware's Templates. Others, such as Rackspace cloud, don't have explicit server templates, but the functionality used to create snapshots for backups can easily be used for templating.

The process of creating a template can start with an operating system image, such as an OS installation ISO file, or it may start with a previously created template image. A server instance is started, changes are made to it, and then it is saved to a snapshot of some kind. This process might be manual, or can be automated, possibly using configuration management tooling to prepare the template before saving it.

Templates may be very simple, with little more than the base operating system, or they can be heavier, with everything needed for a particular server role already installed. The most minimal templating approach is to directly use an OS installation ISO as a template, creating each new server instance by booting and running the OS installation process.

Trade-offs of different approaches are discussed later in this chapter, and ways to implement template packaging are covered in Chapter 7.

Create a new server

Creating a new server involves allocating resources such as CPU, memory, and disk space, and instantiating a virtual machine or hardware server. This phase also usually involves configuring networking, including assigning an IP address and placing the server in the networking architecture—for example, adding it to a subnet. The server may also be added to infrastructure orchestration services such as DNS, a configuration registry, or monitoring (see Chapter 5).

Software and configuration may be installed at this point, particularly those needed for a given role, if they're not installed in the template. In many cases, updates may be run to apply system updates and security patches released after the server template used to create the server was built.

Again, different approaches to handling provisioning activities in templates versus server creation time are discussed in the following sections, as well as in the following chapters.

Update a server

A good server creation process ensures new servers are consistent when they are created. However, this consistency doesn't last. Changes may be made to servers over their lifetime, which can cause them to diverge. And the contents of server templates, and activities that happen on server creation, tend to be continuously updated and improved by the infrastructure team, which means that servers created at different times are likely to be different.

Automated configuration tools such as Ansible, CFEngine, Chef, and Puppet were created to deal with this problem. Chapter 8 goes into this subject in detail.

Replace a server

Some changes may require completely replacing a server, rather than simply updating an existing one. For example, it may not be possible to upgrade a running server to a major new version of an OS. Even for less dramatic changes, it may be easier to completely rebuild a server rather than change it, especially when automation can make rebuilding quicker and more reliable than selectively upgrading parts of it. Immutable infrastructure is a change management strategy that involves rebuilding a server for any configuration change.

Replacing servers seamlessly is a key to continuity strategies, ensuring major changes to infrastructure can happen without interrupting service or losing data. Zero-downtime replacement ensures that a new server is completely built and tested while the existing server is still running so it can be hot-swapped into service once ready.

Replacing a server usually requires updating infrastructure services such as DNS and monitoring. These tools should handle the replacement of a server gracefully, without interrupting service, and without losing the connection of data for services that run across the lifespan of multiple servers. Similarly, data may need to be retained across rebuilds of a server instance.

Zero-downtime changes and data persistence across the server lifecycle are discussed in more detail in Chapter 14.

Immutable Servers: Replacing Servers Instead of Updating Them

The immutable server pattern mentioned in "Server Change Management Models" on page 69 doesn't make configuration updates to existing servers. Instead, changes are made by building a new server with the new configuration.

With immutable servers, configuration is usually baked into the server template. When the configuration is updated, a new template is packaged. New instances of existing servers are built from the new template and used to replace the older servers.

This approach treats server templates like software artifacts. Each build is versioned and tested before being deployed for production use. This creates a high level of confidence in the consistency of the server configuration between testing and production. Advocates of immutable servers view making a change to the configuration of a production server as bad practice, no better than modifying the source code of software directly on a production server.

Immutable servers can also simplify configuration management, by reducing the area of the server that needs to be managed by definition files.

Immutable servers are discussed in more detail in Chapter 8 ("Patterns and Practices for Immutable Servers" on page 143).

Delete a server

Destroying a server may be simple, but infrastructure services need to be updated to reflect its removal. Data may also need to be retained. It's useful to make sure that information about a deleted server is retained after it is deleted. Retaining historical metrics and log data for deleted servers is essential for debugging problems and tracking trends.

Other events in a server's life

The lifecycle phases are the major events for a server, but other interesting events occur.

Recover from failure. Cloud infrastructure is not necessarily reliable. Some providers, including AWS, have an explicit policy (*http://docs.aws.amazon.com/AWSEC2/latest/ UserGuide/instance-retirement.html*) that server instances may be terminated without warning—for example, if the underlying hardware needs to be replaced. Even providers with stronger availability guarantees have hardware failures that affect hosted systems.

As a rule, a team that has responsibility for managing the lifecycle of server instances needs to take responsibility for continuity. Infrastructure as code can be used to make services more reliable than the individual system elements they run on. The "replacement" phase of a server's lifecycle is about replacing servers while maintaining data and service continuity. If this can be done easily and routinely, a bit of extra work can ensure it happens automatically in the face of failure. This is discussed in more detail in Chapter 14.

Resize a server pool. Being able to easily add and remove servers from a pool, such as load-balanced web servers or database nodes, is a handy benefit of being able to build servers repeatably and consistently. Some infrastructure management platforms and orchestration tools offer functionality to do this automatically. This can be done in response to changes in demand (e.g., adding web servers when traffic increases and removing them when it decreases) or on a schedule to match predictable patterns of demand (e.g., shutting down services overnight).

For many services, it's useful being able to easily add and remove capacity even if it's not automated—for example, if someone can use a UI to quickly add and remove servers.

Example 6-1 is a Terraform definition that creates a pool of web servers on AWS. The `aws_autoscaling_group` defines a pool of 2 to 5 servers. The launch configuration (not shown in this example) defines how to create a web server for this pool, with an AMI ID and AWS server type such as "t2.micro". Also not shown here are the rules that tell the AWS platform when to automatically add and remove servers from the pool. As with other platforms, this can be triggered by metrics such as CPU load or network response times, or by events or a schedule.

Example 6-1. Example of a web server pool configuration

```
resource "aws_autoscaling_group" "web-server-pool" {
  min_size = 2
  max_size = 5
  launch_configuration = "${aws_launch_configuration.webserver.name}"
}
```

Reconfigure hardware resources. With many virtualization and cloud platforms, it's possible to change the hardware resources provided to a running server instance. For example, it may be possible to add or remove RAM to a virtual server, or change the number of CPU cores allocated to it. This can be changed in the infrastructure definition and then applied with the infrastructure definition tool (e.g., Terraform, CloudFormation, or Heat).

However, in some circumstances, the change may require rebooting or even rebuilding the server instance. This may be because the infrastructure or tooling doesn't support making that type of change to a running instance. In these situations, the change becomes a server replacement.

A well-implemented server management system will transparently cope with these changes. This is a natural outcome of reliably rebuilding servers in a consistent way and handling continuity across changes to dynamic infrastructure elements.

What Goes onto a Server

It's useful to think about the various things that go onto a server, and where they come from.

 This chapter describes some different models for categorizing the things that go onto a server, but it's important to remember that these kinds of categorizations are never going to be definitive. They're fine as far as they are useful to map out approaches to managing servers. If you find yourself obsessing over the "right" category for a particular thing from your infrastructure, take a step back. It probably doesn't matter.

Types of Things on a Server

One way of thinking of the stuff on a server is as software, configuration, and data (Table 6-1). This is useful for understanding how configuration management tools should treat a particular file or set of files.

Table 6-1. Things found on a server

Type of thing	Description	How configuration management treats it
Software	Applications, libraries, and other code. This doesn't need to be executable files; it could be pretty much any files that are static and don't tend to vary from one system to another. An example of this is timezone data files on a Linux system.	Makes sure it's the same on every relevant server; doesn't care what's inside
Configuration	Files used to control how the system and/or applications work. The contents may vary between servers, based on their roles, environments, instances, and so on. This category is for files managed as part of the infrastructure, rather than configuration managed by applications themselves. For example, if an application has a UI for managing user profiles, the data files that store the user profiles wouldn't be considered configuration from the infrastructure's point of view; instead, this would be data. But an application configuration file that is stored on the filesystem and would be managed by the infrastructure would be considered configuration in this sense.	Makes sure it has the right contents on every relevant server; will make sure it's consistent and correct.
Data	Files generated and updated by the system, applications, and so on. It may change frequently. The infrastructure may have some responsibility for this data (e.g., distributing it, backing it up, replicating it, etc.). But the infrastructure will normally treat the contents of the files as a black box, not caring about what's in the files. Database data files and logs files are examples of data in this sense.	Naturally occuring and changing; may need to preserve it, but won't try to manage what's inside.

The key difference between configuration and data is whether automation tools will automatically manage what's inside the file. So even though some infrastructure tools do care about what's in system logfiles, they're normally treated as data files. When building a new server, you don't expect your provisioning tools to create logfiles and populate them with specific data.

Data is treated as a black box by configuration management. Data that you care about needs to be managed so that it survives what happens to a server. Provisioning a server may involve making sure that the appropriate data is made available—for example, mounting a disk volume or configuring database software so that it replicates data from other instances in a cluster.

Quite a lot of system and application configuration will be treated as data by automated configuration management. An application may have configuration files that specify network ports and other things that the configuration system will define. But it may also have things like user accounts and preferences that get stored in other files. Automated configuration will treat these as data because their contents aren't defined by configuration definitions.

Where things come from

The elements of a given server instance may come from different sources:

Base operating system
> Typically comes originally from an installation image: CD, DVD, or ISO. Often there are optional system components that may be chosen during the OS setup process.

System package repositories
> Most modern Linux distributions support automatically downloading packages from a centralized repository (e.g., RHN/YUM repositories of RPM packages for Red Hat–based distributions, APT repositories of *.deb* packages for Debian-based distributions). Repositories may be hosted or mirrored internally, and/or public repositories may be used. You may add packages not available in the main public repositories.

Language, framework, and other platform repositories
> Many languages and frameworks these days have library formats and repositories to make them available (e.g., RubyGems, Java Maven repositories, Python PyPi, Perl CPAN, NodeJS npm, etc.). The principle is the same as the system package repositories.

Third-party packages
> Things not available in public repositories (e.g., commercial software). May be managed by putting them into internal, private repos.

In-house software packages
> Again, may be put into internal repos. In many cases, these are handled separately—for example, deployment tooling pushes a build onto servers.

It's often best to install third-party and in-house packages from an internal repository so they can be managed and tracked consistently. Some operations teams like to use version control repositories like Git and Perforce to manage these, although some tools are better than others at storing large binary files.

Some teams install these packages manually. In some cases, this can be pragmatic, especially in the short term while automation is still being implemented. However, it obviously doesn't support the principles discussed in this book, such as repeatability.

Another option for distributing packages to servers is within the definition files of a configuration tool. Puppet, Chef, and Ansible all allow files to be bundled with modules, cookbooks, and playbooks. Although this is more repeatable than manual installation, they tend to make configuration definitions unwieldy, so this is really only suitable for a stopgap until a private artifact repository of some sort can be installed.

Caching to Optimize Provisioning

Building servers or templates typically involves downloading software packages and updates. Downloading these from public repositories can take quite a while, often becoming the longest part of the process, and use significant network bandwidth.

Making these files available closer to where templates and servers are built can speed things up dramatically. Ways to do this can include keeping a local repository mirror or caching proxy. Things that can be cached this way include OS installation images, package repositories (APT, YUM, RubyGems, Maven, npm, etc.), and static data files.

As with any performance optimization, take the time to measure the different parts of the process before spending time and effort to optimize it, not to mention adding complexity to your infrastructure.

Server Roles

Different servers will need different things installed on them depending on what they will be used for, which is where the concept of roles comes in. Puppet calls these classes, but the idea is the same. In many models for server roles, a particular server can have multiple roles.

One pattern is to define *fine-grained roles*, and combine these to compose particular servers. For example, one server might be composed of the roles TomcatServer,

MonitoringAgent, BackupAgent, and DevelopmentServer, with each of these roles defining software and/or configuration to be applied.

Another pattern is to have a *role-inheritance hierarchy*. The base role would have the software and configuration common to all servers, such as a monitoring agent, common user accounts, and common configuration like DNS and NTP server settings. Other roles would add more things on top of this, possibly at several levels. Figure 6-2 illustrates the relationships between roles with inheritance.

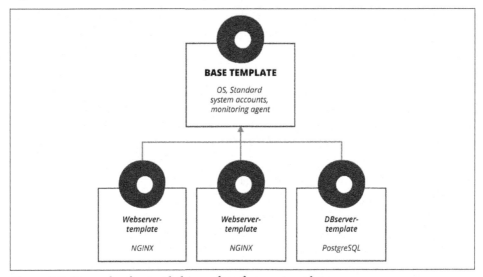

Figure 6-2. Example of a simple hierarchy of server templates

It can still be useful to have servers with multiple roles even with the role inheritance pattern. For example, although production deployments may have separate web, app, and db servers, for development and some test cases, it can be pragmatic to combine these onto a single server.

Different teams will prefer different patterns and strategies for organizing roles. The important thing is how easy the structure is for the team to understand and work with. If the structure becomes awkward and messy, it may be time to reconsider and restructure it.

Patterns for Creating Servers

Most infrastructure management platforms, whether they're a public cloud like AWS or a virtualization product like VMware, can create servers either from a user interface like a web UI or admin application, or by using a programmable API.

Once a new server image has been launched, there are typically changes made on the server itself, which may include installing and configuring software as well as system updates and configuration. Orchestration activities integrate the new server into network and infrastructure services such as DNS.

The source for launching a new server instance might be:

- Cloning an existing server
- Instantiating from a snapshot that was saved earlier from a running server
- Building from a specially prepared server template such as an EC2 AMI
- Booting directly from an OS installation image such as an ISO file from an OS vendor

Antipattern: Handcrafted Server

The most straightforward way to create a new server is to use an interactive UI or command-line tool to specify each of the options needed. This is usually the first thing I do when learning how to use a new cloud or virtualization platform. Even when I've been using a platform for a while and have more sophisticated scripting options available, it's still sometimes useful to use the basic tools to whip up a new VM to try out something new, or to help with debugging a problem by testing different things about how the creation process works.

Example 6-2 uses the AWS command-line tool to create a new server.

Example 6-2. Running a command manually to create a server

```
$ aws ec2 run-instances \
  --image-id ami-12345678 \
  --region eu-west-1 \
  --instance-type t2.micro \
  --key-name MyKeyPair
```

But a manual process is not a sustainable way to routinely create servers.

Manually creating a server relies on someone deciding, for each new server, which options to choose. This is clearly not repeatable, at least not easily and reliably. Even if the same person creates another server later on, he may not remember exactly which options he chose the first time, and a different person is even more likely to configure the server at least a little differently than the first person did. It may be possible to refer back to an existing server to figure out the settings that were used, but this takes time and effort and can still lead to errors.

So manually building servers leads almost immediately to configuration drift and snowflake servers. Server creation is not traceable, versionable, or testable, and is certainly not self-documenting.

Practice: Wrap Server Creation Options in a Script

A script is a simple way to capture the process for creating new servers so that it's easily repeatable. Check the script into a VCS to make it transparent, auditable, reversible, and to open the door to making it testable.

The `aws` command from the previous example could easily be saved in a shell script and committed to version control, taking a first step into infrastructure as code.

Avoid Scripts That Need to Be Edited Every Time

I've seen more than one experienced system administrator new to infrastructure as code write a script that creates a server but needs to be edited every time it's run to set parameters. This may help make part of a manual process a bit easier, but it doesn't really automate the server creation process.

For all but the simplest situations, a script that creates new servers needs to use different options for different situations. The goal should be that, even though the person using the script will need to know what she wants, she shouldn't need to remember the details of how to make it happen. These details, and the logic of how to assemble the various options to give the user what she wants, should be captured in the script.

Example 6-3 is a Bash script that creates a web server in AWS using the awscli tool.

Example 6-3. Script that creates a web server

```
#!/bin/bash

aws ec2 run-instances \
    --image-id ami-12345678 \
    --count 1 \
    --instance-type t2.micro \
    --key-name MyKeyPair \
    --security-groups open-https-port
```

This avoids the need for the person creating a web server to remember which options should be passed. The script could be extended to run a server configuration tool to bootstrap the server once it becomes available, as mentioned in "Patterns for Bootstrapping New Servers" on page 112. Many teams will opt to use an extensible tool designed for provisioning, such as Chef's knife command-line tool or Ansible.

But for more complex infrastructure, a declarative infrastructure definition tool (such as those described in "Working with Infrastructure Definition Tools" on page 50) provisions servers without the need for special scripts.

Antipattern: Hot Cloned Server

My team and I loved cloning servers when we started using virtualization. Nearly every new server we needed was a variation of one we already had running, so cloning was a simple way to create a new server with everything it needs already installed and configured. But as our infrastructure grew, our team realized that our habit of cloning servers was one of the reasons we were suffering from server sprawl and configuration drift.

We found that our servers were wildly different from one another. Whatever differences we had on our web servers were made worse every time we picked one of them —usually the one we thought was most up to date—to create a new server and tweak its configuration.

We tried declaring a particular server to be the master for all cloning, and kept it in the ideal state, with all the latest updates. But of course, whenever we updated the master servers, the servers that we'd created before weren't updated to match.

A server that has been cloned from a running server is not reproducible. You can't create a third server from the same starting point, because both the original and the new server have moved on: they've been in use, so various things on them will have changed.

Cloned servers also suffer because they have runtime data from the original server.

I recall a colleague who was debugging an unreliable Tomcat server and spent several days working on a fix based on strange messages he'd found in the server's logfiles. The fix didn't work. Then he realized that the strange messages hadn't actually been logged on the server he was trying to fix. That server had been cloned from another server, and the messages had come from the original, so he had been wasting several days chasing a red herring.

Pattern: Server Template

Cloning running servers isn't a good way to build servers consistently, but making a snapshot of a server and using that as a template can be. The key difference is that the template is static. Once it is built, it is never run, so it doesn't accumulate changes or data.

Two new servers built from a given template always start out identical, even if the second one is built a week after the first. This is different from cloning from a running server, which will have accumulated some changes between the creation of the first server and the second server a week later.

Of course, even servers created from the same template won't stay consistent. As they run, differences will creep in, so you still need strategies to update servers as discussed in Chapter 8.

Antipattern: Snowflake Factory

Many organizations adopt automated tools to provision servers, but a person still creates each one by running the tool and choosing options for the particular server. This typically happens when processes that were used for manual server provisioning are simply carried over to the automated tools. The result is that it may be quicker to build servers, but that servers are still inconsistent, which can make it difficult to automate the process of keeping them patched and updated.

Consistency is an issue because humans are involved in applying configuration options to a new VM. For example, someone looks at the specification to decide which user accounts to create, which packages to install, and so on. Even when a company is using an expensive, GUI-driven automation tool (arguably, especially when it's using such a tool), it's common that two different people, even people in the same IT team, may choose slightly different options. And it's also entirely likely that requirements are expressed differently by different user teams. So each VM that comes out of this process is at least slightly different from other VMs that are used for very similar purposes.

Patterns for Bootstrapping New Servers

After launching a new server, but before putting it into use, it usually needs to have changes made to it. These may include installing system updates and setting system configuration options, installing and configuring software, and/or seeding data onto the server.

Some teams aggressively minimize the changes that need to be made to a new server by putting as much as possible into the template image. This streamlines the server creation process, although it requires more sophistication in template management. Different patterns for template management will be explored thoroughly in the next chapter.

But many teams do apply configuration during creation, normally by leveraging the same server configuration tooling used for making changes to running servers. For example, if a team runs Ansible, Chef, or Puppet across their server estate, they will normally run it on each newly built server. This will tailor the server to its role and ensure it is up to date with the latest package versions.

Running a configuration tool when creating a server requires bootstrapping to be able to run the tool. There are two main strategies for this: push bootstrapping and pull bootstrapping.

Pushing to Bootstrap

As discussed in Chapter 4 ("Tools for Configuring Servers" on page 64), some tools configure servers using a push model. This involves connecting to the new server over the network from a central server or agent machine, typically using SSH. The bootstrap process may involve installing the configuration tool or agent, initial configuration, and potentially generating a key to register the new server as a configuration client.

Some of this, such as installing the configuration software, can be done on the server template so that it doesn't need to be done when bootstrapping the new server. But server-specific setup still needs to be run. So if this will be done by the tool connecting into the new server, the server will need to have access credentials preinstalled for the connection to work.

Having a single set of login credentials with root privileges preinstalled on every new server may create a security vulnerability. A safer approach is generating a one-off authentication secret when launching a new server. For example, the AWS EC2 API supports creating and assigning a unique SSH key to each new server instance as it is created. Rackspace's cloud automatically assigns a random strong root password when creating a server.

So the server creation process can provide the new server's unique key to the process that bootstraps the server's configuration. The bootstrapping process can also involve locking the new server down further, even disabling keys, passwords, or accounts as appropriate.

Pushing is also sometimes used for updating servers, which will be discussed in Chapter 8 ("Pushing to synchronize" on page 138).

Pulling to Bootstrap

Pull bootstrapping works by configuring a server template image with a script that runs when a new server starts up. The script may download configuration definition files from a repository, retrieve configuration settings from a central registry, or even download the latest configuration software package from a file server in order to configure itself.

Most infrastructure platforms can pass parameters passed by the script or tool that creates a server. This allows the provisioning process to tell the server its role and perhaps set certain parameters that the setup script needs to customize the new server for bootstrapping.

For example, a server may be created from a template that has cloud-init (*https://launchpad.net/cloud-init*) pre-installed, along with a configuration management tool. The provisioning script passes a parameter that specifies the role for the new server.

The setup script on the server uses this parameter to run the configuration tool for the first time, so that the software and configuration for the new server's role is installed on the new server.

Example of pulling to bootstrap

Example 6-4 shows part of an AWS CloudFormation definition file that provisions a server.

This file would be applied using the aws command-line tool, or from a script using the AWS REST API. For this example, the command or API call will pass two parameters. The ServerAmi parameter specifies the AMI of the server template to be used. The ServerRole parameter specifies the role of the server (e.g., *web*, *app*, *db*, etc.).

The "UserData" section of the CloudFormation definition tells cloud-init to execute the script */usr/local/sbin/server-setup.sh* on startup, passing the ServerRole parameter as an argument. This script will have been baked into the AMI and will use the argument passed in to configure the server for the appropriate role.

Example 6-4. AWS CloudFormation template that implements push provisioning

```
"ServerHost" : {
  "Type" : "AWS::EC2::Instance",
  "Properties" : {
    "ImageId" : {
      "Ref" : "ServerAmi"
    },
    "InstanceType" : "t2.small",

    "UserData" : {
      "Fn::Base64" : {
        "Fn::Join" : [ "", [
          "#!/bin/bash\n",
          "/usr/local/sbin/server-setup.sh ",
          { "Ref": "ServerRole" }
        ]
      ]
    }
  }
}
```

Practice: Smoke Test Every New Server Instance

If a server is automatically created, then it can be automatically tested. It's too common to create a new server, hand it over, and only discover there was something wrong with it after people try to use it.

In an ideal world, automation means you can trust that every new server was built without flaws. In the real world, automation scripts are written by human beings, so

---

mistakes are common. Automation scripts are also maintained by human beings, so even after a script has spun up many perfectly good servers, you can never assume the next one will also be perfect.

So it's good sense to sanity check each new server when it's created. Automated server smoke testing scripts can check the basic things you expect for all of your servers, things specific to the server's role, and general compliance. For example:

- Is the server running and accessible?
- Is the monitoring agent running?
- Has the server appeared in DNS, monitoring, and other network services?
- Are all of the necessary services (web, app, database, etc.) running?
- Are required user accounts in place?
- Are there any ports open that shouldn't be?
- Are any user accounts enabled that shouldn't be?

Smoke tests should be triggered automatically. If you rely on a person to manually run the script, it may be overlooked and become less useful over time. This is where using a CI or CD server like Jenkins or GoCD to create servers helps, because it can automatically run these kinds of tests every time.

Smoke tests could be integrated with monitoring systems. Most of the checks that would go into a smoke test would work great as routine monitoring checks, so the smoke test could just verify that the new server appears in the monitoring system, and that all of its checks are green.

Conclusion

This chapter has described approaches and patterns for provisioning servers. The core theme has been what to provision, and in what parts of the server lifecycle. The next chapter will go into more detail of managing server templates.

## CHAPTER 7

Patterns for Managing Server Templates

This chapter builds on the previous chapters on provisioning and server creation to discuss ways to manage server templates.

Using server templates can help to build new servers consistently and repeatably. However, it requires good processes for managing the templates. Templates need to be built and kept up to date with patches and improvements. The process and tooling for this should follow the principles of infrastructure as code. Templates themselves should be built through a repeatable, transparent, self-documenting, and self-testing process.

Stock Templates: Can't Someone Else Do It?

The simplest way to manage templates is to let someone else do it. Many OS vendors and cloud services provide prepackaged, stock templates, like those in Figure 7-1. These will have a base OS installation, plus default configurations, tools, and user accounts to make servers ready to use with the hosting provider. For example, the server template may be configured to use local DNS servers and OS package repositories, and may have utilities installed for finding metadata about the hosting environment.

Using stock images offloads the hassle and complexity of managing your own templates. This can be especially helpful in the early days of setting up and running a new infrastructure. Over time, the team may want to push provisioning activities from server creation into the template, and so decide to move to managing their own templates to gain more control.

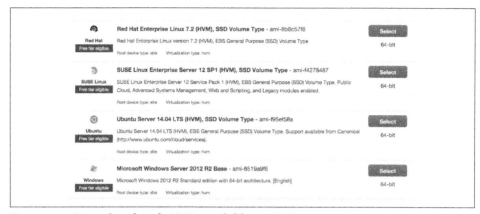

Figure 7-1. Examples of stock AMIs available on AWS

It is important to understand where the stock images you use come from, and what user accounts, software, and security configuration are in place. Make sure the template doesn't have security issues such as well-known passwords or SSH keys. Even if you remove them automatically after a new server boots, attackers actively exploit those brief windows of opportunity.

When using stock server templates, be sure to follow changes and updates to them so your servers are not left with unpatched bugs or vulnerabilities.

The rest of the patterns and practices in this section assume you will be baking your own server templates.

Provisioning Servers Using Templates

A natural question is which configuration elements and software packages should be provisioned in the server template, and which ones should be added when a new server is created. Different teams will have different approaches to this.

Provisioning at Creation Time

One end of the spectrum is minimizing what's on the template and doing most of the provisioning work when a new server is created. New servers always get the latest changes, including including system patches, software package versions, and configuration options.

This approach simplifies template management. There will be very few templates, probably only one for each combination of hardware and OS version used in the infrastructure—for example, one for 64-bit Windows 2016 and one each for 32-bit and 64-bit Ubuntu 14.x. The templates don't need to be updated very often, as there is little on them that changes; and in any case, updates can be applied when servers are provisioned.

Reasons to provision at creation time

This is often appropriate when the team isn't able to invest in sophisticated template management tooling. Teams can manage and update their templates manually, as they don't need to do it very often. Most of the tooling effort goes into configuration management. A single process and a single set of definitions are used both for provisioning new servers and for running regular updates on existing servers.

Keeping templates minimal makes sense when there is a lot of variation in what may be installed on a server. For example, if people create servers by self-service, choosing from a large menu of configuration options, it makes sense to provision dynamically when the server is created. Otherwise, the library of prebuilt templates would need to be huge to include all of the variations that a user might select.

Issues with provisioning at creation time

The main drawback of doing most of the provisioning work every time a new server is created is that it takes longer to create a new server. Repeating the same activities for every new server can be wasteful. Downloading a large number of packages and files every time a new server is created can waste bandwidth.

For infrastructures where automatically creating new servers is a key part of disaster recovery, automatic scaling, and/or deployment, a heavyweight server creation process means these things take more time. Larger-scale disaster-recovery scenarios can be especially painful, if provisioning new servers requires waiting for infrastructure services such as repository servers and configuration servers to be rebuilt first.

Provisioning in the Template

At the other end of the provisioning spectrum is putting nearly everything into the server template. Building new servers then becomes very quick and simple, just a matter of selecting a template and applying instance-specific configuration such as the hostname. This can be useful for infrastructures where new instances need to be spun up very quickly—for example, to support automated scaling.

More extensive provisioning in the template requires more mature processes and tools for building templates.[1] Even if there aren't very many templates, making configuration changes by building new template versions means building them quite

---

1 Building templates has become easier in recent years thanks to tools like Packer (*http://packer.io*) and Aminator (*https://github.com/Netflix/aminator*), which were described in Chapter 4 ("Tools for Packaging Server Templates" on page 65).

often. It's not unusual to build new templates at least weekly, and some teams have new templates being packaged and rolled out multiple times a day.

 Templates and Immutable Servers

Doing all of the significant provisioning in the template, and disallowing changes to anything other than runtime data after a server is created, is the key idea of immutable servers. This was discussed in Chapter 6 ("Immutable Servers: Replacing Servers Instead of Updating Them").

With immutable servers, templates are treated like a software artifact in a continuous delivery pipeline. Any change to a server's configuration is made by building a new version of the template. Each new template version is automatically tested before it is rolled out to production environments. This ensures that every production server's configuration has been thoroughly and reliably tested. There is no opportunity to introduce an untested configuration change to production.

Template versioning is discussed later in this chapter. Managing changes through immutable servers is discussed in Chapter 8 ("Patterns and Practices for Immutable Servers" on page 143). Applying continuous delivery pipelines to infrastructure, including server templates, is the subject of Chapter 12.

Balancing Provisioning Across Template and Creation

Although it's possible to go to either extreme—doing all of the provisioning either in the template building phase or else doing it all when creating a new server—most teams spread provisioning tasks across both phases. There are several things to take into account when deciding how to balance the provisioning work.

One consideration is the cycle time[2] for making a change available in newly created servers. A change that involves rebuilding a template will take longer than a change that is applied when the new server is created.

So it's a good idea to consider how often different elements of a server change. Things that change often may be better done at server creation time, while things that don't change very often can be put into the template.

---

2 "Cycle time" is a term used in Lean processes for measuring the end-to-end time for a particular activity. It is measured for a single work item and starts when the need is identified, and ends when the need has been fulfilled. Cycle time is a key concept for pipelines, as discussed in Chapter 12 ("Measuring Pipeline Effectiveness: Cycle Time" on page 242)

It's also possible to provision elements in both phases. For example, server configuration definitions can be used to install packages and configuration when building templates, and then run again when creating a new server. When something changes in the definitions, they will be applied to new servers even if the template still has the old configuration. Creating new servers will still be quick, because only things that have changed since the template was built will need to be applied. New template versions can be built periodically to roll up the latest changes.

The Process for Building a Server Template

The process for building a template involves:

- Selecting an origin image
- Applying customizations to the image
- Packaging the image into a server template image

Most server templates start from an origin image. This may be a raw OS setup image, a stock image from a vendor, or a previously created server template. Options for choosing and managing origin images are discussed in the next section. An exception to this is when building a Unikernel server template, which involves compiling the server image. Unikernel templates are discussed later in this chapter.

The most straightforward way to apply customizations is to boot the origin image as a server instance and then customize that running server. This may include things like applying system updates, installing common software packages like a monitoring agent, and standard configurations like DNS and NTP servers. It should also include hardening the server by removing or disabling unnecessary software, accounts and services, and applying security policies like local firewall rules.

An alternative to booting the origin image is to mount the origin disk image in another server and apply changes to its filesystem. This tends to be much faster, but the customization process may be more complicated. This approach is discussed later in this chapter.

Once the server is ready, it is "baked," meaning it is saved into a format that can be used to create new servers. This will normally be the server image format supported by the infrastructure platform, such as an Openstack image, AWS AMI, or VMware server template. On some platforms, such as Rackspace Cloud and Openstack, the same server image format is used for backing up servers and booting new servers. Other platforms, including AWS and VMware, have a special version of their server image format for server templates. This is typically the same format under the covers; it simply presents and organizes them differently.

Build Templates Repeatably

The infrastructure as code principles of repeatability and consistency lead to the idea that server templates themselves should be created in a way that is repeatable so that the servers created from them are consistent. The following patterns and practices aim to help with this.

Creating Templates for Multiple Platforms

Some teams run servers on multiple infrastructure platforms. For example, an organization may host some servers in AWS and others in a data center using Openstack. It is useful to make sure that servers in both locations run the same OS versions and patches, and are consistently configured where appropriate.

Even when hosting only uses a single platform, it's convenient to be able to run a consistently built OS image on local virtualization–for example, using Vagrant.

The template building process can be implemented to generate consistent server templates for each supported infrastructure platform. Each time a new template version is built, it should be built for all of the platforms.

Example 7-1 is a snippet from a Packer template. The snippet shows three "builders," each of which creates a server template image for a different platform. The first creates an AWS AMI, the second creates an Openstack image for a private cloud, and the third creates a VirtualBox image that can be used with Vagrant.

Example 7-1. Sample Packer template for multiple platforms

```
{
  ... (common configuration goes here) ...
  "builders": [
    {
      "type": "amazon-ebs",
      "access_key": "abc",
      "secret_key": "xyz",
      "region": "eu-west-1",
      "source_ami": "ami-12345678",
      "instance_type": "t2.micro"
      "ami_name": "our-base "
    },
    {
      "type": "openstack",
      "username": "packer",
      "password": "packer",
      "region": "DFW",
      "ssh_username": "root",
      "image_name": "Our-Base",
      "source_image": "12345678-abcd-fedc-aced-0123456789ab",
```

```
        "flavor": "2"
    },
    {
      "type": "virtualbox-iso",
      "guest_os_type": "Ubuntu_64",
      "iso_url": "http://repo/ubuntu-base-amd64.iso",
      "ssh_username": "packer",
      "ssh_password": "packer"
    }
  ]
}
```

Origin Images

Server templates are usually built by creating an image from a running server. This involves starting a server from some kind of origin image, making customizations to the server, and then snapshotting the server to a new template image. There are several options for the origin image.

Antipattern: Hot Cloned Server Template

As mentioned previously ("Antipattern: Hot Cloned Server" on page 111), you shouldn't create a new server by hot cloning a running server. This is also true for creating server templates.

If you want servers to be reproducible, then you also want templates to be reproducible. So the process involved in starting, customizing, and snapshotting a server to make a template should be completely controlled and reproducible.

Templates should be created from a clean server, one that has never been used for any other purpose. This way the only history and runtime data on a new server is left over from the process of setting up the template, not from any kind of production use.

Baking a Template from an OS Installation Image

An OS installation image, such as ISO file from the OS vendor, provides a clean, consistent starting point for building a server template. The template building process starts by booting a server instance from the OS image and running the automated setup process (such as Red Hat's Kickstart). The server instance can then be customized before saving an image to use as a template.

This tends to be an option for virtualization platforms, but most IaaS cloud platforms don't provide an easy way to boot servers directly from an ISO. In these cases, the most viable option is building from a stock image.

Baking a Template from a Stock Image

As discussed earlier in this chapter, most dynamic infrastructure platforms provide stock server images that can be used to build servers and customized templates. These images may be provided by the platform's vendor, by the OS vendor, or even by third parties or user communities. Amazon AWS has the AMI marketplace with server templates built and supported by a variety of vendors.

A stock image can be used directly to create a server, as described earlier. But it's generally preferable to use it as a starting point to build a customized template. Packages and configurations needed for the team's own infrastructure can be added.

A vendor's stock images are often intended to be useful for many needs, so it's a good idea to strip out unwanted packages. For example, a number of popular images have multiple server configuration packages preinstalled—Puppet, Chef, etc.—to make it easy for different teams to get started with them.

Stripping out unused packages, user accounts, services, and configuration will make servers more secure. It also reduces their resource footprint, so they take less disk space and memory to run, and should also reduce the startup time for new servers.

When considering a stock server template, it's critical to be confident in the provenance of everything on the template. Be sure that the packages and configuration are from reliable sources, with strong processes to ensure they are secure, legally licensed, and safe.

Just Enough Operating System (JEOS)

The just-enough operating system approach, or JEOS (*http://bit.ly/ 1PjGAD9*), pares the system image down to the bare essentials. This is mainly intended for building virtual appliances, containers, and embedded systems, but for a highly automated infrastructure, it's a good idea to consider how far you can strip the OS down.

As mentioned in the discussion of containers in Chapter 4, there are a number of OS distributions that have been created specifically to minimize and simplify server installations. Examples include:

- Red Hat Atomic (*http://red.ht/1TJKn9k*)
- CoreOS (*https://coreos.com/using-coreos/*)
- Microsoft Nano (*http://bit.ly/1TXII2d*)
- RancherOS (*http://rancher.com/rancher-os/*)
- Ubuntu Snappy (*https://developer.ubuntu.com/en/snappy/*)
- VMware Photon (*http://vmw.re/1Zd2Pe4*)

Building a Template from a Unikernel

Unikernels are machine images that are specially built to run a process in a single address space. Rather than starting a complete OS image and customizing it, the OS image is compiled together with the application, including the minimal set of OS libraries needed. This machine image can then be booted as a virtual machine or built into a container image, such as a Docker image.

Unikernel server templates can bring efficiencies in terms of resource usage, startup times, and security. As of 2016 Unikernels are new, and the ecosystem of tooling, knowledge, and practices hasn't fully developed. So this approach may be more complex to implement and maintain than the alternatives.

Customizing a Server Template without Booting It

The process of booting the origin server image as a server instance, applying customizations, and then shutting down the instance to bake the template image can be slow. An alternative is to use a source image that is mountable as a disk volume—for example, an EBS backed AMI in AWS. A longer-running server can mount a copy of the origin image as a disk volume and then make customizations to the files on the image. This may use chroot to make sure that package management tools and other scripts see the image's relative paths correctly.

Once the customizations have been made to the disk volume, it is unmounted and then converted to the relevant server image for use as a server template.

This process is much faster than booting to customize, which makes it particularly useful for teams who build templates frequently, such as those using immutable servers.

Another advantage is that there should be little or no pollution of the template server image from having been booted and run for a short period. For example, booting and customizing the template will inevitably create system log entries and may leave temporary files and other cruft.[3]

The main drawback of this method is that it can be a bit more complex. It may not be as easy to use the same server configuration tools and definition files that are used for running servers, at least not without some extra work. And not all infrastructure platforms provide a way to mount server image volumes onto another server, in which case this approach may simply not be possible.

---

3 Cruft is anything that is left over, redundant, and getting in the way.

Tools for Building Server Templates without Booting

Netflix's Aminator tool builds AWS AMIs by mounting the origin image as a disk volume. The company's blog post on Aminator (*http://techblog.netflix.com/2013/03/ami-creation-with-aminator.html*) describes the process quite well. Packer offers the amazon-chroot builder (*https://www.packer.io/docs/builders/amazon-chroot.html*) to support this approach.

Updating Server Templates

Server templates become stale over time as packages fall out of date and configuration improvements are found. Although patches and updates can be applied each time a new server is created, it takes longer and longer to do so as time goes on. Regularly refreshing templates keeps everything running smoothly.

Reheating a Template

One way to refresh a template is to use the previous version of the template as the origin. Updates and improvements can be applied and saved to a new template version. Often this is as simple as running a subset of the normal server configuration definitions.

One drawback of this approach is that templates can accumulate cruft. When something like a software package is removed from a definition, it isn't automatically removed from server templates. Even if it is, there may be leftover files, dependent packages, or even orphaned user accounts. Ensuring that all of these are removed from new versions of a template is difficult if it needs to be done explicitly.

Baking a Fresh Template

The other approach for refreshing templates is to rebuild a fresh template from the same origin as the previous version, such as the OS installation image or the stock image. If a new version of the origin becomes available (e.g., an OS update), then the new template can be built using that.

Frequently building fresh templates is easy with a well-automated process. It can also simplify the configuration that needs to be run, as the origin image is more predictable and doesn't include any cruft from previous template versions.

Versioning Server Templates

It's important to point out that "updating" a template really means building a new template image to be used instead of the old one. The old template image should never be overwritten. The reasons for this are similar to the reasons for using version

---

control for files: the ability to troubleshoot and roll back if you find problems with changes, and visibility of what changes were made and when.

Traceability of Server Templates

It should be possible to trace any running server instance back to the template version used to build it. The template version can then be traced back to the origin image and any scripts and definition files used to build that template.

Figure 7-2 shows a running server named webserver-qa-2.1.2-032. This was built from the server template named webserver-template-2.1.2. The materials used to build this template were a Packer template file (*webserver-packer-2.1.json*) and an Ubuntu installation ISO image (*ubuntu-14.04.4-server-amd64.iso*).

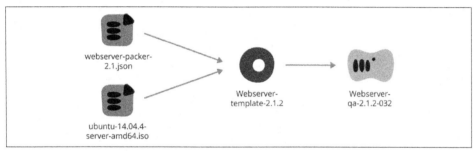

Figure 7-2. Tracing a running server to the template and its inputs

The benefits of this level of versioning and traceability include:

- Aids debugging problems, because it is easy to see what changes have been made, who made them, and hopefully why they were made.
- Makes it possible to accurately rebuild any existing server, or even previous versions of servers.
- Creates confidence in testing, as it is possible to view the results of the automated testing that was run against the template version used to create any server.
- Makes it easy to identify which existing servers need to be replaced due to out-of-date versions.

Implementing template versioning

Some infrastructure platforms, including EC2, directly support tracing instances to their original image. However, few fully support versioning of server templates, so teams need to implement at least part of the versioning themselves.

One approach is to store the template version in a tag on the template image, if the platform supports it. Servers started from the template can also have the template ID and version stored in tags, to provide traceability.

For platforms that don't offer tagging, the template version number can be included in the template name. This might also work to include the template version number in the server name. For example, a server created from template `webserver-template-2.1.2` could be named `webserver-qa-2.1.2-032`. The naming convention for the server includes the template name ("webserver") as the first field before the dash. The template version is also included in the server name ("2.1.2"), and then a unique number for the server is appended with a dash ("-032").

If neither of this options is viable, the fields could be added to servers in the configuration registry (assuming you're using one) or in some other centrally stored location or log.

Example Naming Convention

On several projects, I have named templates with the format `$\{TEMPLATE_ROLE}-$\{YYYYMMDDHHSS}`. The `${TEMPLATE_ROLE}` is the name of the template type, which might be something like "base", "centos65", "dbserver" or something else, depending on what kinds of templates my team uses. The datestamp string gives us a unique version number each time we build a new version of that particular template. When creating a new server, the creation script will know the template type to use, usually based on the server role, and will either select the latest version number, or else choose the appropriate version number based on which template has been promoted to the relevant stage of the pipeline (see Chapter 12 for more on promoting templates).

Removing old templates

It's usually important to clean out older template versions to save storage space. Teams that update templates frequently (e.g., those using immutable servers) will find that this consumes massive amounts of storage if they don't prune them.

A rule of thumb is to keep the templates that were used to create the servers running in your infrastructure to ensure you can rapidly reproduce the server in a pinch.

Retaining Templates for Legal Reasons

Some organizations have a legal requirement to be able to reproduce, or at least prove the provenance, of their infrastructure, for
some number of years later. Because they use so much storage,
archiving server templates may be a difficult and expensive way to
meet this requirement.

If your templates are built automatically, it may be a viable alternative to simply archive the scripts and definitions used to build the
templates, as well as to reference the original third-party images
used to build from.

Check with appropriate auditors and/or experts. Often, the kind of
traceability and regularity that comes with infrastructure as code is
far better for compliance regimes than what most IT organizations
consider "best practice."

Building Templates for Roles

We've discussed the use of server roles in "Server Roles" on page 107. It may be useful
to create a separate server template for each role, with the relevant software and configuration baked into it. This requires more sophisticated (i.e., automated) processes
for building and managing templates but makes creating servers faster and simpler.

Different server templates may be needed for reasons other than the functional role
of a server. Different operating systems and distributions will each need their own
server template, as will significant versions. For example, a team could have separate
server templates for CentOS 6.5.x, CentOS 7.0.x, Windows Server 2012 R2, and Windows Server 2016.

In other cases, it could make sense to have server templates tuned for different purposes. Database server nodes could be built from one template that has been tuned
for high-performance file access, while web servers may be tuned for network I/O
throughput.

Pattern: Layered Template

Teams that have a large number of role-based templates may consider having them
build on one another. For example, a base server template may have the optimiza-
tions, configuration, and software common to all servers in the infrastructure. The
base template would be used as the origin image to build more specific role-based
templates for web servers, app servers, and the like.

Layered templates fit well, conceptually at least, with a change management pipeline
(see Chapter 12), because changes to the base image can then ripple out to automatically build the role-specific templates. This is illustrated in Figure 7-3. But although

this appeals to techie-minded love of structuring and ordering things, in practice it isn't always useful. In fact, it can actually make the end-to-end process of making a change and getting the usable template longer.

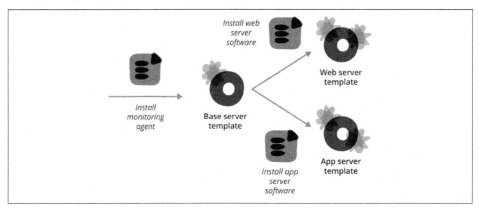

Figure 7-3. Multistage process for building layered templates

However, layering can be useful when the base template is updated much less often than the role templates. For example, a team using the immutable server pattern may bake each new build of their application into a new template, which can mean building templates many times a day when the application is being actively developed. Building these templates from a base template that already has all of the heavy changes on it can speed up the application build-and-test cycle.

This is especially helpful when the base template can be built in a way that makes building role templates much quicker—for example, by stripping it down to a minimal system so that it boots and bakes very quickly.

Sharing Base Scripts for Templates

One of the motivations for layering is to get consistency when various role templates share common base elements. However, a more efficient alternative to layering is to simply share common scripts or configuration definitions that are used to customize a server before it is baked into a template.

For example, base scripts may install common utilities, a monitoring agent, and common configuration settings, as shown in Figure 7-4. Each role template is built completely from the stock server image, adding all of the base elements and the role-specific elements in a single stage.

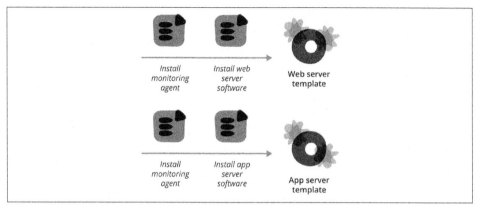

Figure 7-4. Single-stage process for building templates with shared base scripts

Automating Server Template Management

It's straightforward to automate the end-to-end process of building a template, from spinning up a server, applying updates, and then baking the template and making it available for use. "Tools for Packaging Server Templates" on page 65 in Chapter 4 describes tooling that can be used for building templates.

Customizing Servers Before Baking

Tools like Packer that automate the end-to-end template building process typically allow you to trigger scripts or configuration management tools to run on the server to customize it before baking it into a template.

Teams using a server configuration tool like Ansible, Chef, or Puppet for running servers may prefer to run the same tool to build the template. The tool would run after the instance has been started from the source instance, running an appropriate set of configuration definitions before the server is then baked to a template image.

On the other hand, the configuration applied when building a template is often straightforward enough that a set of simple shell or batch scripts can do the job. This is especially likely for teams who use immutable servers, as they probably don't use a server configuration tool at all.

Full-blown configuration management tools are intended for a more complex use case: continuously synchronizing configuration on running servers whose state may change between runs. But configuring a template is a one-off, with a known starting state: a clean stock image or freshly installed OS.

Practice: Automatically Test Server Templates

Automatically building templates leads naturally to automatically testing them. Every time a new template is built, the automation tooling can use it to spin up a new VM, run tests to make sure it's correct and compliant, and then mark the template as ready for use. Scripts that create new servers can then automatically select the newest template that has passed its tests.

As with any automated testing, it's important to keep test suites pared down to those that add real value. The goal is to catch common errors and keep confidence in the automation. Designing an effective testing regime is the topic of Chapter 11.

Conclusion

This chapter, along with Chapters 5 and 6, has focused on aspects of server provisioning. The next chapter moves onto ways of keeping servers updated.

## CHAPTER 8

Patterns for Updating and Changing Servers

Dynamic infrastructure makes it easy to create new servers, but keeping them up to date once they've been created is harder. This combination often leads to trouble, in the shape of a sprawling estate of inconsistent servers. As seen in earlier chapters, inconsistent servers are difficult to automate, so configuration drift leads to an unmanageable spaghetti infrastructure.

So a processes for managing changes to servers is essential to a well-managed infrastructure. An effective change management process ensures that any new change is rolled out to all relevant existing servers and applied to newly created servers. All servers should be up to date with the latest approved packages, patches, and configuration.

Changes to servers should not be allowed outside the automated process. Unmanaged changes lead to configuration drift and make it difficult to quickly and reliably reproduce a given server. If changes are routinely made by bypassing the automation, then this is a sign that the processes need to be improved so that they are the easiest and most natural way for team members to work.

The process for updating servers should be effortless so that it can scale as the number of servers grows. Making changes to a server should be a completely unattended process. A person may initiate a change, for example, by committing a change to a configuration definition. Someone may also manually approve a change before it is applied to certain parts of the infrastructure. But the change should roll out to servers without someone "turning a handle" to make it happen.

Once a well-oiled server change process is in place, changes become fire and forget. Commit a change, and rely on tests and monitoring to alert the team if a change fails or causes an issue. Problems can be caught and stopped before they're applied to important systems, and even those that slip through can be rapidly rolled back or corrected.

Characteristics of an effective server change process:

- The automated process is the easiest, most natural way for team members to make changes.
- Changes are rolled out to all of the relevant existing servers.
- Servers that are meant to be similar are not allowed to drift into inconsistency.
- Changes are applied as an unattended process.
- The effort involved in a change is the same, regardless of how many servers are affected by it.
- Errors changes are made visible quickly.

This chapter drills into the main server change management models that were introduced in Chapter 4 ("Server Change Management Models" on page 69) and then describes patterns and practices for implementing them.

Models for Server Change Management

The four models for making configuration changes servers are ad hoc, configuration synchronization, immutable servers, and containerized servers.

Ad Hoc Change Management

The traditional approach has been to leave servers alone unless a specific change is required. When a change is needed, someone may edit a file by hand or write a one-off script to make the change. Many teams who use a configuration management tool like Chef, Puppet, or Ansible still only run it when they have a particular change to make.

As discussed throughout this book, this tends to leave servers inconsistently configured, which in turn makes it difficult to use automation reliably and comprehensively. In order to run an automated process across many servers, the state of those servers needs to be generally consistent to start with.

Continuous Configuration Synchronization

Most server configuration tools are designed to be used in a continuous synchronization model. This means that the tool runs on an unattended schedule, usually at least once an hour. Each time the tool runs, it applies or reapplies the current set of definitions. This ensures that any changes made between runs are brought back into line, preventing configuration drift.

Continuous synchronization helps to maintain the discipline for a well-automated infrastructure. The tool will run no matter what, so the team must keep the definitions working correctly. The shorter the time between configuration runs, the more quickly issues with the configuration definitions are found. The more quickly issues are found, the more quickly the team can fix them.

However, writing and maintaining configuration definitions takes work, so there is a limit to how much of a server's surface area can be reasonably managed by definitions. Any areas not explicitly managed by configuration definitions may be changed outside the tooling, which leaves them vulnerable to configuration drift.

Immutable Servers

The so-called immutable server approach is the practice of making configuration changes to a server by building an entirely new server, rather than by making changes to the existing server.[1] This ensures that any change can be tested before being put into production, whereas a change made to running infrastructure could have unexpected effects.

The configuration of a server is baked into the server template, so the contents of a server are predictable. They are defined by whatever is on the origin image for the template, combined with the set of script and/or configuration definitions run as a part of building the template image. The only areas of a server that aren't predictable, and tested, are those with runtime states and data.

Immutable servers are still vulnerable to configuration drift, as their configuration could be modified after they've been provisioned. However, the practice is normally combined with keeping the lifespan of servers short, as with the Phoenix. So servers are rebuilt as frequently as every day, leaving little opportunity for unmanaged changes. Another approach to this issue is to set those parts of a server's filesystems that should not change at runtime as read-only.

Immutable Servers Aren't Really Immutable

Using the term "immutable" to describe this pattern can be misleading. "Immutable" means that a thing can't be changed, so a truly immutable server would be useless. As soon as a server boots, its runtime state changes—processes run, entries are written to logfiles, and application data is added, updated, and removed.

---

1 My colleague Peter Gillard-Moss and former colleague Ben Butler-Cole used immutable servers when they worked on the ThoughtWorks' Mingle SaaS platform (*http://thght.works/1Vw3GY8*).

It's more useful to think of the term "immutable" as applying to the server's configuration, rather than to the server as a whole. This creates a clear line between configuration and data. It forces teams to explicitly define which elements of a server they will manage deterministically as configuration and which elements will be treated as data.

Containerized Servers

Standardized methods for packaging and distributing lightweight containers create an opportunity to simplify server configuration management. With this model, each application or service that runs on a server is packaged into a container, along with all of its dependencies. Changes to an application are made by building and deploying a new version of the container. This is the immutable infrastructure concept, applied at the application level.

The servers that host containers can then be greatly simplified. These host servers can be stripped down to a minimal system that only includes the software and configuration needed to run containers. Host servers could be managed using configuration synchronization or the immutable server model; but in either case, because there isn't much to them, their management should be simpler than for more complex, frequently changing servers.

As of this writing, very few organizations have converted their infrastructure as radically as this. Most are using containers for a minority of their applications and services. Containers are useful for applications that change frequently, such as software developed in-house. And infrastructure teams are finding that at least some core services work better running directly on the host rather than inside containers. But assuming containerization continues to mature and becomes a standard way to package applications for distribution, then this could become a dominant model for infrastructure management.

General Patterns and Practices

There are a number of practices and patterns that can be relevant with different server change management models.

Practice: Minimize Server Templates

The less you have on your servers to start with, the less you need to manage afterward. This is also a good idea for security, performance, stability, and troubleshooting. This can be done during the template building process, as discussed in the previous chapter.

Practice: Replace Servers When the Server Template Changes

When a server template is updated and new servers are created from it, the new servers may be different from existing servers that were created from previous versions of the template. For example, the template may be changed to use a new version of the OS distribution, which includes updates to libraries and other server elements that aren't explicitly managed by configuration definitions.

If servers are kept in use for a long time—months for example—and templates are updated several times, a team can end up with a fair bit of configuration drift that continuous synchronization won't resolve.

So it's a good practice to replace running servers whenever the template used to build them is updated, as illustrated in Figure 8-1. This should be done progressively rather than in a disruptive big bang. For example, a new template can be applied to test environments, then promoted to more sensitive environments. See Chapter 12 for more on this. Also, members of a server cluster can be replaced sequentially, to avoid disrupting service. See Chapter 14 for ideas on this.

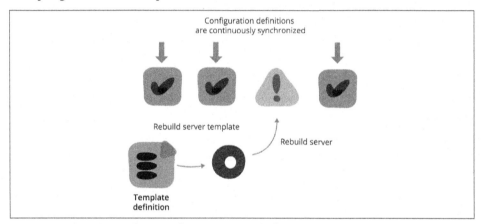

Figure 8-1. Server templates with continuous synchronization

Pattern: Phoenix Servers

Some organizations have found that routinely replacing servers, even when the server template hasn't been updated, is a good way to combat configuration drift. In effect, this achieves the goal of having 100% of your machine's surface area automatically managed. Any changes that happen to parts of the server not managed by configuration definitions that are continuously synchronized will be reset when the server is rebuilt from the server template.

This is implemented by setting a maximum lifespan for all servers, and having a process that runs on a schedule to rebuild servers older than this limit. This process should ensure that service is not interrupted—for example, by using zero-downtime replacement patterns (see "Zero-Downtime Changes" on page 282 in Chapter 14).

Patterns and Practices for Continuous Deployment

Continuous synchronization involves regularly running a process to apply the current configuration definitions to a given server. This process can work in one of two different ways. With the push model, a central process controls the schedule, connecting to individual servers to send and apply the configuration. With the pull model, a process on the server itself runs, downloading and applying the latest configuration definitions.

Pushing to synchronize

Many server configuration tools have a master server that pushes configuration to the servers it manages. Push configuration may need a client running on each managed server, which receives commands from the server on a network port or message bus. Other systems use remote command protocols like SSH to connect and execute configuration commands, in which case client software may not be needed. In either case, it's a central server that decides when it's time to synchronize and then orchestrates the process.

Ansible, for example, connects over SSH, copies scripts onto the target server, and executes them. The only requirement for a machine to be managed by Ansible is an SSH daemon and the Python interpreter.

An advantage of the push approach is that it gives centralized control over when and where to apply configuration changes. This can help if changes need to be orchestrated across an infrastructure in a certain order or with certain timings. Ideally you should design systems with loose coupling that avoids the need for this type of orchestration, but in many cases it's difficult to avoid.

Pulling to synchronize

Pull configuration uses an agent installed on the managed server to schedule and apply changes. It could be a scheduled Cron job, or else a service that runs its own scheduler. The client checks a master or some central repository to download the latest configuration definitions, and then applies them.

The pull model has a simpler security model than the push model. With the push model, each managed server needs to expose a way for the master to connect and tell it how to configure itself, which opens up a vector for a malicious attack. Most tools implement an authentication system, often using certificates, to secure this, but of course this requires managing keys in a secure way. Ansible's use of SSH lets it take advantage of a widely used authentication and encryption implementation rather than inventing its own.

With a pull system, there is still a need to ensure the security of the central repository that holds the configuration definitions, but this is often simpler to secure. Managed servers don't need to make any ports or login accounts available for an automated system to connect.

Depending on the design of the configuration tool, a pull-based system may be more scalable than a push-based system. A push system needs the master to open connections to the systems it manages, which can become a bottleneck with infrastructures that scale to thousands of servers. Setting up clusters or pools of agents can help a push model scale. But a pull model can be designed to scale with fewer resources, and with less complexity.

Pattern: Masterless Configuration Management

Many teams find it effective to scrap the idea of a centralized server, even when the configuration tool they're using supports it. The main reasons for doing this are to improve stability, uptime, and scalability.

The approach is to run the configuration management tool in offline mode (e.g., chef-solo rather than chef-client), using copies of configuration definitions that have been downloaded to the managed server's local disk.

Doing this removes the master server as a potential point of failure. The definitions still need to be downloaded, but they can be hosted as static files. This can scale very well with minimal resources; object storage services (discussed in "Object storage" on page 27) work very well for this.

Another way teams implement the masterless pattern is by bundling the definitions into a system package like an *.rpm* or *.deb* file and hosting it in their private package repository. They run a script from Cron, which executes yum update or apt-get update to download and unpack the latest definitions before running the configuration tool.

Practice: Apply Cron

A team that uses a server configuration tool such as Ansible, Chef, or Puppet to continuously synchronize configuration can use the same tool when building server templates and also when bootstrapping new servers. This allows configuration definitions to be reused and ensures that newly built templates and newly created servers have the latest configurations. See Figure 8-2.

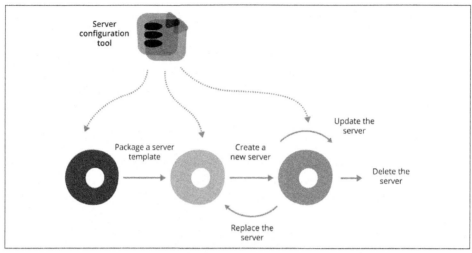

Figure 8-2. Using the same configuration tool across the server lifecycle

Packaging the template
> Apply a subset of configuration definitions that are common to all server roles built from the particular template.

Creating the server
> Apply all of the definitions for the new server's role. This prepares the server for its specified role and also applies any changes that were made to the common definitions since the server template was packaged.

Updating the server
> The configuration definitions are regularly applied to keep the server's configuration in line and up to date.

Continuous Synchronization Flow

With continuous synchronization, configuration definitions are applied and repeatedly reapplied to a server. Figure 8-3 shows this process. After a configuration definition has been applied to a server, assuming nothing has changed, then the repeated runs of the tool won't make any changes. When a definition is changed and made available, then the configuration tool will make the change to the server the next time it runs.

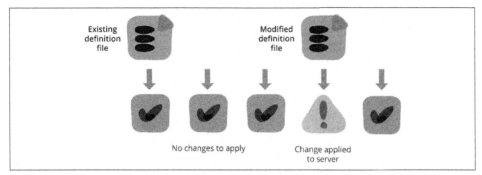

Figure 8-3. Making a change with configuration synchronization

This process ensures that changes made outside of the automation are reverted, as shown in Figure 8-4. When someone makes a manual change on the server that conflicts with a configuration definition, the next time the configuration process runs, it reapplies the definition, reverting the manual change.

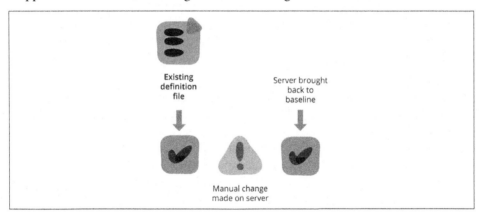

Figure 8-4. Reverting a manual change with configuration synchronization

The Unconfigured Country

When using continuous synchronization, it's important to be aware that the majority of a server will not be managed by the configuration definitions that are applied on every run. As shown in Figure 8-5, configuration definition files can only cover a fraction of the surface area of a server's configuration.

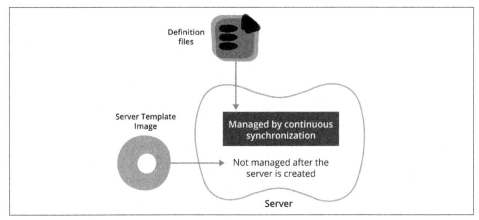

Figure 8-5. Sources of things on a server

The majority of a server's configuration actually comes from the server template (e.g., AMI, OS installation disc, etc.) used to create the server. Once the server is up and running, this is essentially unmanaged. This is often not a problem. The fact that you haven't written a configuration definition to manage a particular part of the server probably means you're happy with what's on the server template and that you don't need to make changes to it.

But these unmanaged areas do leave the door open to configuration drift. If someone finds the need to change the configuration in an unmanaged part of a server, they may be tempted to make it manually rather than going through the hassle of writing a new configuration definition. This then means that particular change isn't captured in a way that ensures it will always be made where it's needed. It can also create a snowflake server, where an application works on some servers but not others, but nobody remembers why.

Why unmanaged areas are unavoidable

An obvious solution to this issue is to make sure configuration definitions cover everything on the system. But this simply isn't realistic with the current generation of configuration tools. There are two major obstacles. One is that there are too many things on a server than can be realistically managed with current tools. The other is that current tools can't prevent unwanted things from being added to a system.

First, consider how much stuff would need to be managed. As discussed in the sidebar "How Many Things Are on a Linux Server" on page 143, even using a pared-down Linux server image leaves a huge number of files. Writing and maintaining configuration definitions to explicitly manage every one of these is a ridiculous amount of work.

How Many Things Are on a Linux Server

I built some fresh VMs to see how many files are on a typical server, before adding applications and services. I did this with CentOS 6.6, using *CentOS-6.6-x86_64-minimal.iso*, and then with CoreOS version 607.0.0, to see how a JEOS distribution compares.

Running `find /etc -type f | wc -l` shows the configuration files on the server. My CentOS VM had 712 files, while CoreOS had only 58.

I then ran a similar find command across root folders that tend to include files managed by configuration definitions and/or packages, but which don't normally have transient or data files.

The folders I included in this were: */bin*, */etc*, */lib*, */lib64*, */opt*, */sbin*, */selinux*, and */usr*.

My CentOS VM had 38,496 files, and my CoreOS VM had 4,891.

So while a JEOS server can dramatically reduce the number of files that might need to be managed, there are still quite a few.

Even if you declare everything that exists on a given server, maybe by taking a snapshot of it, there are still the things that you *don't* want on it. This is a literally infinite set of things you'd have to write definitions to exclude—"on web server machines, ensure there is no installation of MySQL, no Oracle, no websphere application server, and so on."

You could handle this with a white-listing approach, deleting everything on the system that isn't explicitly declared. But there are many transient files and data files that are needed for the server to work properly, but which can't be predicted ahead of time. You would need to make sure that data files, logs, temp files, and the like are all protected. Current server configuration tools simply don't support this.

This isn't to say that this can't or won't be made much easier than it is with current tools. And most teams get along just fine without an obsessive level of control over every element of their servers.

Patterns and Practices for Immutable Servers

Once an immutable server is created from its server template, its configuration files, system packages, and software are not modified on the running server instance. Any changes to these things are made by creating a new server instance. However, servers are vulnerable to configuration drift if left running for long periods, so teams using immutable servers tend to keep their lifespan short, following the phoenix pattern described earlier in this chapter.

Teams using immutable servers need more mature server template management because of the need to build new templates quickly and often.

Of course, immutable servers aren't truly immutable. Aside from transitory runtime state, there is often a need to maintain application and system data, even as servers come and go.[2]

Server Image as Artifact

One of the key drivers for adopting immutable servers is strong testing. Once a server template is created and tested, there is a smaller chance for untested changes and variation to happen on a production server. Runtime state and data will change, but system libraries, configuration files, and other server configuration won't be updated or revised at runtime, as can happen with continuous synchronization. Change management pipelines (as described in Chapter 12) can help to ensure the quality of a template.

Simplifying Confirmation Management Tooling with Immutable Servers

Many teams that embrace the immutable model find they can simplify the tooling they use to configure servers when preparing a server template. Ansible, Chef, Puppet, and similar tools are designed to be run continuously, which adds some complexity to their design and use. They need to be able to apply configuration definitions to servers that may be in different states when the tools run, including running repeatedly when the configuration has already been applied.

But configuration, which is always done to a server template, can make assumptions about the starting state of the server when they run. For example, a new template may always be built using a base OS installation image. It's common for teams to use a series of fairly simple shell scripts to configure server templates, which reduces their tooling and maintenance overhead.

Immutable Server Flow

Figures 8-6 and 8-7 show the typical flow for making a change with immutable servers. The existing servers have been built from the server template image generated from the first version of the server template definition file—for example, a Packer template file.

---

2 Chapter 14 explores ways to manage data that needs to persist across the lifespan of individual servers.

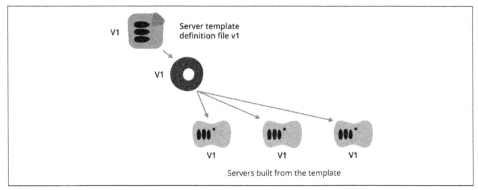

Figure 8-6. Immutable server flow (part one)

A change is needed, so the template definition file is changed and then used to package a new version of the server template image. This image is then used to build new servers to replace the existing servers.

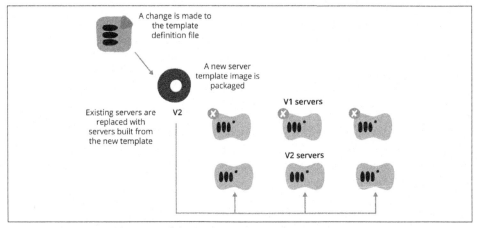

Figure 8-7. Immutable server flow (part two)

The process for replacing a running server with a new one will ideally be done without interrupting services provided by the server.[3]

Bootstrap Configuration with Immutable Servers

The purest use of immutable servers is to bake everything onto the server template and change nothing, even when creating server instances from the template. But

---

3 Patterns for doing this are discussed in Chapter 14 ("Zero-Downtime Changes" on page 282).

some teams have found that for certain types of changes, the turnaround time needed to build a new template is too slow.

An emerging practice is to put almost everything into the server template, but add one or two elements when bootstrapping a new server. This might be a configuration setting that is only known when the server is created, or it might be a frequently changing element such as an application build for testing.[4]

A small development team using continuous integration (CI) or continuous delivery (CD) is likely to deploy dozens of builds of their application a day, so building a new server template for every build may be unacceptably slow. Having a standard server template image that can pull in and start a specified application build when it is started is particularly useful for microservices.

This still follows the immutable server pattern, in that any change to the server's configuration (such as a new version of the microservice) is carried out by building a new server instance. It shortens the turnaround time for changes to a microservice, because it doesn't require building a new server template.

However, this practice arguably weakens the testing benefits from the pure immutable model. Ideally, a given combination of server template version and microservice version will have been tested through each stage of a change management pipeline.[5] But there is some risk that the process of installing a microservice, or making other changes, when creating a server will behave slightly differently when done for different servers. This could cause unexpected behavior.

So this practice trades some of the consistency benefits of baking everything into a template and using it unchanged in every instance in order to speed up turnaround times for changes made in this way. In many cases, such as those involving frequent changes, this trade-off works quite well.

Example of a Team's Microservice Application Standards

A number of teams I've worked with have used the pattern of standardized application deployments. They typically develop multiple microservice applications and want to be able to add and change these applications without needing to change the infrastructure. They do this by having conventions around how an application is packaged, deployed, and managed by the infrastructure. The infrastructure can then deploy and run any application developed according to these standards.

The following are some of the standards agreed by one team.

---

4 Cloud-init is a useful tool for handling these simple bootstrap activities, as discussed in Chapter 6 ("Pulling to Bootstrap" on page 113).

5 As described in Chapter 12.

Applications are packaged as a tarball (*.tar.gz* file), including certain files at root level:

- A JAR file named *SERVICEID-VERSION.jar*, where *VERSION* follows a format matching the regular expression (\d+)\.(\d+)\.(d+)
- A configuration file named *SERVICEID-config.yml*
- A shell script named *SERVICEID-setup.sh*

To deploy the application, the server provisioning script will download the artifact from a URI passed in the environment variable SERVICE_ARTEFACT_URI. It will then extract the contents of the artifact to the directory */app/SERVICEID*, which will be owned by a user account named SERVICEID. It will also create a file in this same directory named *SERVICEID-env.yml*, which contains some configuration information specific to the environment.

The provisioning script also runs the *SERVICEID-setup.sh* script, which can carry out any initialization activities needed before the application is started. Finally, the provisioning script creates and enabled a service startup script as */etc/init.d/SERVICE-NAME*, which starts the application by running the startup command java -jar /app/SERVICEID/SERVICEID-VERSION.jar server.

Developers can build an application based on these standards and know that it will work seamlessly with the existing infrastructure and tooling.

Transactional Server Updates

Another approach with potential is transaction server updates. This involves package management tooling that supports updating all of the packages on a server to a defined set of versions as an atomic transaction. If any of the updates fail, the entire set of updates is rolled back. This ensures that the server's configuration, at least as far as system packages, don't end up in an untested state. The server will either be updated to the new, completely tested state, or reverted to the existing state, which was presumably tested previously.[6]

This approach has a lot in common with immutable servers, and also with containers.

---

6 NixOS (*http://nixos.org/*) is a Linux distribution that provides atomic updates and rollbacks of groups of packages, using the Nix package management tool.

Practices for Managing Configuration Definitions

Teams moving to infrastructure as code, especially those using continuous synchronization, find that working with configuration definitions for their toolchain becomes a core activity.[7] This section discusses a few practices specifically useful for managing configuration definitions for configuring servers.

Practice: Keep Configuration Definitions Minimal

Code, including configuration definitions, has overhead. The amount of time your team spends writing, maintaining, testing, updating, debugging, and fixing code grows as the amount of code grows. This overhead grows exponentially, considering each piece of code has interactions with at least some other code. These interactions may be deliberate (i.e., one piece of code may depend on another) or unintentional (i.e., two pieces of code happen to affect common parts of the system in a way that can create conflicts).

Teams should strive to minimize the size of their codebase. This doesn't mean writing code that uses the least number of lines as possible, an approach that can actually make code harder to maintain. Rather, it means avoiding the need to write code whenever possible. Most of what is configured on a server is undeclared; it comes from the server template used to create a server, rather than being explicitly defined in a configuration definition.

This is a good thing. As a rule, an infrastructure team should only write and maintain configuration definitions to cover areas that really require explicit, continuous configuration. This will include parts of the system that need to change quite often, and those that most need to be protected from unwanted, unmanaged changes.

A useful approach to implementing automated configuration is to start small, writing definitions for the things you need most. Over time you'll discover changes that are needed, so you can add definitions for those. You should also keep a constant eye out for definitions that are no longer needed and so can be pruned.

Of course, there is a trade-off between minimizing configuration definitions and leaving areas of the servers unmanaged, with the potential for configuration drift.

---

7 Chapter 10 explains a number of software development practices that are useful for infrastructure developers.

Organizing Definitions

Configuration definitions, as with any code, seem to enjoy becoming a large, compli-cated mess over time. It takes discipline and good habits to avoid this. Once an infra-structure team gets a handle on the basics of writing and using a server configuration tool, they should invest time in learning how to use the tool's features for modulari-zation and reuse.

The goal is to keep individual modules or definition files small, simple, and easy to understand. At the same time, the overall organization needs to be clear so anyone with a reasonable understanding of the tool can quickly find and understand the sec-tions of definitions that are involved in a given part of the system.[8]

Some server configuration tools have evolved tools that help to manage groups of configuration definitions as packages or libraries. These libraries can be developed, versioned, published, and installed independently from one another. They typically have a dependency management system, so installing one library will automatically trigger other libraries to be installed if they are needed.

Examples of Package Management Tools for Configuration Definitions

A few examples of tools to manage libraries of configuration defi-nitions include Berkshelf (*http://berkshelf.com*) for Chef, and Librarian-puppet (*http://bit.ly/Lib-puppet*) and r10k (*http://bit.ly/ r10k-puppet*) for Puppet.

Practice: Use Test-Driven Development (TDD) to Drive Good Design

A common misunderstanding of TDD is that it's just a way to make sure automated tests get written as code is developed. But developers and teams who become effective at TDD find that its main value is in driving clean, maintainable code design.

The way this works with configuration definitions is ensuring that every module has a set of unit tests for testing that module in isolation. If the tests are written and maintained with good discipline, they make it clear when a module is becoming too large or complicated, because the tests become more difficult to update and to keep working as the definitions are updated. Tests also reveal when a module is too tightly coupled to its dependencies, because this makes it difficult to set up self-contained tests.[9]

---

8 Chapter 10 gives more ideas about how to do this.

9 Chapters 10 and 11 go into the software engineering and test automation practices behind this.

Conclusion

This chapter, along with the previous two, have focused on provisioning and updating individual servers. The next chapter will pull the focus out to larger sections of infrastructure, looking at how to manage environments and interrelated systems and services.

CHAPTER 9

Patterns for Defining Infrastructure

Most of Part II of this book has focused on provisioning and configuring servers. This chapter will look at how to provision and configure larger groups of infrastructure elements. As infrastructure grows in size, complexity, and number of users, it becomes harder to achieve the benefits of infrastructure as code:

- The larger scope of what may be affected by a given change makes it difficult to make changes frequently, quickly, and safely.

- People spend more time on routine maintenance and firefighting, and less on making more valuable improvements to services.

- Allowing users to provision and manage their own resources can risk disruption to other users and services.

The typical reaction is to centralize control over infrastructure. This leads to more time spent on meetings, documentation, and change process, and less time spent on activities that add value to the organization.

But an alternative to centralizing control is to design infrastructure to minimize the scope of impact of a given change. An effective approach to defining, provisioning, and managing infrastructure will enable changes to be made frequently and confidently even as the size of the infrastructure grows. This in turn allows ownership of application and service infrastructure to be safely delegated.

What Is a Stack?

A stack is a collection of infrastructure elements that are defined as a unit (the inspiration for choosing the term stack comes mainly from the term's use by AWS CloudFormation).

A stack can be any size. It could be a single server. It could be a pool of servers with their networking and storage. It could be all of the servers and other infrastructure involved in a given application. Or it could be everything in an entire data center. What makes a set of infrastructure elements a stack isn't the size, but whether it's defined and changed as a unit.

The concept of a stack hasn't been commonly used with manually managed infrastructures. Elements are added organically, and networking boundaries are naturally used to think about infrastructure groupings.

But automation tools force more explicit groupings of infrastructure elements. It's certainly possible to put everything into one large group. And it's also possible to structure stacks by following network boundaries. But these aren't the only ways to organize stacks.

Rather than simply replicating patterns and approaches that worked with iron-age static infrastructure, it's worth considering whether there are more effective patterns to use.

This chapter is concerned with ways of organizing infrastructure into "stacks" to support easier and safer change management. What are good ways of dividing infrastructure into stacks? What is a good size for a stack? What are good approaches to defining and implementing stacks?

Environments

The term "environment" is typically used when there are multiple stacks that are actually different instances of the same service or set of services. The most common use of environments is for testing. An application or service may have "development," "test," "preproduction," and "production" environments. The infrastructure for these should generally be the same, with perhaps some variations due to scale.

Keeping multiple environments configured consistently is a challenge for most IT organizations, and one which infrastructure as code is particularly well suited to address.

Antipattern: Handcrafted Infrastructure

It's not unusual for teams that automatically provision and configure their servers to manually define surrounding infrastructure elements, such as networking and storage. This is especially common when using virtualized servers with non-virtualized storage and networking. Quite often, teams will script server creation but use an interactive interface to configure networking and allocate storage.

For example, setting up a database cluster for a new environment may involve someone allocating disk space on a storage area network (SAN), and then configuring firewall rules and selecting IP addresses for the servers in the cluster.

Changes made manually with an interactive GUI or tool aren't easily repeatable, and lead to inconsistency between environments. A firewall change made by hand in a test environment may not be made the same way for the production environment.

Organizations that work this way often find they need to take extra time to manually test and inspect each environment after it's built. Signs that this is an issue is if it is common practice to allocate time on project plans for correcting mistakes after setting up new environments, or else that it's common for implementation schedules to slip due to unexpected errors.

Snowflake Environments

As with snowflake servers, an environment that is "special" can be difficult to rebuild, which makes it scary to change and improve. It's very common to see this for infrastructure services like monitoring, and other internally facing services such as bug tracking systems. Resist the temptation to treat setting up this kind of system as a one-off task that isn't worth properly automating.

Defining Infrastructure Stacks as Code

Figure 9-1 illustrates a stack with a simple web server cluster with frontend networking.

The Terraform file excerpt in Example 9-1 shows how this stack might be defined on AWS. The definition file would be committed to a VCS so that it can be easily rebuilt or replicated.

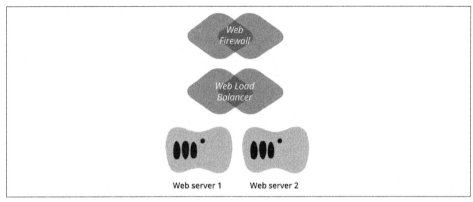

Figure 9-1. A simple environment

The first two blocks each define a web server, specifying the server template (AMI) and the size of the server. The third block defines a load balancer (ELB). This defines the port to take requests on and forward them to, and references to the server instances defined in the earlier blocks as the destination for requests. The ELB block also refers to the security group, defined in the last block of the example, which is the firewall rule to allow traffic in.[1]

Example 9-1. Terraform definition for a simple stack

```
resource "aws_instance" "web_server_1" {
  ami = "ami-47a23a30"
  instance_type = "t2.micro"
}

resource "aws_instance" "web_server_2" {
  ami = "ami-47a23a30"
  instance_type = "t2.micro"
}

resource "aws_elb" "web_load_balancer" {
  name = "weblb"

  listener {
    instance_port = 80
    instance_protocol = "http"
    lb_port = 80
    lb_protocol = "http"
  }
```

---

1 Note that this is not a well-designed example. In practice, you should use a dynamic pool of servers—an autoscaling group in AWS—rather than statically defined ones. It's preferable to have the AMIs defined as variables so they can be changed without having to edit and push changes to this definition file.

```
  instances = [
    "${aws_instance.web_server_1.id}",
    "${aws_instance.web_server_2.id}"
  ]

  security_groups = ["${aws_security_group.web_firewall.id}"]
}
resource "aws_security_group" "web_firewall" {
  name = "web_firewall"

  ingress {
      from_port = 80
      to_port = 80
      protocol = "tcp"
      cidr_blocks = ["0.0.0.0/0"]
  }
}
```

Antipattern: Per-Environment Definition Files

A simplistic way of managing multiple, similar environments is to have a separate definition file for each environment, even when the environments are used to run different instances of the same application or service.

With this approach, a new environment can be made by copying the definition file from another environment and editing it to reflect differences such as networking details. When a fix, improvement, or other change is made, it is made by hand to each of the separate definition files.

This dependency on manual effort to keep multiple files up to date and consistent is the weakness of per-environment definition files. There is no way to ensure that changes are made consistently. Also, because the change is made manually to each environment, it isn't possible to use an automated pipeline to test and promote the change from one environment to the next.

Pattern: Reusable Definition Files

A more effective approach is to use a single definition file across all of the environments that represent the same application or service. The file can be parameterized to set options specific to each environment. This makes it easy to build and run multiple instances of an infrastructure stack.

The earlier Terraform definition (Example 9-1) can be modified to use environment-specific parameters. Example 9-2 shows part of the previous example, adding tags to the servers to indicate the environment. A variable environment is declared, signalling that it should be provided to the Terraform command-line tool. This variable is then used to set the value of a tag on the AWS EC2 instance.

Example 9-2. Parameterized Terraform environment definition

```
variable "environment" {}

resource "aws_instance" "web_server_1" {
  ami = "ami-47a23a30"
  instance_type = "t2.micro"
  tags {
    Name = "Web Server 1"
    Environment = "${var.environment}"
  }
}

resource "aws_instance" "web_server_2" {
  ami = "ami-47a23a30"
  instance_type = "t2.micro"
  tags {
    Name = "Web Server 2"
    Environment = "${var.environment}"
  }
}
```

The definition tool is run separately for each environment.

First for QA:

```
$ terraform apply -state=qa-env.tfstate -var environment=qa
```

Then the tool is run again for PROD:

```
$ terraform apply -state=prod-env.tfstate -var environment=prod
```

This creates two sets of servers, and assuming the load balancer is similarly parameterized, it creates separate ELBs as well.

Separate State Files or IDs per Environment

These Terraform command-line examples use the `-state` parameter to define a separate state data file for each environment. Terraform stores information about infrastructure that it manages in a state file. When managing multiple instances of an infrastructure with a single definition file, each instance needs to have its state stored in a separate file.

Other definition tools, such as CloudFormation, store the state server side and allow each instance to be identified by a parameter (`StackName`, in the case of CloudFormation).

Practice: Test and Promote Stack Definitions

A reusable, parameterized definition file can be reliably tested before being applied to production infrastructure. Rather than making a networking configuration change directly to a production environment, the change can be made to the relevant definition file, and applied to a test environment first. Automated tests can validate whether there are any errors or issues with the change. Once testing has been carried out, the change can be safely rolled out to the production infrastructure.

Because the process for applying the configuration is automated, there is a far higher confidence in the reliability of testing. The ease of creating and modifying a test environment also lowers barriers. When people need to manually set up and run tests, they are tempted to skip it when they're in a hurry, telling themselves it's a small change that shouldn't break anything.

This leads to test environments that aren't configured consistently with production, which makes testing less reliable. This in turn gives more reason not to bother with testing. This is the automation fear spiral (see "Automation Fear" on page 9) all over again. Using a single definition file across environments makes it trivial to keep the environments consistently configured.

Simplifying Change Management Process for Environments

In larger organizations with a need for strong governance around changes to infrastructure, making a configuration change and rolling it out across the pipeline of test, staging, and production environments can be lengthy.

Making a single change may require a separate change process for each environment, with detailed designs, tickets, change requests, and change reviews. In many cases, different people may implement the same change in different environments. When this is a manual process, no amount of documentation or inspection can guarantee the change will be implemented consistently.

The proper use of a reusable environment definition, in conjunction with an automated pipeline, can make this process simpler, faster, and more consistent. The amount of process overhead needed can be dramatically reduced. What's more, because changes, and the process used to apply them, are explicitly defined in files and managed in a VCS, it is easy to provide traceability and assurance that legal and other requirements are being complied with.

Self-Service Environments

Another benefit of parameterized environment definitions is that new instances can be easily created.

For example, development and testing teams don't need to coordinate access to shared environments, slowing their pace of work. A new environment can be built in minutes. Environments can even be created and destroyed on demand.

This can also be used with standard services, such as a ticketing application like JIRA. Each team can easily be given their own instance, avoiding the need to coordinate configuration changes across multiple teams.

Environment and service instances defined through a common definition file can be provisioned through self-service. Rather than requiring infrastructure team members to take time to set up services and infrastructure, a team can use a predefined, well-tested template to spin up their own instance.

It's important that self-service provisioning be supported by a process for updates. When a change is made to a shared infrastructure definition, it should be rolled out to all existing instances. A change management pipeline can ensure that changes are tested before being rolled out to teams using them, and that they are applied and tested to test environments for applications before being applied to production environments.

Organizing Infrastructure

An infrastructure is normally composed of a variety of interrelated stacks. Some stacks share infrastructure like networking devices. Others have interdependencies that require networking connections between them. And there is normally a continuous stream of changes that need to be made to some or all stacks, which can potentially create issues.

This section looks at some ways to organize infrastructure stacks to address these concerns.

Antipattern: Monolithic Stack

When first adopting an infrastructure definition tool, it's easy to create large, sprawling infrastructure in a single definition. Different services and applications, even different testing environments, can all be defined and managed together.

This simplifies integration of different elements of the infrastructure, and sharing them. In the monolithic stack shown in Figure 9-2, the shared pool of web servers needs to be configured to access two different pools of content management system (CMS) servers. Having all of these configured in one file is convenient. If a new CMS server is added to the definition, it can be referred to by the web servers and network routing.

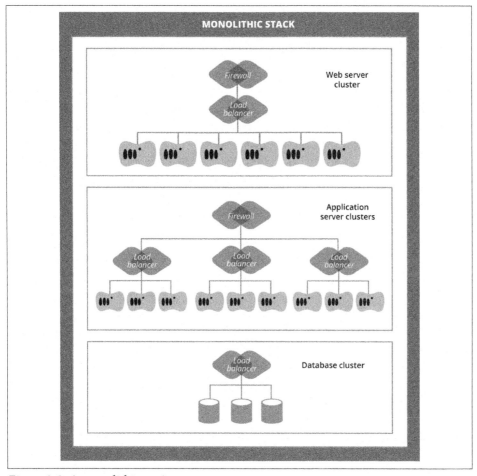

Figure 9-2. A monolithic environment

The difficulty of a monolithic definition is that it becomes cumbersome to change. With most definition tools, the file can be organized into separate files. But if making a change involves running the tool against the entire infrastructure stack, things become dicey:

- It's easy for a small change to break many things.
- It's hard to avoid tight coupling between the parts of the infrastructure.
- Each instance of the environment is large and expensive.

- Developing and testing changes requires testing an entire stack at once, which is cumbersome.

- If many people can make changes to the infrastructure, there is a high risk someone will break something.

- On the other hand, if changes are limited to a small group to minimize the risk, then there are likely to be long delays waiting for changes to be made.

You know your infrastructure definition is becoming monolithic when people become afraid to make a change. When you find yourself considering adding organizational processes to coordinate and schedule changes, stop! There are ways to organize your infrastructure to make it easier and safer to make changes. Rather than adding organizational and process complexity to manage complex infrastructure designs, redesign the infrastructure to eliminate unnecessary complexity.

Avoid "Lift and Shift" When Migrating Infrastructure

Organizations that have existing, static infrastructure will have become accustomed to their architectural patterns and implementations. It's tempting to assume these are still relevant, and even necessary, to keep when moving to a dynamic infrastructure platform.

But in many cases, applying existing patterns will, at best, miss out on opportunities to leverage newer technology to simplify and improve the architecture. At worst, replicating existing patterns with the newer platforms will involve adding even more complexity.

It can be difficult to see "outside the box" of an existing, proven infrastructure implementation, but it's well worth the effort.

Dividing an Application Environment into Multiple Stacks

Multitier applications can be divided into multiple stacks to allow each tier to be changed independently. Figure 9-3 shows a stack each for web servers, application servers, database cluster, and networking.

These stacks have interdependencies. The web server stack needs to be added to the firewall and subnets defined in the network stack. It also needs to know the IP address of the load balancer VIP for the application server stack, so the web servers can be configured to proxy requests to the application server. The application server stack will similarly need the IP addresses of the database cluster.

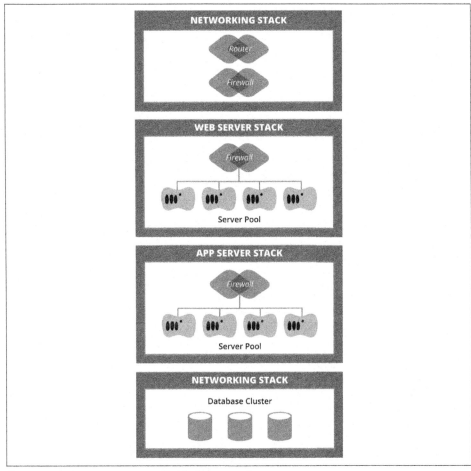

Figure 9-3. An environment divided into stacks

Example 9-3 shows parts of a Terraform definition[2] for the web server stack from Figure 9-3. It assumes the networking stack, application server stack, and database stack are all defined in separate files, and each built and updated separately.

So this definition only defines the infrastructure elements that are specific to the web server pool, including the autoscaling group and load balancer. Changes can be made to this file and applied, with only minimal coupling to the other stacks in an environment.

---

2 In the interests of clarity, this example excludes a number of arguments that would be needed for it to actually work.

Example 9-3. Web server stack definition

```
# Declare a variable for passing the app server pool's IP address
variable "app_server_vip_ip" {}

# Define the web server pool
resource "aws_autoscaling_group" "web_servers" {
  launch_configuration = "${aws_launch_configuration.webserver.name}"
  min_size = 2
  max_size = 5
}

# Define how to create a web server instance for the pool
resource "aws_launch_configuration" "webserver" {
  image_id = "ami-12345678"
  instance_type = "t2.micro"
  # Pass the IP address of the app server pool so it can be used
  # by the server configuration tool
  user_data { app_server_vip_ip = "${app_server_vip_ip}" }
}

# Define the load balancer for the web server pool
resource "aws_elb" "web_load_balancer" {
  instances = [ "${aws_asg.web_servers.id}" ]
  listener {
    instance_port = 80
    instance_protocol = "http"
    lb_port = 80
    lb_protocol = "http"
  }
}
```

Managing Configuration Parameters Between Stacks

A basic, and not very scalable technique for coordinating information between infrastructure stacks is to have a script that runs the definition tool for all of the different stacks. It makes sure to run them in the appropriate order, and captures the outputs of each stack so they can be passed as variables to other stacks. However, this is brittle, and loses the advantage of being able to run the definition tool independently for different stacks.

This is where a configuration registry[3] comes in handy. It provides a structured way to capture information about a stack, and make it available in a central location for other stacks to use.

---

3 As described in Chapter 3 ("Configuration Registries" on page 55), there are different types of tooling and approaches that can be used for a configuration registry.

Many infrastructure definition tools have built-in support for setting and fetching values from a registry.

Example 9-4 modifies Example 9-3 to use a Consul configuration registry. It finds the IP address of the application server stack's load balancer VIP in the registry, looking up the key path *myapp/${var.environment}/appserver/vip_ip*. Using *var.environment* allows this definition file to be shared across multiple environments, each storing its own app server VIP in a unique location.

Example 9-4. Application server stack definition using a registry

```
# The "environment" parameter must be passed in
variable "environment" {}

# Import keys from the Consul registry
resource "consul_keys" "app_server" {
  key {
    name = "vip_ip"
    path = "myapp/${var.environment}/appserver/vip_ip"
  }
}

resource "aws_launch_configuration" "webserver" {
  image_id = "ami-12345678"
  instance_type = "t2.micro"
  # Pass the IP address of the app server pool so it can be used
  # by the server configuration tool
  user_data { app_server_vip_ip = "${consul_keys.app_server.var.vip_ip}" }
}
```

Lightweight registry approaches for sharing configuration between stacks

Some teams prefer to use a lightweight registry (discussed in "Lightweight Configuration Registries" on page 56) although it may require more work to implement than an off-the-shelf tool. For example, the script that runs the definition tool might fetch structured registry files (e.g., JSON or YAML files) from a static file sharing service (e.g., an AWS S3 bucket), and pass it as parameters for applying the stack definition. The output of the definition tool is then captured and stored in the file sharing service, where it will be used for other stacks.

This can be highly scalable and robust, because it can take advantage of standard tools and techniques for hosting static files, including caching and distribution.

Packaging the outputs of a stack into a system package, like an RPM or .*deb* file, is another technique that leverages existing, well-proven tooling, as does committing the output files into a VCS.

Sharing Infrastructure Elements

By itself, the preceding example of splitting a single application environment into several stacks may not be especially useful. Most definition tools only apply changes to the part of the stack that has actually changed, anyway. So if you are making a change to the web server tier, having the other tiers defined in separate files doesn't buy much. Worse, you've seen how much complexity is added to the system in order to pass information between stacks.

However, dividing stacks makes more sense as the size and complexity of the infrastructure grows.

One use is to make it easier for different application environments to share infrastructure resources. Figure 9-4 shows two applications sharing a single frontend stack, including a pool of web servers, and also sharing a database stack. Each application might have its own database schema and virtual web host in each of these stacks. The application stacks are independently managed.

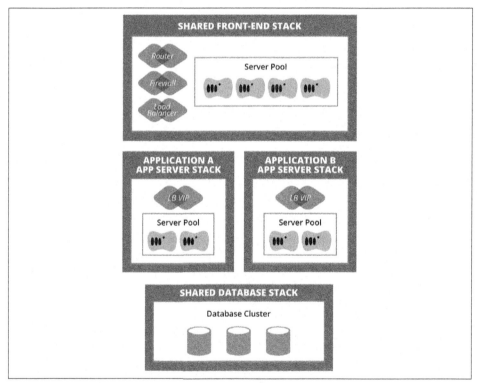

Figure 9-4. Two application environments sharing stacks

Pitfalls of sharing infrastructure elements

Sharing stacks should be avoided whenever possible, because it creates dependencies that can make changes expensive and risky.

Sharing is usually driven by hardware such as networking devices and storage. Hardware devices tend to be expensive, and changing them may be high effort. But virtualized and cloud infrastructure, driven by automated configuration, makes it cheaper and easier to give each application dedicated resources.

The overhead of changes to infrastructure increases exponentially with the number of applications and services that share it. This overhead is reflected in time, cost, and risk.

In Example 9-4 with the database cluster shared between two applications, a change to the cluster, such as upgrading the database server, affects both applications. The change needs to be coordinated for both of these, which can make scheduling the upgrade more challenging.

Both applications may need to be taken offline, have their schemas updated, brought up, and then tested. If things go wrong, both applications may be offline for an extended time. If one application works fine after the upgrade but the other doesn't, both will need to be rolled back.

Because changing shared infrastructure has a higher risk, organizations must put more effort into planning and managing the change. This can involve meetings, documentation, and project plans. A larger number of people need to schedule time for planning, implementation, and testing. Project managers and analysts get involved to handle all of this. Entire teams and departments may be created to oversee this type of process.

One indication that this is an issue is when a simple change takes several months and a budget running as high as five and six figures. Another indication is when the organization is still running outdated versions of key system and middleware, having been unable to muster the time and money to carry out upgrades that impact many applications and services.

But by allocating dedicated infrastructure to each application, upgrades can be carried out in more manageable chunks, with less overhead.

At a glance, upgrading the database for each application one at a time may seem less efficient than upgrading a single shared instance all in one go. But upgrading the database for a single application has a much smaller risk area. Automation can cut the time and improve the reliability of the upgrade process. The upgrade can be made even more reliable by having it automatically applied and tested in a test environment first.

This is another case where automation and dynamic infrastructure, when used the right way, can dramatically simplify the change process while also making it less risky.

Practice: Manage Application Code and Infrastructure Code Together

The default approach in many organizations is to manage the definitions for a given application's infrastructure separately from the code for that application. Application code is kept in its own VCS project, and infrastructure definitions are kept in another. Often, each is managed by a separate team. This follows the tradition of separating development and operations concerns, but can add technical and organizational overhead.

Consider a change that involves both the application and its infrastructure. An application might read environment-specific configuration options from a file that is added to the system by a server configuration definition, such as an Ansible playbook. The file contains the IP address of the database server, which may be different in each environment the application is deployed to. If the playbook is managed in a separate VCS repository from the application code, then a new version of the application may be deployed to an environment that hasn't had a new configuration option added to the file yet.

Dividing ownership of an application from the configuration of its infrastructure between teams adds even more complexity. In addition to technical integration issues, the time and work of both teams need to be coordinated. When the infrastructure is shared by multiple development teams, you see the same problems described earlier in this chapter ("Pitfalls of sharing infrastructure elements" on page 165).

It's certainly possible to manage the dependencies between an application and its infrastructure even when they are managed separately, and by separate teams. But this involves adding complexity, including technical mechanisms and organizational processes.

An alternative is to manage application software and its supporting infrastructure as a single concern.[4] Putting the definitions for the application-specific infrastructure elements into the same project folder as the development code, as shown in Example 9-5, makes it easy to manage, test, and deliver them as a unit.

---

4 My former colleague Ben Butler-Cole put it well: "Build systems, not software."

Example 9-5. Project structure with combined application and infrastructure code

```
./our-app
./our-app/build.sh
./our-app/deploy.sh
./our-app/pom.xml
./our-app/Vagrantfile
./our-app/src
./our-app/src/java
./our-app/src/java/OurApp.java
./our-app/src/infra
./our-app/src/infra/terraform
./our-app/src/infra/terraform/our-app.tf
./our-app/src/infra/ansible
./our-app/src/infra/ansible/roles
./our-app/src/infra/ansible/roles/our_app_server
./our-app/src/infra/ansible/roles/our_app_server/files
./our-app/src/infra/ansible/roles/our_app_server/files/service.sh
./our-app/src/infra/ansible/roles/our_app_server/tasks
./our-app/src/infra/ansible/roles/our_app_server/tasks/main.yml
./our-app/src/infra/ansible/roles/our_app_server/templates
./our-app/src/infra/ansible/roles/our_app_server/templates/config.yml
```

Managing application and infrastructure definitions together means they can be tested together. The preceding project structure includes configuration to build and deploy the application to a local virtual machine with Vagrant. This allows developers, testers, and operations people to run the application in a server that is configured the same way as the production servers. Changes and fixes can be made and tested locally with a high level of confidence.

A good rule of thumb for what code can and should be managed together is to consider the scope of a typical change. If it's common for changes to involve modifying code that lives in different VCS repositories, then putting them into the same repository is likely to simplify the process for making a change.

Approaches to Sharing Definitions

With many development teams, there are often benefits from sharing infrastructure code. Getting the balance right between sharing good code and keeping team agility can be tricky.

Central code libraries are a common approach to sharing infrastructure definitions and code. Most server configuration tools support using a centralized library for cookbooks or modules. So all of the application teams in an organization could use the same Puppet module for building and configuring nginx web servers, for example. Improvements and upgrades can be made to the module, and all of the teams can take advantage of it.

Of course, this risks the pitfalls of shared infrastructure, as a change can potentially impact multiple teams. The overhead and risks this creates often discourages frequent updates.

A few approaches that some teams use to get around this:

Versioning of shared modules
Teams can opt-in to updates as they are released, so they can adopt newer versions of modules as time permits.

Copy rather than share
Teams maintain templates for application and infrastructure code, and copy the files as needed to create new applications, and fold in improvements as they become available.

Optional sharing
Teams use a shared module, but have the option to write alternative modules if it makes more sense for their needs.

Overridable modules
Modules are designed in a way that makes it easy for application teams to customize them and override behavior as needed.

As a rule, sharing functionality and definitions makes more sense for things where the requirements are truly common, don't change very often, and are low risk to change. It also makes sense when there is a clear, easy way for teams to customize and override the shared capability.

As an example, many organizations find that the base operating system distribution can be shared fairly easily. So a server template with the base OS can be centrally created and made available to teams. Teams are able to customize this base, either by building a new template that layers changes onto the base template ("Pattern: Layered Template" on page 129), or by writing server configuration definitions (Chef, Puppet, etc.) that makes changes to the base image when provisioning a new server instance.

In those rare cases where a team needs a different base image (e.g., if they're running third-party software that requires a different OS distribution) then they will ideally have the option to create and manage their own images, potentially sharing them with other teams.

Practice: Align Infrastructure Design with the Scope of Change

Clearly there are trade-offs to consider when deciding how to split infrastructure into stacks. A division that makes sense in one organization may not make sense in another, depending on the team structures and on the services that the infrastructure supports.

However, a good guiding principle when considering the breakdown is the scope of change. Consider the types of changes that are made often, and those that are the most difficult and risky. Then look at the parts of the infrastructure that are impacted by each of those changes. The most effective structures will put those parts together.

Keeping the scope of a change together simplifies the technical integration, which in turn simplifies the design and implementation of the systems involved. Simplified design is easier to understand, test, secure, support, and fix. "Pitfalls of sharing infrastructure elements" on page 165 outlined the reasoning behind this principle.

When it's not possible to keep the infrastructure affected by a change in a single stack, or within a single team, then it's important to make the interfaces between them simple. Interfaces should be designed to be tolerant, so that a change or problem with one side of the integration doesn't break the other side.

Teams that provide services to other teams should make sure those other teams can customize and configure them without involving the providing team. The model for this is public cloud vendors. These vendors provide APIs and configuration, rather than having a central team make configuration changes on behalf of their customers.

When considering different types of changes and their scope, it's important to cast a wide net. It's important to optimize the most common and simple changes, such as creating a new server of a standard type, or using a Chef cookbook for a common service following the most common use case. But also consider the changes that don't fit into the common use cases. These are the ones that can take the most work to implement if the infrastructure design is not aligned to make them simple.

Example: An Infrastructure Design for Microservices

Microservices is proving to be a popular style of software architecture for deploying to the cloud. Its approach of breaking systems into small-ish, independently deployable pieces of software aligns well with the approach to defining infrastructure described in this chapter. Figure 9-5 describes a design for implementing infrastructure for an example microservices-based application on AWS.

A typical microservice may be composed of an application and a corresponding database schema. The microservice application is deployed to a pool of application servers implemented as an AWS autoscaling group.

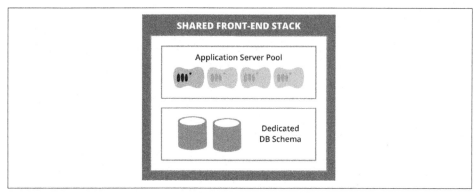

Figure 9-5. Deployable parts of a microservice

The Terraform definition in Example 9-6 can be used to create a pool of application servers running a microservice application. When it is run, parameters are passed in giving it the name and version of the microservice to run, and the name of the environment to run it in. This single definition can be used multiple times to create multiple microservices in multiple environments.

Terraform passes the contents of the `user_data` string to the new server instance using the EC2 API. The AMI `ami-12345678` has the cloud-init tool (*https://launch pad.net/cloud-init*) preinstalled.[5]

Cloud-init automatically runs when a new server instance boots, examines the contents of the `user_data` string, and runs the */usr/local/sbin/microservice-bootstrap.sh* script, passing it the arguments `environment`, `microservice_name`, and `microser vice_version`. The *microservice-bootstrap.sh* script is written by the infrastructure team and is built into the AMI image as part of the template building process. This script uses the `microservice_name` and `microservice_version` arguments to download and install the relevant microservice application package. It may also use the `environment` argument to look up configuration parameters in a configuration registry.

---

5 Cloud-init has become a standard tool; most stock server images for cloud platforms have it preinstalled and configured to run at startup.

Example 9-6. Terraform definition for a microservice autoscaling group

```
variable "microservice_name" {}
variable "microservice_version" {}
variable "environment" {}

resource "aws_launch_configuration" "abc" {
  name = "abc_microservice"
  image_id = "ami-12345678"
  instance_type = "m1.small"
  user_data = "#!/bin/bash
/usr/local/sbin/microservice-bootstrap.sh \
  environment=${var.environment} \
  microservice_name=${var.microservice_name} \
  microservice_version=${var.microservice_version}"
}

resource "aws_autoscaling_group" "abc" {
  availability_zones = ["us-east-1a", "us-east-1b", "us-east-1c"]
  name = "abc_microservice"
  max_size = 5
  min_size = 2
  launch_configuration = "${aws_launch_configuration.abc.name}"
}
```

Each microservice application can use this definition, or one similar to it, to define how it is to be deployed in an environment. This definition doesn't define the networking infrastructure for the application. Although each application could define its own AWS VPC, subnets, security groups, and so on, this duplication is potentially excessive as the system grows. These elements should not need to change very often, and should not be very different between applications. So this is a good candidate for sharing.[6]

Figure 9-6 shows the elements of an AWS infrastructure that might be managed in their own global stack.

---

6 Sharing these kinds of network structures is also recommended by Amazon. See this presentation from Gary Silverman (*http://www.slideshare.net/gsilverm/aws-vpc-in*) for typical Amazon recommendations.

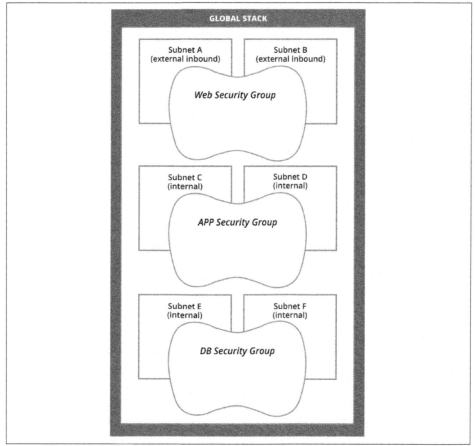

Figure 9-6. Global stack for microservices

This stack would have its own Terraform definition file, which is applied separately for each environment. The IDs of the infrastructure elements provisioned by Terraform will be recorded in a configuration registry.

Each microservice application then has its own Terraform definition file, similar to the preceding example. The microservice infrastructure would also add an ELB to route traffic to the autoscaling group, and an RDS definition to create a database schema instance for the application. The definition would also reference the configuration registry to pull in the IDs for the subnets and security groups to assign the various parts of the infrastructure to. The result would look like Figure 9-7.

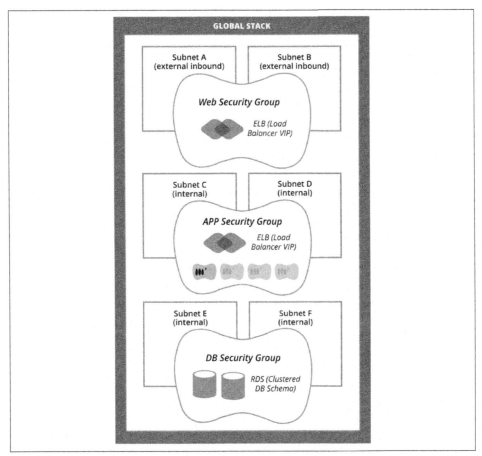

Figure 9-7. Microservice application stack

This architecture is appropriate for a set of microservices that don't need to be segregated from one another. In other situations, segregation might be needed. For example, if a payment service involves handling credit card details, it would be subject to PCI-DSS regulations. In this case, putting the payment service into its own global stack makes it easier to keep it segregated. This can then be managed with more tightly controlled processes to ensure and demonstrate compliance.

Reverse-Engineered Definitions Versus Build-Forward Ones

One popular feature for a definition tool is a way to point it at existing infrastructure and automatically generate definition files. This offers a quick way to start using a tool like Terraform, Cloud-Formation, or Heat for teams that already have extensive infrastructure in place.

The risk with this approach is that there is no guarantee the tool will actually be able to rebuild the infrastructure if needed. There may be aspects of the infrastructure that the tool did not detect, or perhaps doesn't even support.

The best way to have confidence in the ability to reliably rebuild infrastructure is to "build forward." That is, write the definition files to match the existing infrastructure, and then run them to create new instances of the infrastructure. The new instances can be tested to make sure they work correctly. Then, the old infrastructure should be replaced by the newly built infrastructure.

If your team does not believe the old infrastructure can safely be replaced by infrastructure that has been built from scratch using the automated definition tools, then this is a sign of a snowflake or even fragile infrastructure ("Fragile Infrastructure" on page 8). Consider rebuilding elements of the legacy infrastructure using infrastructure as code, one piece at a time, until the entire infrastructure can be easily and reliably rebuilt with confidence.

Automatically generating configuration definitions from existing infrastructure can be useful for learning about infrastructure. Generated definitions can even be used as a starting point for automatically built infrastructure. But don't make the mistake of considering them a useful recovery point for handcrafted infrastructure.

Running Definition Tools

Engineers can run definition tools from their local workstation or laptop to manage infrastructure. But it's better to ensure that infrastructure is provisioned and updated by running tools from centrally managed systems, such as an orchestration agent. An orchestration agent is a server that is used to execute tools for provisioning and updating infrastructure. These are often controlled by a CI or CD server, as part of a change management pipeline.

There are a number of reasons to run definition tools from an agent:

- The agent server can itself be automatically built and configured, ensuring that it can be reliably rebuilt in an emergency situation.
- It avoids relying on snowflake configuration for executing the tool, which often happens when tools are installed and run on an engineer's desktop.
- It avoids dependency on a particular person's desktop.
- It makes it easier to control, log, and track what changes have been applied, by whom, and when.
- It's easier to automatically trigger the tool to be applied for a change management pipeline.
- It removes the need (or temptation) to keep credentials and tools for changing infrastructure on a laptop, which could be lost or stolen.

Running a tool locally is fine for working with sandbox infrastructure ("Using the Virtualization Platform for Sandboxes" on page 266) to develop, test, and debug automation scripts and tooling. But any infrastructure used for important purposes, including change management, should be run from centralized agents.

Conclusion

Part II of this book built on the technical concepts from Part I to outline patterns and practices for using automation tooling effectively for infrastructure as code. It should have provided clear guidance on good approaches, as well as pitfalls to avoid.

Part III will explore a variety of practices that can help to make this work. These will delve into practices and techniques derived from software development, testing, and change management.

Practices

## CHAPTER 10

Software Engineering Practices for Infrastructure

The enabling idea of Infrastructure as Code is that the systems and devices used to run software can be treated as if they, themselves, are software. This makes it possible to use tools and working practices that have been proven in the software development world. This chapter examines specific software engineering practices that many teams have found to work well for developing and maintaining infrastructure.

The main theme of the software engineering practices covered in this chapter is building quality into the system. Quality is not a separate practice from development, a testing activity that happens after a system has been built. Quality must be an integral part of the way in which developers—including infrastructure developers—plan, design, implement, and deliver systems.

Some of the principles that support quality in developing software and infrastructure include:[1]

- Start delivering working, useful code early.
- Continue to deliver in small, useful increments.
- Build only what is necessary at the moment.
- Build each increment as simply as possible.
- Ensure each change is well designed and implemented.

---

[1] These are inspired by the Agile Manifesto (*http://agilemanifesto.org/*), particularly the Twelve Principles of Agile Software (*http://agilemanifesto.org/principles.html*). Occasionally people propose creating a manifesto for DevOps or Infrastructure as Code. However, the existing Agile Manifesto applies just as well to developing infrastructure as it does to developing applications.

- Get feedback on every change as early as possible.

- Expect requirements will change as you and your users learn.

- Assume everything you deliver will need to change as the system evolves.

This chapter explains how to use practices from continuous integration (CI) and continuous delivery (CD) to support these principles. It also looks at practices for using a version control system (VCS), which is a prerequisite for both CI and CD.

Building on Software Engineering Practices

The remaining chapters in this book build on the core software engineering practices from this one. Chapter 11 covers testing, in particular how to design, implement, and maintain a well-balanced suite of automated tests. Chapter 12 explains how a change management pipeline, the core mechanism for CD, is used to put these software engineering and testing practices into use. Chapter 13 outlines the workflows that people can use to work with the tools on a day-to-day basis to develop, test, and debug automated infrastructure as code. Chapter 14 focuses on how dynamic infrastructure creates new challenges and offers new techniques for keeping services running reliably. Finally, Chapter 15 closes the book by explaining how teams and organizations can build and run IT operations using infrastructure as code.

Note for Experienced Software Developers

Experienced software developers who are experienced with agile and Extreme Programming (XP) (*http://www.extremeprogramming.org/*) practices like test-driven development (TDD) and CI may find the contents of this chapter familiar. Even so, it should be worth at least skimming the contents, as there are some notes on how these specifically apply to infrastructure development.

System Quality

Good software engineering practices produce high-quality code and systems. Too often, quality is seen as a simple matter of functional correctness. In reality, high quality is an enabler of change. The true measure of the quality of a system, and its code, is how quickly and safely changes are made to it.

Poor-Quality Systems Are Difficult to Change

A seemingly simple change can take much more time than seems reasonable and cause far more problems than it should. Even the people who wrote the code have difficulty understanding how a given part of the codebase works when looking at it. Code that is difficult to understand is difficult to change without creating unexpected problems. That simple change may require pulling apart large sections of code, which can drag on and create even more of a mess. Users and managers are left puzzled and frustrated by how ineffective the team seems.

The same is often true with infrastructure, even without automation. Different people have built, changed, updated, optimized, and fixed various parts of the systems involved over time. The whole interrelated web of parts can be precarious, any change to one part can potentially break one or more others.

High-Quality Systems Are Easier and Safer to Change

Even someone new to the team can understand how any piece of it works when they look into it. The impact of a change is generally clear. Tools and tests are in place that quickly surface problems caused by a change.

Systems like this need only minimal technical documentation. Typically, most members of the team can quickly draw the parts of the system's architecture that are relevant to a particular conversation. Newcomers with relevant technical knowledge are brought up to speed by a combination of conversations, poking through the code, and getting their hands dirty by working on the system.

Infrastructure Quality Through Code

Defining a system as infrastructure as code and building it with tools doesn't make the quality any better. At worst, it can complicate things. A mess of inconsistent, poorly maintained definition files and tooling can be combined with ad hoc manual interventions and special cases. The result is a fragile infrastructure where running the wrong tool can do catastrophic damage.

What infrastructure as code does is shift the focus of quality to the definitions and tooling systems. It is essential to structure and manage automation so that it has the virtues of quality code: easy to understand, simple to change, with fast feedback from problems. If the quality definitions and tools used to build and change infrastructure is high, then the quality, reliability, and stability of the infrastructure itself should be high.

Fast Feedback

A cornerstone of high-quality systems is fast feedback on changes. When I make a mistake in a change to a configuration definition, I'd like to find out about that mistake as quickly as possible.

The shorter the loop between making a change and being notified it causes a problem, the easier it is to find the cause. If I know I made a mistake in the work I've done over the past few minutes, I can find it quickly. If a problem crops up in a massive set of changes I've spent a few weeks on, there is quite a lot of code to go through.

Ideally I'd like to be notified of my mistake before it's been applied to an important system, which is the goal of CI and CD. At worst, I'd like good monitoring to flag a problem quickly after it's been applied, so my teammates and I can resolve it with as little damage as possible.

VCS for Infrastructure Management

As discussed in Chapter 1, a version control system (VCS) is a core part of an infrastructure-as-code regime. A VCS provides traceability of changes, rollback, correlation of changes to different elements of the infrastructure, visibility, and can be used to automatically trigger actions such as testing. This section will discuss some software engineering practices around using a VCS.

What to Manage in a VCS

Put everything in version control that is needed to build and rebuild elements of your infrastructure. Ideally, if your entire infrastructure were to disappear other than the contents of version control, you could check everything out and run a few commands to rebuild everything, probably pulling in backup data files as needed.

Some of the things that may be managed in VCS include:

- Configuration definitions (cookbooks, manifests, playbooks, etc.)
- Configuration files and templates
- Test code
- CI and CD job definitions
- Utility scripts
- Source code for compiled utilities and applications
- Documentation

Things that might not need to be managed in the VCS include the following:[2]

- Software artifacts should be stored in a repository (e.g., a Maven repository for Java artifacts, an APT or YUM repository, etc.). These repositories should be backed up or have scripts (in VCS) that can rebuild them.

---

2 Some of these reference "Types of Things on a Server" on page 105 in Chapter 6.

- Software and other artifacts that are built from elements already in the VCS don't need to be added to the VCS themselves, if they can be reliably rebuilt from source.

- Data managed by applications, logfiles, and the like don't belong in VCS. They should be stored, archived, and/or backed up as relevant. Chapter 14 covers this in detail.

- Passwords and other security secrets should never (never!) be stored in a VCS. Tools for managing encrypted keys and secrets in an automated infrastructure should be used instead.

Continuous Integration (CI)

Continuous integration (http://martinfowler.com/articles/continuousIntegration.html) is the practice of frequently integrating and testing all changes to a system as they are being developed. CI tools, such as Bamboo (*https://www.atlassian.com/software/bamboo*), Jenkins (*https://jenkins-ci.org*), SnapCI (*https://snap-ci.com*), TeamCity (*https://www.jetbrains.com/teamcity*), TravisCI (*https://travis-ci.org*), and others, can be used to enable this practice.

However, it's important to note that continuous integration is not the practice of using a CI tool, but is rather the practice of frequently integrating and testing all changes as they are made. All of the developers on a team commit their changes to the trunk of the codebase. Every time a commit is made, the CI tool builds the codebase and runs an automated test suite.

This gives fast feedback when a change doesn't build correctly, or when it causes a test to fail. Because the tests are run on every commit, it's immediately clear which set of changes caused the issue. The more frequently developers commit, the smaller the changeset is. The smaller a changeset is, the faster and easier it is to find and fix problems.

Continuously Testing Branches Is Not Continuous Integration

Many development teams use a CI tool but don't use it to continuously integrate and test changes. Running the test suite on a schedule (e.g., nightly, or even hourly) gives feedback on a slower loop than running it on every commit throughout the day.

Rather than continuously integrating changes, many development teams commit changes to separate branches in their VCS. The goal is usually to allow people to spend time finishing a large change before they worry about making it work with any changes that other people are working on.[3] However, as illustrated in Figure 10-1, the more changes someone makes on a branch without merging, the more work will be required to merge, test, debug, and fix the changes after merging.[4]

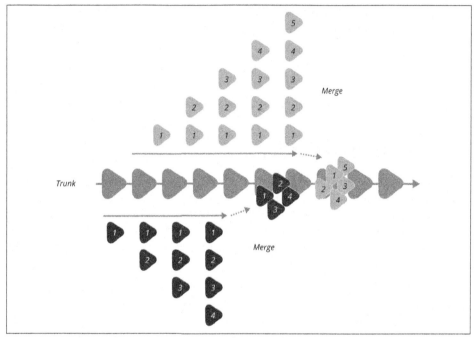

Figure 10-1. Delaying merges builds up work

Although a CI tool can be used to run tests automatically on commits made to each separate branch, the integrated changes are only tested together when the branches are merged. Some teams find that this works well for them, generally by keeping branches very short-lived.

With continuous integration, on the other hand, everyone commits their changes to the same trunk, and tests are run against the fully integrated codebase. Conflicts are found as soon as they are committed, which can save a great deal of work. Figure 10-2 shows how this works, and Table 10-1 summarizes several common branching strategies.

---

3 Branching is also used to separate changes so they can be released separately. However, there are more effective ways to do this, as discussed in Chapter 12 ("Practice: Prove Production Readiness for Every Change" on page 237)

4 Paul Hammant has a good blog post (*http://paulhammant.com/2013/04/05/what-is-trunk-based-development/*) on issues with branching.

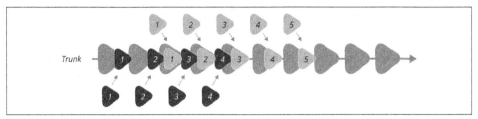

Figure 10-2. Merging every commit simplifies the process

Branching Fail

On one project, two of my colleagues were working on different aspects of the authentication code of a system, each making their changes to a separate branch. Although they did not actually change the same files, the changes turned out to be incompatible. They only discovered the problem when they both committed their changes, a few days before they were expected to deploy the new version of their system. Fixing it required ripping out and rewriting several weeks' worth of changes.

If my colleagues had committed their changes to trunk rather than to branches, they would have uncovered the issue much earlier, and saved a lot of time and effort.

The more frequently changes are committed to the shared trunk, the smaller they are, the fewer conflicts will arise, the easier testing is, and the less there is to fix.

Table 10-1. Common branching strategies

Branching strategy	Description
Feature branching	When a person or small group starts working on a change to the codebase, they can take a branch so they can work on it in isolation. This way, their work in progress is less likely to break something in production. When the change is complete, the team merges their branch back into trunk.
Release branching	When a new release is deployed to production, a branch is taken to reflect the current version in production. Bugfixes are made on the release branch and merged to trunk. Work on the next release is done on trunk.
Continuous integration	All work is done and committed to trunk. Continuous integration is used to ensure every commit is fully tested, and a continuous delivery pipeline can be used to ensure changes are only applied to production after being fully validated.

Who Broke the Build?

In order for continuous integration to be effective, every failure of a build or test in the CI system must be addressed immediately. Ignoring, or not noticing, when a build fails allows errors to pile up, and becomes confusing and difficult to untangle later. So a failed run in the CI tool triggers a "stop the line" situation. Development teams call this a *broken build*, or a *red build*.[5]

Nobody else in the team should commit any changes until the error is fixed, to make it easier to resolve. When commits are added to a broken build, it can be difficult to debug the original cause and untangle it from the following changes.

The person whose commit triggered the failure should prioritize fixing it. If the change isn't fixed quickly, then it should be reverted in VCS so the CI job can run again and hopefully return to a green status.

Build Monitors

Teams need immediate visibility of the status of their CI jobs. It's common to use an information radiator (see "What Is An Information Radiator?" on page 88) in the team's work area, and desktop tools that show pop-up notifications when a build fails. Email isn't very effective for this, as it tends to get filtered and ignored. A broken build needs to be a "red alert" that stops everyone until they know who is working to fix it.

Because fixing broken builds immediately is so critical, avoid falling into the habit of ignoring failing tests. If people become used to working when the build is red, the team gets zero value from CI. Nobody will notice when there is a real problem, so there will be no fast feedback loop.

Ignoring Tests That Fail

A related bad habit is disabling or commenting out tests that fail "for now" just to get things moving. Fixing a failing test should be your immediate priority. Getting a particular change released may be important, but your test suite is what gives you the ability to release quickly. If you allow your tests to degrade, you are undermining your ability to deliver.

Stamp out flaky tests: tests that routinely fail once, then pass when run another time. Randomly failing tests condition the team to ignore red builds. People think "it's always red, just run it again." Legitimate problems aren't noticed right away, after which you need to sift through the various commits to figure out where the real failure came from.[6]

---

5 Martin Fowler quotes Kent Beck (*http://martinfowler.com/articles/continuousIntegration.html#FixBroken BuildsImmediately*) as saying, "Nobody has a higher priority task than fixing the build."

6 Quarantining nondeterministic tests can be a useful strategy, if used in moderation. See Martin Fowler's article, "Eradicating Non-Determinism in Tests" (*http://martinfowler.com/articles/nonDeterminism.html*).

Test-driven development (TDD) and self-testing code are essential for CI. Chapter 11 discusses using these practices to develop tests alongside the code and configuration definitions that they test. Together, TDD and CI are a safety net that makes sure you catch mistakes as you make them, rather than being bitten by them weeks later.

CI for Infrastructure

CI with infrastructure as code involves continuously testing changes made to definition files, scripts, and other tooling and configuration written and maintained for running the infrastructure. Each of these should be managed in a VCS. Teams should avoid branching, to avoid building up an increasing "debt" of code that will need to be merged and tested. Each commit should trigger some level of testing.

In Chapter 11, we'll consider the test pyramid, which is a way of organizing different layers of testing for the infrastructure and systems (see "Structuring the Test Suite: The Test Pyramid" on page 198).

Continuous Delivery (CD)

Continuous integration addresses work done on a single codebase. Multiple developers working on the same code continuously merge their work so that issues are immediately surfaced and resolved. Continuous delivery[7] expands the scope of this continuous integration to the entire system, with all of its components.

The idea behind CD is to ensure that all of the deployable components, systems, and infrastructure are continuously validated to ensure that they are production ready. It is used to address the problems of the "integration phase."

The Problem with the Integration Phase

With the integration phase approach, different people and/or teams work on their piece of the project in isolation. Different applications and services are each built separately. The final production infrastructure is a separate stream of work. There may even be multiple streams of work for different parts of the infrastructure: database, application servers, networking, and so on.

These pieces are only brought together and properly tested once they're finished. The idea behind this is that the interfaces between the pieces can be defined well enough that everything will "just work." This idea is proven wrong again and again.[8]

---

7 *Continuous Delivery (http://amzn.to/1p9XYv1)*, by Jez Humble and David Farley (Addison-Wesley), is the canonical resource on the subject.

8 The LEGO integration game (*http://tastycupcakes.org/2011/10/continuous-integration-with-lego/*) is a fun way to demonstrate the differences between late integration and continuous integration.

It's critical that, throughout development, software is continuously deployed to test environments that accurately reflect their final production deployment environment. This deployment should be done in the exact same way in every environment, with all of the same restrictions applying to the test environments that will apply to production.

Carrying out frequent test deployments ensures that the deployment process is well proven. If any changes are made to the application that will break deployment to production, they will break deployment to the test environment first. This means they can be immediately fixed. Following this practice rigorously makes deployment to production a trivial exercise.

The Twelve-Month Continuous Delivery Project

I worked on a project at a large enterprise that took twelve months before the first release into production. We insisted on frequently deploying to a "controlled" environment, with production constraints, several times a weeks. We created an automated process that was agreed to be suitable for production, including needing a human to manually enter a password to confirm it was suitable.

Many people in the organization resisted this rigorous process. They thought it would be fine to deploy to less restricted environments, where developers had full root access and could make whatever configuration changes they needed to get their code working. They found it frustrating that some of us insisted on stopping and fixing failed deployments to the controlled environment—surely we could worry about that later?

But we got the deployments working smoothly. When the release phase came, the organization's release management teams scheduled a six-week transition phase for getting the "code complete" build ready for production release. The first step of this plan called for the production support team to spend two weeks getting the software installed on the pre-production environment, which would identify the work and changes needed to make the software ready for production use.

The support team got the software deployed and working in pre-production in a few hours, rather than two weeks. They decided that the work to prepare the production environment would also be less than one day. They were delighted—they saved over five weeks of work. Even better, fixes and improvements demanded by the business after go-live could be whipped through the release process, and everyone was confident the software was rock-solid.

Deployment Pipelines and Change Pipelines

Continuous delivery for software is implemented using a deployment pipeline. A deployment pipeline is an automated manifestation of a release process. It builds the application code, and deploys and tests it on a series of environments before allowing it to be deployed to production.

The same concept is applied to infrastructure changes. I use the term "change pipeline" when talking about pipelines for infrastructure, to make it clear that I'm not just talking about deploying application software.

A pipeline typically applies tests with increasing levels of complexity. The earlier stages focus on faster and simpler tests, such as unit tests, and testing a single service. Later stages cover broader sections of a system, and often replicate more of the complexities of production, such as integration with other services.

It's important that the environments, tooling, and processes involved in applying changes and deploying software are consistent across all of the stages of the pipeline. This ensures that problems that might appear in production are discovered early.

Test environments should be locked down just like production. Allowing privileges in test that aren't allowed in production only paves the road to failed production deployments. If production constraints make it hard to make changes as easily as necessary in test environments, then either find deployment solutions that work easily within those constraints, or find better ways to satisfy the goals of the constraints.

At the organization I mentioned in my story ("The Twelve-Month Continuous Delivery Project" on page 188), deploying to production required a sensitive password to be manually entered. We created a mechanism so someone could enter the password while triggering the deployment job in the Jenkins console. We automated this process for test stages where the password wasn't needed, but the script and job ran the exact same scripts. This allowed us to emulate the production constraint with a consistent, repeatable process.

This story illustrates that manual approvals can be incorporated into a CD process. It's entirely possible to accommodate governance processes that require human involvement in making changes to sensitive infrastructure. The key is to ensure that the human involvement is limited to reviewing and triggering a change to be applied. The process that actually applies the change should be automated, and should be exactly the same for each environment it is applied to.

Continuous Delivery Is Not Continuous Deployment

One misconception about CD is that it means every change committed is applied to production immediately after passing automated tests. While some organizations using continuous delivery do take this continuous deployment approach, most don't. The point of CD is not to apply every change to production immediately, but to ensure that every change is ready to go to production.

There is still a decision about when to actually push a given change or release to production. This decision can be made by a human, but is then carried out by the tooling. It's even possible to implement authorization and auditing of the decision process.

The great thing about CD is that the decision to go live becomes a business decision, not a technical one. The technical validation has already been done: it happens on every commit.[9]

The act of rolling out a change to production is not a disruptive event. It doesn't even require the technical team to stop working on the next set of changes. It doesn't need a project plan, handover documentation, or a maintenance window. It just happens, repeating a process that has been carried out and proven multiple times in testing environments.

For infrastructure teams, continuous delivery means that changes to infrastructure are comprehensively validated as they are made. Changes needed by users, such as adding new servers to a production environment, can be made without involvement by the infrastructure team, because they already know exactly what will happen when somebody clicks the button to add a new web server.

Code Quality

Over time, an infrastructure codebase grows and can become difficult to keep well maintained. The same thing happens with software code, and so many of the same principles and practices used by developers can be used by infrastructure teams.

Clean Code

In the past few years, there has been a renewed focus on "clean code"[10] and software craftsmanship, which is as relevant to infrastructure coders as to software developers. Many people see a trade-off between pragmatism (i.e., getting things done) and engineering quality (i.e., building things right). This is a false dichotomy.

Poor-quality software, and poor-quality infrastructure, is difficult to maintain and improve. Choosing to throw something up quickly, knowing it probably has problems, leads to an unstable system, where problems are difficult to find and fix. Adding or improving functionality on a spaghetti-code system is also hard, typically

---

9 Jez Humble has written an article about this, called "Continuous Delivery vs Continuous Deployment" (*http://continuousdelivery.com/2010/08/continuous-delivery-vs-continuous-deployment/*).

10 See Robert "Uncle Bob" Martin's *Clean Code: A Handbook of Agile Software Craftsmanship* (*http://www.amazon.com/Clean-Code-Handbook-Software-Craftsmanship-ebook/dp/B001GSTOAM*) (Prentice-Hall).

taking surprisingly long to make what should be a simple change, and creating more errors and instability.

Craftsmanship is about making sure that what you build works right, and ensuring that loose ends are not left hanging. It means building systems that another professional can quickly and easily understand. When you make a change to a cleanly built system, you are confident that you understand what parts of the system the change will affect.

Clean code and software craftsmanship are not an excuse for over-engineering. The point is not to make things orderly to satisfy a compulsive need for structure. It isn't necessary to build a system that can handle every conceivable future scenario or requirement.

Much the opposite. The key to a well-engineered system is simplicity. Build only what you need, then it becomes easier to make sure what you have built is correct. Reorganize code when doing so clearly adds value—for instance, when it makes the work you're currently doing easier and safer. Fix "broken windows" when you find them.

Practice: Manage Technical Debt

Technical debt is a metaphor for problems in a system that have been left unfixed. As with most financial debts, your system charges interest for technical debt. You might have to pay interest in the form of ongoing manual workarounds needed to keep things running. You may pay it as extra time taken to make changes that would be simpler with a cleaner architecture. Or charges may take the form of unreliable or hard-to-use services for your users.

Software craftsmanship is largely about avoiding technical debt. Make a habit of fixing problems and flaws as you discover them, which is preferably as you make them, rather than falling into the bad habit of thinking it's good enough for now.

This is a controversial view. Some people dislike technical debt as a metaphor for poorly implemented systems, because it implies a deliberate, responsible decision, like borrowing money to start a business. But it's worth considering that there a different types of debt. Implementing something badly is like taking a payday loan to pay for a vacation: it runs a serious risk of bankrupting you.[11]

---

11 Martin Fowler talks about the Technical Debt Quadrant (*http://martinfowler.com/bliki/TechnicalDebtQuadrant.html*), which distinguishes between deliberate versus inadvertent technical debt, and reckless versus prudent technical debt.

Managing Major Infrastructure Changes

The engineering practices recommended in this book are based on making one small change at a time (see "Small Changes Rather Than Batches" on page 16). This can be challenging when delivering large, potentially disruptive changes.

For example, how do you completely replace a key piece of infrastructure like a user directory service? It may take weeks or even months to get the new service working and fully tested. Swapping the old service out for a new one that isn't working properly would cause serious problems for your users and for you.

The key to delivering complex work in an agile way is to break it down into small changes. Each change should be potentially useful, at least enough that someone can try it out and see an effect, even if it's not ready for production use.

I find it useful to think in terms of capabilities. Rather than defining a task like "implement a monitoring check for SSH," I try to define it in terms such as "make sure we'll be notified when SSHD is not available on a server." For larger projects, a team can define progress in terms of capabilities.

There are a number of techniques for incrementally building major changes to a production system. One is to make small, nondisruptive changes. Slowly replace the old functionality, bit by bit. For example, Chapter 8 discussed implementing automated server configuration incrementally. Choose one element of your servers and write a manifest (or recipe, playbook, etc.) to manage that. Over time, you can add further configuration elements piece by piece.

Another technique is to keep changes hidden from users. In the case of replacing a user directory service, you can start building the new service and deploy it to production, but keep the old service running as well. You can test services that depend on it selectively. Define a server role that uses the new user directory, and create some of these servers in production that won't be used for critical services, but which can be tested. Select some candidate services that can be migrated to the new directory at first, perhaps ones that are used by the infrastructure team but not by end users. Table 10-2 summarizes some techniques for hiding unfinished changes in production code.

Table 10-2. Some techniques for deploying a system with changes that aren't ready yet

Technique	Description
Feature hiding	Deploy the changed code, but don't make it visible to users or systems. In many cases, this is simply a matter of not configuring other systems to integrate with the new feature.
Feature toggles	Implement a configuration setting that turns the changed feature or code off in the production environment.
Branch by abstraction	When replacing an existing component, deploy both the new and the old component. Use configuration, such as a feature toggle, so that the older version of the component is used in the production environment, while enabling the newer version to be used in relevant test environments.

The important point is to make sure that any change that will take a while to implement is continuously being tested out, during development.

Feature Toggles

Feature toggles[12] are a technique for testing changes to an existing script. The new changes are added with some conditional logic so that they're only used when a configuration setting is "toggled." For software or tools that use a configuration registry, different environments can have the feature toggled on in test environments, and off for production.

Clean Up Unused Toggles

A common problem with using feature toggles and similar techniques is that it complicates the codebase of the system. Over time, this tends to accumulate a large amount of conditional code and configuration options that aren't needed any more.

It's a trap to think that removing feature toggles is unnecessary work, or that configuration options should be left in "just in case." These add complexity, increasing the time to understand the system and debug errors. Defects love to hide in code that people assume isn't used.

An optional feature that is no longer used, or whose development has been stopped, is technical debt. It should be pruned ruthlessly. Even if you decide later on that you need that code, it should be in the history of the VCS. If, in the future, you want to go back and dust it off, you've got it in the history in version control.

---

12 Using feature toggles effectively is a deep topic. My colleague Pete Hodgson covers many aspects of the subject in an article (*http://martinfowler.com/articles/feature-toggles.html*). Ryan Breen has also written about experiences using feature toggles at scale (*http://lifeinvistaprint.com/techblog/configuration-management-git-consul/*).

Conclusion

This chapter reviewed some core software development practices and how they relate to working with infrastructure as code. The underlying theme of these practices is quality. In order to ensure the quality of systems and the code that defines them, quality must be a first-order concern.

Teams that prioritize the quality of their systems, by getting continuous feedback and acting on it immediately, create a virtuous cycle. They have the confidence to routinely make the small fixes and tweaks that keep their systems humming smoothly. This gives them additional time to spend on the more satisfying, higher-order work rather than fighting fires.

The next chapter covers further specifics on automated testing.

## CHAPTER 11

Testing Infrastructure Changes

The previous chapter described how software engineering practices such as CI and CD can be applied with infrastructure as code. A major theme of that chapter was managing quality. This chapter drills into specifics of testing, especially automated tests. Automated testing is essential to be able to continuously test changes to a system. But many teams find building and maintaining an automated test suite difficult to sustain. This chapter looks at approaches used by teams who do manage to establish and keep up automated testing regimes.

The purpose of testing is to help get work done quickly. Sadly, in many organizations testing is seen as something that slows work down. There is a common misconception that quality and delivery speed are opposing forces that must be traded off, one against the other. This mindset leads to the idea that automation can speed the delivery process by making the act of testing a system go faster.

These misconceptions—testing as the enemy of delivery speed, and automation as a silver bullet to make testing go faster—lead to expensive, failed test automation initiatives.

The reality is that system quality is an enabler of delivery speed. Investing less time to find and fix problems results in a fragile system. Fragile systems are difficult to change, so changes are time consuming and risky.

The goal of automated testing is to help a team keep the quality of their system high by identifying errors as soon as they are made so they can be immediately fixed. A team with strong discipline around continuously testing and fixing is able to make changes quickly and with confidence.

A strong, well-balanced automated testing regime leads to:

- Fewer errors discovered in production
- Faster fixes when errors are discovered
- The ability to make frequent changes and improvements

In other words, good testing results in faster delivery and higher quality.

The Agile Approach to Testing

Many organizations have a process that separates implementation and testing into different phases of work, usually carried out by separate teams. Agile processes encourage teams to integrate testing with implementation to shorten the feedback loop (Figure 11-1). Testing takes place continuously, as changes are made. This is done by testers and developers working closely together, combined with automated testing.

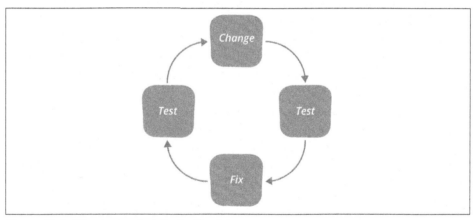

Figure 11-1. The change-test-fix feedback loop

So the most useful goal for test automation isn't to reduce the length of a project's testing phase, but to embed testing and fixing activities into the core workflow. As someone works on a change to the system, whether it's a change to application code or to infrastructure definitions, they continuously test. They test to make sure their change works as they expect. They test to make sure their change doesn't break other parts of the system. And they test to make sure they aren't leaving any loose ends to cause problems later on.

People test so they can fix each problem right away, while they're still working on the changes. Everything is still fresh in their mind. Because the scope of the changes are very small, problems are quick to find and fix.

Automating Tests for Fast Feedback

Teams whose testing process is based around separate implementation and test phases often attempt to adopt automation by automating their test phase. This is often a project owned by the QA team, which aims to create a comprehensive regression test suite that replicates what they have been doing manually. There are several reasons why these automation efforts tend to be disappointing.

One problem is that automated test suites built by a separate testing team tend to focus on high-level testing. This is because tools marketed at test teams tend to be UI-focused, because they are seen as replacing manual testing driven through the UI.

While UI level tests are an essential part of an automated test suite, they are more expensive to develop, slower to run, and require more work to maintain as the systems they test evolve. So a test suite needs to be well balanced. The test pyramid described later in this chapter offers a model for designing a well-balanced test suite.

However, a key to successful test automation is for the entire team to be involved in planning, designing, and implementing it, rather than making it the responsibility of an isolated group.

The Pitfall of Big Bang Test Automation Projects

Initiatives to implement automated testing often bite off more than they can chew. This leads to difficulties keeping up with ongoing development, because the system is a constantly moving and changing target. Before the massive test suite is complete, the system has changed. Once the test suite is built, the system will immediately change again. So tests tend to be constantly broken, and the nirvana of a complete test suite is never achieved.

Aiming for the goal of a complete, finished test suite is doomed to fail. Instead, the goal of an automation initiative should be to embed the habit of continuously writing tests as a part of routine changes and implementation work. So the outcome of an automated testing initiative is not a completed test suite, but a set of working habits and routines.

When automated testing has been successfully adopted by a team, tests are written or updated whenever a change is made to the system. CI and CD regimes run the relevant tests for every change continuously, as discussed in Chapter 10. The team responds immediately to fix failing tests.

Organically Building a Test Suite

The way to start an initiative that results in good testing habits is not to attempt to build a full test suite to cover the existing functionality. Instead, write tests for each new change as it comes up. When a bug is found, write a test that exposes that bug, and then fix it. When a new feature or capability is needed, begin implementing tests as you go, possibly even using test-driven development (TDD), as described later in this chapter.

Building the test suite organically as a part of making routine changes forces everyone to learn the habits and skills of sustainable, continuous testing. Again, the outcome to aim for is not a "finished" test suite, but the routine of testing each change. A test suite will emerge from this approach, almost as a by-product. Interestingly, the test suite that emerges will be focused on the areas of the system that most need tests: the ones that change and/or break the most.

Structuring the Test Suite: The Test Pyramid

Managing a test suite is challenging. The tests should run quickly, be easy to maintain, and help people quickly zero in on the cause of failures. The testing pyramid is a concept for thinking about how to balance different types of tests to achieve these goals (Figure 11-2).

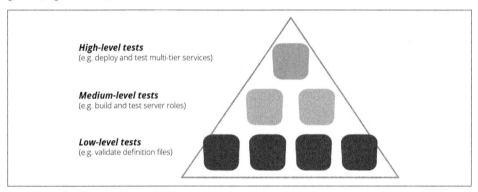

Figure 11-2. The test pyramid

The pyramid puts tests with a broader scope toward the top, and those with a narrow scope at the bottom. The lower tiers validate smaller, individual things such as definition files and scripts. The middle tiers test some of the lower-level elements together —for example, by creating a running server. The highest tiers test working systems together—for example, a service with multiple servers and their surrounding infrastructure.

There are more tests at the lower levels of the pyramid and fewer at the top. Because the lower-level tests are smaller and more focused, they run very quickly. The higher-level tests tend to be more involved, taking longer to set up and then run, so they run slower.

Avoiding an Unbalanced Test Suite

A common problem with automated test suites is the ice-cream cone, or inverted pyramid, as seen in Figure 11-3. This happens when there are too many high-level tests when compared with lower-level tests.

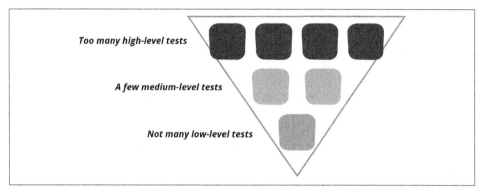

Figure 11-3. The inverted testing pyramid

A top-heavy test suite is difficult to maintain, slow to run, and doesn't pinpoint errors as well as a more balanced suite.

High-level tests tend to be brittle. One change in the system can break a large number of tests, which can be more work to fix than the original change. This leads to the test suite falling behind development, which means it can't be run continuously.

Higher-level tests are also slower to run than the more focused lower-level tests, which makes it impractical to run the full suite frequently. And because higher-level tests cover a broad scope of code and components, when a test fails it may take a while to track down and fix the cause.

This usually comes about when a team puts a UI-based test automation tool at the core of their test automation strategy. This in turn often happens when testing is treated as a separate function from building. Testers who aren't involved in building the system don't have the visibility or involvement with the different layers of the stack. This prevents them from developing lower-level tests and incorporating them into the build and change process. For someone who only interacts with the system as a black box, the UI is the easiest way to interact with it.

Long Test Runs Are a Sign of an Unbalanced Test Suite

In order for CI and CD to be practical, the full test suite should run every time someone commits a change. The committer should be able to see the results of the test for their individual change in a matter of minutes. Slow test suites make this difficult to do, which often leads teams to decide to run the test suite periodically—every few hours, or even nightly.

If running tests on every commit is too slow to be practical, the solution is not to run the tests less often, but instead to fix the situation so the test suite runs more quickly. This usually involves rebalancing the test suite, reducing the number of long-running tests and increasing the coverage of tests at the lower levels.

This in turn may require rearchitecting the system being tested to be more modular and loosely coupled, so that individual components can be tested more quickly.

Practice: Test at the Lowest Level Possible

UI and other high-level tests should be kept to a minimum, and should only be run after the lower level tests have run. An effective test suite runs a small number of end-to-end journey tests, touching the major components of the system and proving that integration works correctly. Specific features and functionality are tested at the component level, or through unit tests.

Whenever a higher-level test fails, or a bug is discovered, look for ways to catch the issue at the lowest possible level of testing. This ensures that the error will be caught more quickly and that it's very clear exactly where the failure is. If an error can't be detected at the unit-test level, move up a layer of the stack and try to catch it there. Essentially, a test at any level above a unit test should be testing an interaction that only happens when the components at that level are integrated.

So if there is a problem in component A, then the test for that component should catch it, rather than an integration test that runs across components A, B, and C. Tests should fail when testing A, B, and C only when they have a found an error in the way those components work together, even when each component is correct in itself.

As an example, let's say you discover that an application error happens because of an error in a configuration file managed by Chef. Rather than testing whether the error appears in the running application, you should write a test for the Chef recipe that builds the configuration file.

Testing for the error in the UI would involve starting a VM, could require setting up a database and other services, and then building and deploying the application built.

A change that caused a problem in the application might cause dozens of tests to fail, which makes it difficult to understand exactly what has gone wrong.

Instead, write a test that runs whenever the Chef recipe changes. The test can use a tool like ChefSpec (*https://docs.chef.io/chefspec.html*) that can emulate what happens when Chef runs a recipe, without needing to apply it to a server. This runs much more quickly, and when it fails there is a very narrow area to look at to find the cause.

The ChefSpec example (Example 11-1) creates a `Runner` object, which is an emulator for running the recipe. Each `it ... do ... end` block is an individual test, checking that the template file has been created, or that it has the correct attributes.[1]

Example 11-1. ChefSpec sample test

```
require 'chefspec'

describe 'creating the configuration file for login_service' do
  let(:chef_run) { ChefSpec::Runner.new.converge('login_service_recipe') }

  it 'creates the right file' do
    expect(chef_run).to create_template('/etc/login_service.yml')
  end

  it 'gives the file the right attributes' do
    expect(chef_run).to create_template('/etc/login_service.yml').with(
      user:    'loginservice',
      group:   'loginservice'
    )
  end

  it 'sets the no_crash option'
    expect(chef_run).to render_file('/etc/login_service.yml').
        with_content('no_crash: true')
  end
end
```

Practice: Only Implement the Layers You Need

The testing pyramid suggests that there should be tests at multiple integration levels for every component. But which layers you implement will depend on the particular system and its needs. It's important to avoid over-complicating the test suite.

There is no formula for what types of tests should be used for an infrastructure codebase. It's best to start out with fairly minimal tests, and then introduce new layers and types of testing when there is a clear need.

---

1 Note that this example probably violates the recommendation later in this chapter to not write reflective tests ("Anti-Pattern: Reflective Tests" on page 213).

Practice: Prune the Test Suite Often

Maintaining an automated test suite can be a burden. It gets easier as a team becomes more experienced, and writing and tweaking tests becomes routine. But there is a tendency for the test suite to grow and grow. Writing new tests becomes a habit, so teams need a corresponding habit of removing tests to keep the suite manageable. It's of course helpful to avoid implementing unnecessary tests in the first place.

Practice: Continuously Review Testing Effectiveness

The most effective automated testing regimes involve continuously reviewing and improving the test suite. From time to time, you may need to go through and prune tests; remove layers or groups of tests; add a new layer or type of tests; add, remove, or replace tools; improve the way you manage tests; and so on.

Whenever there is a major issue in production or even in testing, consider running a blameless post-mortem (*https://codeascraft.com/2012/05/22/blameless-postmortems/*). One of the mitigations that should always be considered is adding or changing tests, or even removing tests.

Some signs that you should consider revamping your tests:

- Do you spend more time fixing and maintaining certain tests than you save from the problems they catch?
- Do you often find issues in production?
- Do you often find issues late in the process, such as when releasing?
- Do you spend too much time debugging and tracing failures in high-level tests?

Code Coverage for Infrastructure Unit Tests

Avoid the temptation to set targets for code coverage for infrastructure unit tests. Because configuration definitions tend to be fairly simple, an infrastructure codebase may not have as many unit tests as a software codebase might. Setting targets for unit test coverage—a much-abused practice in the software development world—will force the team to write and maintain useless test code, which makes maintaining good automated testing much harder.

Implementing a Balanced Test Suite

There is a variety of tooling available to implement automated infrastructure testing. In many cases, tools designed for software testing can be directly adopted and applied to infrastructure. Some of these tools have been extended to add infrastructure-specific functionality. For example, Serverspec (*http://serverspec.org/*) extends the RSpec (*http://rspec.info/*) Ruby-based testing tool with features for checking server configuration.

Different tools may be needed for different types of testing at different levels of the pyramid. It's important to avoid getting hung up on the tooling. Avoid choosing a tool and basing your testing strategy around it. Instead, analyze your systems and components to decide how you need to approach testing them. Then find tools to carry out your approach. As with any part of your infrastructure, assume that you will change parts of your test tooling over time.

Figure 11-4 shows an example application, *LoginService*, which will be used throughout this chapter to illustrate the implementation of a balanced test suite. LoginService uses two types of servers: a database server and an application server. Each server type has a Puppet manifest to configure it, and a Packer template to build an AMI for it. A CloudFormation definition file is used to define the surrounding infrastructure for the service.

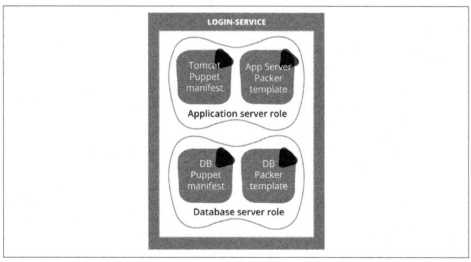

Figure 11-4. LoginService architecture

Figure 11-5 shows a test pyramid for the LoginService, giving a rough idea about levels of testing that may be appropriate.

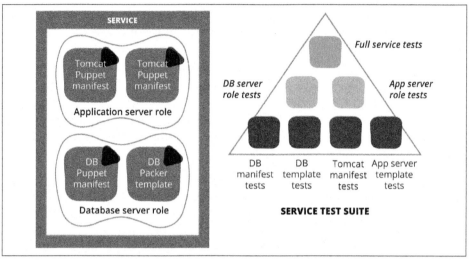

Figure 11-5. An example service and its test pyramid

Low-Level Testing

The following sets of files are all managed in VCS:

- Application server Puppet manifest
- Database server Puppet manifest
- Application server Packer template
- Database server Packer template
- CloudFormation file

Each of these definition files is managed in a VCS and is independently testable. When a change is committed, the CI server pulls the relevant files from the VCS and runs some validation on it.

A change to either one of the Puppet manifests triggers some validation for the manifest:

- Syntax checking
- Static analysis
- Unit testing

All of these tests can be run quickly, because they don't have complex setup requirements. They don't require actually creating a server and applying the manifest. They tend to find simple mistakes very quickly.

Without this layer of tests, a simple syntax mistake might not be found until several minutes have been spent creating a virtual machine and fully configuring it. And at that point, tracing a problem down to the specific error can take a while. It's much nicer to have a quick check that immediately tells you about the error.

Syntax Checking

Many tools that use configuration definition files, including Puppet, Packer, and CloudFormation, have a syntax checking mode that can be used to implement this kind of check. In Example 11-2, the puppet command-line tool is being used to validate the *appserver.pp* file.

Example 11-2. Running Puppet's syntax checking

```
$ puppet parser validate appserver.pp
```

Static Code Analysis

Static code analysis tools work by parsing code or definition files without executing them. Lint (*https://en.wikipedia.org/wiki/Lint_(software)*) is the archetypal static analysis tool, originally written to analyze C code. Static code analysis tools are available for a growing number of infrastructure definition file formats, like puppet-lint (*http://puppet-lint.com*) and Foodcritic (*http://www.foodcritic.io*) for Chef.

Static analysis can be used to check for common errors and bad habits which, while syntactically correct, can lead to bugs, security holes, performance issues, or just code that is difficult to understand.

Many of the things that static analysis tools check for can seem trivial or pedantic. But the most effective infrastructure and development teams tend to be rigorous about good coding hygiene. Forcing yourself to change your coding habits to keep definitions and scripts consistent and clean results in more reliable systems. Those small bits of messy code and trivial bugs accumulate and create unreliable infrastructure and services.

Unit Testing

A unit test in software code executes a small subsection of a program, on the order of a one or two classes, to make sure that they run correctly. Most infrastructure tools have some kind of unit testing tool or framework, such as rspec-puppet (*http://rspec-puppet.com/*) and ChefSpec (*https://docs.chef.io/chefspec.html*). Saltstack even comes with its own built-in unit testing support (*https://docs.saltstack.com/en/latest/topics/tutorials/writing_tests.html*).

Tools like this allow a particular configuration definition to be run without actually applying it to a server. They usually include functionality to emulate other parts of a system well enough to check that the definition behaves correctly. This requires ensuring that each of your definitions, scripts, and other low-level elements can be independently executed. Restructuring things to make test isolation possible may be challenging, but results in a cleaner design.

A pitfall with unit testing is that it can lead to reflective testing (as described in "Anti-Pattern: Reflective Tests" on page 213). Don't fall into the trap of thinking that you must have unit tests covering every line of your configuration definitions. This idea leads to a mass of brittle tests that are time consuming to maintain and have little value for catching problems.

Mid-Level Testing

Once the quicker validation has been run, different pieces can be assembled and tested together. For the LoginService example described earlier, this might involve building an application server template using the Packer template and the Puppet manifest. The validation process would be to create a server instance using the new template, and then run some tests against it. Figure 11-6 shows how mid-level tests for the application server role map to that part of the system architecture.

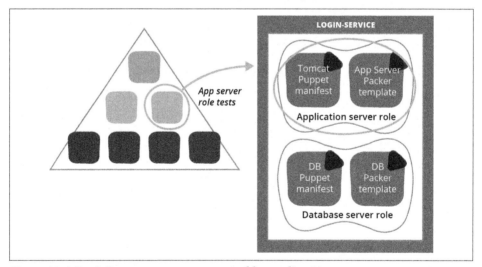

Figure 11-6. LoginServer components covered by application server tests

Example 11-3 shows a Serverspec snippet that tests whether there is a service named `login_service` running.

Example 11-3. Serverspec to validate the login service is running

```
describe service('login_service') do
  it { should be_running }
end
```

The flow to set up and run this test (and presumably others) is illustrated in Figure 11-7. At this point, each of the pieces involved in building the application server template has been validated on its own. Tests at the middle level should not be proving the correctness of the individual components, but rather should be proving that they work correctly when integrated together.

For example, the Puppet manifest may make assumptions about packages that have been installed by the base operating system. If someone updates the version of the operating system in the template, the packages may change, which may cause problems for the Puppet manifest. This level of testing is the first point where you can catch this kind of error.

Other failures you would like to discover at this stage are those uncovered because the system is now using an actual server instance, rather than having unit testing software emulate the environment the manifest is applied to.

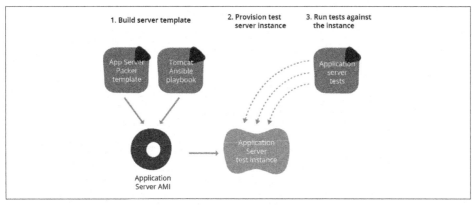

Figure 11-7. Flow for testing the LoginService application server

Creating Test Infrastructure

Tests at this level will need to create test instances of the relevant infrastructure. For the LoginService appserver test, this is a test server. But other tests may need to test other things, such as networking configuration or data persistence. Scripts or definitions that manage network configuration will require the ability to stand up at least emulated pieces of infrastructure.

This should be done using the same infrastructure platform technology used by the things being tested. Cloud style infrastructure allows test tooling to draw from a pool of resources, to spin up servers, networking elements, and so on, as needed. For teams using a more limited set of resources (e.g., a set of physical hardware dedicated to the project), this requires an investment to ensure there is enough capacity to run this kind of testing.

Test infrastructure should be baselined before each test. If possible, new instances should be provisioned from scratch, using the same definitions, tooling, and processes that are used to provision the infrastructure in production. The resources are then disposed of after the test is complete. This requires the infrastructure provisioning process to be quick so that the testing process doesn't run overly long.

If testing happens on a fixed set of infrastructure, the instances should be cleared down and reconfigured from scratch. This avoids situations where cruft builds up across test runs, polluting the test environment.

Locally Virtualized Test Infrastructure

In more constrained environments, or just to optimize the time for testing, it's often useful to run tests on a locally virtualized environment like Vagrant, rather than on the main infrastructure platform. If the CI agents that run tests are built in a way that supports hosting virtual machines, then they can spin up local VMs to validate server configuration.

The important criteria is how useful this is in actually catching problems quickly. In many cases, a Vagrant box running the same OS, built and provisioned using the same tools and definitions, is an accurate enough representation of a VM running on the production infrastructure.

Don't Get Hung Up on the Language

Teams often prefer testing tools written in the same language they are using for their infrastructure management scripts and tooling. This is sensible when people using the tool must write tests in that same language. It can also be useful for writing extensions. For example, knowing (or learning) Ruby is helpful when using RSpec-based tools.

But the implementation language is less important when using tools where tests are defined using a DSL that is more abstracted from it. If the team doesn't have much exposure to the underlying language, it should be less of a consideration when choosing the tool.

Tooling for Managing Test Infrastructure

There are a variety of tools that make it easier to automatically create server instances, or other infrastructure context, for the purposes of testing. Test Kitchen (*http://*

kitchen.ci/) is designed to make it easy to manage test servers on different infrastructure platforms in order to apply and test configuration. It was written specifically for Chef but is also used for testing Puppet and other tools. Kitchen Puppet (*https://github.com/neillturner/kitchen-puppet*) was written to support testing Puppet manifests with Test Kitchen.

Higher-Level Tests

The higher levels of the test suite involve testing that multiple elements of the infrastructure work correctly when integrated together. This is illustrated in Figure 11-8. End-to-end testing for a particular service integrates all of the elements needed to deliver that service. This potentially includes integrating external systems as well.

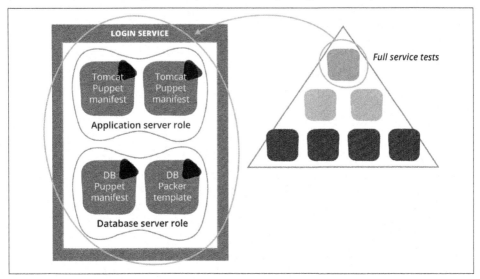

Figure 11-8. LoginServer components covered by high level tests

The considerations for testing at this level are similar to those for testing at the middle tiers. For example, a test instance of the relevant infrastructure needs to be provisioned, preferably by building it from scratch, or at least reliably setting it to a baseline, before applying the configuration.

For higher-level infrastructure, it becomes more difficult to emulate the infrastructure without using the same infrastructure platform as production. In any case, this is typically the point where accurately reproducing production infrastructure becomes essential, because this is probably the last stage of testing to be carried out before production.

This level of testing doesn't tend to need much special tooling that isn't already used elsewhere. The infrastructure should be provisioned using the same tooling and definitions that are used for the production infrastructure. Testing can often be carried out using a mix of tools as appropriate. The types of tools used for mid-level validation, like Serverspec, are often appropriate here. Simple scripts using `curl` can validate that connectivity works correctly.

In some cases, it may be useful to use general-purpose behavior-driven development (BDD[2]) and UI testing tools.[3] This type of testing is particularly useful to test more complex interactions involving a web UI.

Because this tier of testing is the slowest to set up and run, it's crucial to keep the tests rigorously pruned. Tests at this level should be the minimum needed to find problems that can't be found through lower level testing.

Example 11-4 uses a Serverspec that will be executed from the application server. It proves that the database server is reachable from the application server. This will catch any errors with the firewall rule configuration.

Example 11-4. Serverspec to validate connectivity

```
describe host('dbserver') do
  it { should be_reachable.with( :port => 5432 ) }
end
```

Securely Connecting to a Server to Run Tests

Automatically tests that remotely logging into a server can be challenging to implement securely. These tests either need a hard-coded password, or else an SSH key or similar mechanism that authorizes unattended logins.

One approach to mitigate this is to have tests execute on the test server and push their results to a central server. This could be combined with monitoring, so that servers can self-test and trigger an alert if they fail.

Another approach is to generate one-off authentication credentials when launching a server to test. This requires support in the infrastructure platform—for example, the ability to assign an SSH key to a server instance when creating it. The automated test script would generate a new key, apply it when spinning up a test server, and then use it to log in and run tests. The credentials never need to be shared or stored. If they are compromised, they don't give access to any other servers.

---

2 See behavior-driven development (*http://dannorth.net/introducing-bdd/*).

3 Such as Selenium (*http://www.seleniumhq.org/*).

Testing Operational Quality

People managing projects to develop and deploy software have a bucket of requirements they call non-functional requirements, or NFRs (*https://en.wikipedia.org/wiki/Non-functional_requirement*); these are also sometimes referred to as cross-functional requirements (CFRs). Performance, availability, and security tend to be swept into this bucket.

NFRs related to infrastructure can be labeled operational qualities for convenience. These are things that can't easily be described using functional terms: take an action or see a result. Operational requirements are only apparent to users and stakeholders when they go wrong. If the system is slow, flaky, or compromised by attackers, people notice.

Automated testing is essential to ensuring operational requirements. Every time a change is made to a system or its infrastructure, it's important to prove that the change won't cause operational problems. The team should have targets and thresholds defined which it can write tests against.

Operational testing can take place at multiple tiers of the testing pyramid, although the results at the top tiers are the most important. These tests measure and validate performance, security, and other characteristics of the system when all of the pieces are in place end to end. So this is the level where operational targets are normally set.

However, it can be useful to have operational quality tests at lower levels of the pyramid. Care should be taken to avoid complicating the test suite with low value tests. But when some parts of the system tend to be the weak link in delivering the right level of operational quality, it can be useful to push testing down to that level.

For example, if a particular application tends to be the slowest part of the end-to-end system, putting application-level tests around it can be useful. Components that the sluggish application integrates with can be mocked or stubbed (as in "Techniques to Isolate Components for Testing" on page 213) so the performance of the application can be measured on its own.

Automated security tests can take the form of static analysis tools that look for common programming errors that lead to vulnerabilities. They can also check for versions of packages or libraries that have known vulnerabilities. There are many tools available for scanning systems and infrastructure for security issues,[4] many of which can be automated and made part of a regular testing suite.

---

4 A few examples include BDD-Security (*http://www.continuumsecurity.net/bdd-intro.html*), Burp Suite (*https://portswigger.net/burp/*), Gauntlt (*http://gauntlt.org/*), Vega (*https://subgraph.com/vega/*), and ZAP (*https://www.owasp.org/index.php/OWASP_Zed_Attack_Proxy_Project*).

Monitoring as Testing

There is a close relationship between monitoring and automated testing, both of which are ways of detecting problems with a system. Testing is aimed at detecting problems when making changes, before they are applied to production systems. Monitoring is aimed at detecting problems in running systems. Chapter 14 explores ways of combining testing and monitoring in more detail ("Continuous Monitoring through the Pipeline" on page 296).

Managing Test Code

The tooling for writing and running tests should be treated the same as everything else in the infrastructure. Team members need to apply the same time, effort, and discipline to maintaining high-quality test code and systems.

It should be possible to configure testing agents or software in a way that is repeatable, reproducible, transparent, and has all of the other qualities expected with infrastructure as code.

"Version All the Things" on page 15 applies to tests just as it applies to infrastructure definitions. Tests should be stored in an externalized format that can be committed to a VCS, rather than hidden inside a proprietary black-box tool. This way, a change to a test can automatically trigger a test run in CI, proving that it works.

Practice: Keep Test Code with the Code It Tests

Tests should be managed together with the code of the thing they test. This means putting them together in your VCS, and promoting them together through your pipeline until they reach the stage where they're run. This avoids a mismatch of test to code.

For example, if you write some tests to validate a Chef cookbook, they may need to change when there's a change to the cookbook. If the tests are stored separately, you may end up running an older or newer version of the tests against a different version of the cookbook. This leads to confusion and flaky builds, because it's unclear whether there is really an error in the cookbook or just a test mismatch.

A variation of this is to keep them in the same VCS, but to package and promote them separately. Version numbers can be used to correlate tests. For example, playbooks might be packaged as *app-server-config-2.101.rpm*, and the corresponding tests packaged as *app-server-tests-2.101.tgz*. This helps ensure the correct version of tests are always used, without needing to include test scripts in the configuration package.

Anti-Pattern: Reflective Tests

A pitfall with low-level infrastructure tests is writing tests that simply restate the configuration definitions. Example 11-5 is a Chef snippet that creates the configuration file from the earlier test example.

Example 11-5. Simple definition to be tested

```
file '/etc/login_service.yml'
  owner ourapp
  group ourapp
end
```

Example 11-6 is a snippet from the earlier ChefSpec unit test example.

Example 11-6. Test that the definition created the file

```
describe 'creating the configuration file for login_service' do
  # ...
  it 'gives the file the right attributes' do
    expect(chef_run).to create_template('/etc/login_service.yml').with(
      user:   'ourapp',
      group:  'ourapp'
    )
  end
```

This test only restates the definition. The only thing it proves is whether the Chef developers have correctly implemented the `file` resource implementation, rather than proving anything useful about what you've written yourself. If you're in the habit of writing this kind of test, you will end up with quite a few of them, and you'll waste a lot of effort editing every piece of configuration twice: once for the definition, once for the test.

As a rule, only write a test when there's some complexity to the logic that you want to validate. For the configuration file example, it may be worth writing that simple test if there is some complex logic that means the file may or may not be created.

For example, maybe `login_service` doesn't need a configuration file in most environments, so you only create the file in a few environments where the default configuration values need to be overridden. In this case, you would probably have two unit tests: one that ensures the file is created when it should be, and another that ensures it isn't created when it shouldn't be.

Techniques to Isolate Components for Testing

In order to effectively test a component, it must be isolated from any dependencies during the test.

As an example, consider testing an nginx web server's configuration.[5] The web server proxies requests to an application server. However, it would be nice to test the web server configuration without needing to start up an application server, which would need the application deployed to it, which in turn needs a database server, which in turn needs data schema and data. Not only does all of this make it complex to set up a test just to check the nginx configuration, there are many potential sources of error aside from the configuration being tested.

A solution to this is to use a stub server instead of the application server. This is a simple process that listens on the same port as the application server and gives responses needed for the tests. This stub could be a simple custom application that is deployed just for the test—for example, a Ruby Sinatra web app. It could also be another nginx instance or a simple HTTP server written in the infrastructure team's favorite scripting language.

It's important for the stub server to be simple to maintain and use. It only needs to return responses specific to the tests you write. For example, one test can check that requests to */ourapp/home* returns an HTTP 200 response, so the stub server handles this path. Another test might check that, when the application server returns a 500 error, the nginx server returns the correct error page. So the stub might answer a special path like */ourapp/500-error* with a 500 error. A third test might check that nginx copes gracefully when the application server is completely down, so this test is run without the stub in place.

A server stub should be quickly started, with minimum infrastructure required. This enables running it in complete isolation as part of a larger test suite.

Test Doubles

Mocks, fakes, and stubs are all types of "test doubles." A test double replaces a dependency needed by a component or service being tested, to simplify testing. These terms tend to be used in different ways by different people, but I've found the definitions used by Gerard Meszaros in his xUnit patterns book (*http://xunitpatterns.com/*) to be useful.[6]

---

5 This example was inspired by Philip Potter's blog post about testing web server configuration (*https://gdstech nology.blog.gov.uk/2015/03/25/test-driving-web-server-configuration/*) at GDS (UK Government Digital Services).

6 Martin Fowler's bliki Mocks Aren't Stubs (*http://martinfowler.com/articles/mocksArentStubs.html*) is a useful reference to test doubles and is where I learned about Gerard Meszaros' book.

Refactoring Components so They Can Be Isolated

Oftentimes, a particular component can't be easily isolated. Dependencies to other components may be hardcoded or simply too messy to pull apart. One of the benefits of writing tests while designing and building systems, rather than afterward, is that it forces you to improve your designs. A component that is difficult to test in isolation is a symptom of design issues. A well-designed system should have loosely coupled components.

So when you run across components that are difficult to isolate, you should fix the design. This may be difficult. Components may need to be completely rewritten, libraries, tools, and applications may need to be replaced. As the saying goes, this is a feature, not a bug. In order to make a system testable, it needs a clean design.

There are a number of strategies for restructuring systems. Refactoring[7] is an approach that prioritizes keeping the system fully working throughout the process of restructuring the internal design of a system.

Managing External Dependencies

It's common to depend on services not managed by your own team. Some elements of the infrastructure, such as DNS, authentication services, or email servers, may be provided by a separate team or an external vendor. These can be a challenge for automated testing, for a number of reasons:

- They may not be able to handle the load generated by continuous testing, not to mention performance testing.
- They can have availability issues that affect your own tests. This is especially common when vendors or teams provide test instances of their services.
- There may be costs or request limits that make them impractical to use for continuous testing.

Test doubles can be used to stand in for external services for most testing. Your test suite can first run tests with the system using test doubles. Only after these tests have passed should the test suite move on to test integration with external services. This way, if a test fails with the integrated systems, the correctness of your own code has already been proven. So you can be sure the test failure is caused either by problem with the other service, or with the way you've integrated with it.

---

7 Martin Fowler has written about refactoring (*http://martinfowler.com/books/refactoring.html*) as well as other patterns and techniques for improving system architecture. The Strangler Application (*http://martin fowler.com/bliki/StranglerApplication.html*) is a popular approach I've seen on a number of projects.

You should ensure that, if an external service does fail, it's very clear that this is the issue. Any integrations with third parties, and even those between your own services, should implement checking and reporting that makes it immediately visible when there is an issue. This should be made visible through monitoring and information radiators for all environments. In many cases, teams implement separate tests and monitoring checks that report on connectivity with upstream services.

Wasted Time

I recall spending over a week with one team, poring over our application and infrastructure code to diagnose an intermittent test failure. It turned out that we were hitting a request limit in our cloud vendor's API. It's frustrating to waste so much time on something that could have been caught much more quickly.

Test Setup

By now you may be tired of hearing about the importance of consistency, reproducibility, and repeatability. If so, brace yourself: these things are essential for automated testing. Tests that behave inconsistently have no value. So a key part of automated testing is ensuring the consistent setup of environments and data.

For tests that involve setting up infrastructure—building and validating a VM, for example—the infrastructure automation actually lends itself to repeatability and consistency. The challenge comes with state. What does a given test assume about data? What does it assume about configuration that has already been done to the environment?

A general principle of automated testing is that each test should be independent, and should ensure the starting state it needs. It should be possible to run tests in any order, and to run any test by itself, and always get the same results.

So it's not a good idea to write a test that assumes another test has already been run. For example, Example 11-7 shows two tests. The first tests the installation of nginx on the web server, the second tests that the home page loads with expected content.

Example 11-7. Tests that are too tightly coupled

```
describe 'install and configure web server' do
  let(:chef_run) { ChefSpec::SoloRunner.converge(nginx_configuration_recipe) }

  it 'installs nginx' do
    expect(chef_run).to install_package('nginx')
  end
end
```

```
describe 'home page is working' do
  let(:chef_run) { ChefSpec::SoloRunner.converge(home_page_deployment_recipe) }

  it 'loads correctly' do
    response = Net::HTTP.new('localhost',80).get('/')
    expect(response.body).to include('Welcome to the home page')
  end
end
```

This example looks reasonable at a glance, but if the 'home page is working' test is run on its own, it will fail, because there will be no web server to respond to the request.

You could ensure that the tests always run in the same order, but this will make the test suite overly brittle. If you change the way you install and configure the web server, you may need to make changes to many other tests which make assumptions about what has happened before they run. It's much better to make each test self-contained, as in Example 11-8.

Example 11-8. Decoupled tests

```
describe 'install and configure web server' do
  let(:chef_run) { ChefSpec::SoloRunner.converge(nginx_configuration_recipe) }

  it 'installs nginx' do
    expect(chef_run).to install_package('nginx')
  end
end

describe 'home page is working' do
  let(:chef_run) {
    ChefSpec::SoloRunner.converge(nginx_configuration_recipe,
                                  home_page_deployment_recipe)
  }

  it 'loads correctly' do
    response = Net::HTTP.new('localhost',80).get('/')
    expect(response.body).to include('Welcome to the home page')
  end
end
```

In this example, the second spec's dependencies are explicit; you can see that it depends on the nginx configuration. It's also self-contained—either of these tests can be run on their own, or in any order, with the same result every time.

Managing Test Data

Some tests rely on data, especially those that test applications or services. As an example, in order to test a monitoring service, a test instance of the monitoring server may be created. Various tests may add and remove alerts to the instance, and emulate situations that trigger alerts. This requires thought and care to ensure tests can be run repeatably in any order.

For example, you might write a test that adds an alert and then verifies that it's in the system. If this test runs twice on the same test instance, it may try to add the same alert a second time. Depending on the monitoring service, the attempt to add a duplicate alert may fail. Or, the test may fail because it finds two alerts with the same name. Or the second attempt to add the alert may not actually work, but the validation finds the alert added the first time, so does not tell you about a failure.

So some rules for test data:

- Each test should create the data it needs.
- Each test should either clean up its data afterward, or else create unique data each time it runs.
- Tests should never make assumptions about what data does or doesn't exist when it starts.

Persistent test environments tend to drift over time, so that they're no longer consistent with production. Immutable servers (as described in "Patterns and Practices for Immutable Servers" on page 143) help ensure a clean and consistent test environment for every test run.

Roles and Workflow for Testing

Infrastructure teams tend to find testing a challenge. The typical system administrator's QA process is as follows:

1. Make a change
2. Do some ad hoc testing (if there's time)
3. Keep an eye on it for a little while afterward

On the flip side, not many testers understand infrastructure very well. As a result, most infrastructure testing tends to be superficial.

One of the big wins of agile software development was breaking down the silos between developers and testers. Rather than making quality the responsibility of a separate team, developers and testers share ownership. Rather than allocating a large block of time to test the system when it's almost done, agile teams start testing when they start coding.

There is still controversy over what the role of a quality analyst (QA) or tester should be, even within an agile team. Some teams have decided that, because developers write their own automated tests, there is no need for a separate role. Personally, I find that even in a highly functioning team, QAs bring a valuable perspective, expertise, and a talent for discovering the gaps and holes in what I build.

There are some guidelines for how to manage testing with a team.

Principle: People Should Write Tests for What They Build

Having a separate person or team write automated tests has several negative effects. The first one is that delivering tested work takes longer. There is delay in handing over the code, then a loop while the testers work out what the code should do, write the tests, and then try to understand whether test failures are because they've gotten the test wrong, because of an error in the code, or a problem with the way the work was defined. If the developer has moved on to another task, this creates a constant stream of interruptions.

If a team does have people who specialize in writing automated tests, they should work with the developers to write the tests. They could pair[8] with the developer for the testing phase of work, so the developer doesn't move on to something else but stays with the work until the tests are written and the code is right. But it's better still if they pair during development, writing and running the tests while writing the code.

The goal should be to help the developers become self-sufficient, able to write automated tests themselves. The specialist may carry on working with the team, reviewing test code, helping to find and improve testing tools, and generally championing good practice. Or they may move on to help other teams.

The Test-Writing Habit

Many teams struggle to make writing tests a routine habit. It's a lot like exercising, in that it's unpleasant to do when you aren't used to it. It's easy to find excuses to skip doing it, promising yourself you'll make up for it later. But if you push yourself to do it, over time it becomes easier. Eventually, the habit becomes embedded enough that you feel uncomfortable writing code or configuring systems without writing tests.

Principle: Everyone Should Have Access to the Testing Tools

Some automated testing tools have expensive per-user licensing models. Typically, this means only a certain few individuals are able to write and run tests with the tool,

---

8 For more on pair programming, see the XP website (*http://www.extremeprogramming.org/rules/pair.html*). Martin Fowler has also written about the topic in his article "Pair Programming Misconceptions" (*http://martinfowler.com/bliki/PairProgrammingMisconceptions.html*).

because buying licenses for everyone on the team is too expensive. The problem with this is that it creates longer feedback loops.

If the people writing and fixing code aren't able to run and observe tests themselves, it takes more time to reproduce and debug failures. The engineer must reproduce and fix the error blindly, without being able to run the failing test. This leads to a few rounds of "fixed it," "still fails," "how about now?", "that broke something else," and so on.

There are many powerful test automation tools, with large communities of free and commercial support, which are either free or cheap enough to be used without adding waste and pain to the delivery process.[9]

The Value of a Quality Analyst

A person with deep expertise and enthusiasm for quality assurance is a huge asset to any engineering team. They often act as a champion for testing practices. They help people to think about work that is being planned or discussed.

Team members should consider how to define each task so that it's clear where it begins and ends and how to know that it's been done correctly. Surprisingly often, simply having this conversation before starting the work saves an enormous amount of time and wasted effort.

Some quality engineers have expertise with automated testing tools. Their skills are best harnessed by teaching, coaching, and supporting the other team members in using these tools. It's important to avoid the trap of letting this expert do all of the work of writing the tests. This risks becoming a test silo and leaves the team disengaged from their own work.

Another strength that many testers bring is a talent for exploratory testing. These people can take any system and immediately discover the gaps and holes.

---

9 A few examples include Cucumber (*https://cucumber.io/*), RSpec (*http://rspec.info/*), and Selenium (*http://docs.seleniumhq.org/*).

The Three Amigos Conversation

Many agile teams find it useful to have a "three amigos" conversation[10] before starting on an item of work. This involves the person doing the work, the stakeholder who has requested the work (the "product owner" in agile parlance), and the person who will test it. This is a useful way to make sure everyone understands what is expected from the work, and to clarify any questions. This same group also meets once the item is complete, to review it, identify any tweaks or fixes needed, and then sign it off.

It's important that this be a conversation, rather than documentation or a request system ticket. Documentation and tickets become formalities to get out of the way, rather than a meaningful human interaction.

It should also be noted that the scope of the three amigos conversation is a small piece of work (what developers call a "story"), that will take at most a few days to complete. Larger chunks of work also need conversations, but the three amigos conversations are specific and targeted.

Test-Driven Development (TDD)

Test-driven development, or TDD (*http://martinfowler.com/bliki/TestDrivenDevelopment.html*), is a core practice of Extreme Programming.[11] The idea is that, because writing tests can improve the design of what you build, you should write the test before you write the code you test. The classic working rhythm is *red-green-refactor:*[12]

Red
Write a test for the next change you want to make, run the test, and see that it fails.

Green
Implement and test the definitions until the test passes.

Refactor
Improve the new and old definitions to make it well structured.

---

10 More on the Three Amigos pattern can be found in a talk by George Dinwiddie (*http://www.infoq.com/interviews/george-dinwiddie-three-amigos*).

11 Extreme Programming (*http://www.extremeprogramming.org/*), sometimes referred to simply as XP, is one of the more popular agile development methodologies. It focuses on involving the users of a system in the process of building it, and continuous testing and reviews of work. The premise of the name is that, because testing and user involvement are useful, they should be done more intensively than previous methodologies.

12 See "Red-Green-Refactor" (*http://www.jamesshore.com/Blog/Red-Green-Refactor.html*).

Writing the test first forces you to think about the code you're about to write. What should it do and how will you know it works? What are the inputs and outputs? What errors could happen, and how should they be handled? Once you've got a clear test, implementing the changes to make the test pass should be easy.

Running the test before writing the code proves that it's a valid test. If the test passes before you've implemented the change, then clearly you need to rethink your test.

"Refactoring" is making changes to improve existing code without changing the behavior. This is an important technique for improving code quality, and automated tests are a safety net that assure you that you haven't accidentally broken working code.

Take It One Test at a Time

I once met a team that was struggling to get started with TDD, because they thought they needed to write *all* of the tests for a component before they started coding the system itself. TDD is not about switching around the phases of a waterfall. It is about writing tests and code together, one small piece at a time.

Conclusion

Automated testing is possibly the most challenging aspect of infrastructure as code, while also being the most important for supporting a reliable and adaptable infrastructure. Teams should incorporate testing habits into their routine. The next chapter explains how to create change management pipelines to support these habits.

## CHAPTER 12

Change Management Pipelines for Infrastructure

Previous chapters have discussed the use of continuous integration (CI) to automatically test changes to scripts, tools, and configuration definitions, as they are committed to source control. They have also mentioned continuous delivery (CD), which builds on this to provide assurance that all of the elements of a system work correctly after a change.

This chapter explains how to implement continuous delivery for infrastructure by building a change management pipeline.

A deployment pipeline[1] is used in CD to manage the deployment and testing of software to a series of validation stages whenever there is a change to the codebase. The validations ensure that the codebase is production ready and that it will deploy correctly and reliably. The same automated process is used to deploy and configure the software in each environment, including production, to prevent the classic "worked in test; failed in live" issues that arise from inconsistencies and manual processes.

The point of CD and the software deployment pipeline is to allow changes to be delivered in a continuous flow, rather than in large batches. Changes can be validated more thoroughly, not only because they are applied with an automated process, but

---

1 Jez Humble and David Farley explained the idea of a deployment pipeline (*http://martinfowler.com/bliki/DeploymentPipeline.html*) in their book *Continuous Delivery* (*http://www.amazon.com/Continuous-Delivery-Deployment-Automation-Addison-Wesley/dp/0321601912*) (Addison-Wesley), building on experiences from a ThoughtWorks client project (*http://blog.magpiebrain.com/2009/12/13/a-brief-and-incomplete-history-of-build-pipelines/*). Humble defines a deployment pipeline as an "automated manifestation of your process for getting software from version control into the hands of your users" (*http://www.informit.com/articles/article.aspx?p=1621865&seqNum=2*).

also because changes are tested when they are small, and because they are tested immediately after being committed. The result, when done well, is that changes can be made more frequently, more rapidly, and more reliably.

Continuous Change Management

Continuous delivery for infrastructure could be characterized as continuous change management or continuous provisioning (*http://www.heavywater.io/blog/2015/02/17/continuous-provisioning/*). The point is to create a process that is optimized to quickly and rigorously validate a continuous flow of small changes.[2]

An infrastructure change management pipeline is no different from a software deployment pipeline. Many people use the term "deployment pipeline" for pipelines that apply infrastructure changes. I like to use the term "change management pipeline" just to emphasize its relevance to infrastructure. A software deployment pipeline has been described as the automated manifestation of your software release process.[3] A change management pipeline could be described as the automated manifestation of your infrastructure change management process.

A change management pipeline works by:

- Immediately and thoroughly testing each change to prove whether it is production ready.
- Testing the elements of the system affected by a change progressively. This aligns with the test pyramid discussed in the previous chapter.
- Enabling manual validation activities, like exploratory testing, user acceptance testing (UAT), and approvals, where appropriate.
- Applying changes to production systems easily, quickly, and with low risk and impact. This happens by making sure that the process for applying the changes is fully automated and works the same way in all environments.

---

2 The idea of continuous change management, and how it relates to governance and controls, is explored more in Chapter 15 ("Governance through Continuous Change Management" on page 322).

3 I've paraphrased Jez Humble from "Continuous Delivery: Anatomy of the Deployment Pipeline" (*http://www.informit.com/articles/article.aspx?p=1621865&seqNum=2*)

Pipelines with Human Oversight

Many people assume that because an automated pipeline is triggered whenever a change is committed to the codebase, changes will be automatically rolled out to production without human intervention. Although some organizations do implement their pipelines this way, most have at least one stage in their pipeline that is manually triggered. Often, multiple changes are committed and validated in the pipeline before being applied to production.

Benefits of a Change Management Pipeline

Teams who embrace the pipeline as the way to manage changes to their infrastructure find a number of benefits:

- Their infrastructure management tooling and codebase is always production ready. There is never a situation where extra work is needed (e.g., merging, regression testing, and "hardening") to take work live.

- Delivering changes is nearly painless. Once a change has passed the technical validation stages of the pipeline, it shouldn't need technical attention to carry through to production unless there is a problem. There is no need to make technical decisions about how to apply a change to production, as those decisions have been made, implemented, and tested in earlier stages.

- It's easier to make changes through the pipeline than any other way. Hacking a change manually—other than to bring up a system that is down—is more work, and scarier, than just pushing it through the pipeline.

- Compliance and governance are easy. The scripts, tools, and configuration for making changes are transparent to reviewers. Logs can be audited to prove what changes were made, when, and by whom. With an automated change management pipeline, a team can prove what process was followed for each and every change. This tends to be stronger than taking someone's word that documented manual processes are always followed.

- Change management processes can be more lightweight. People who might otherwise need to discuss and inspect each change can build their requirements into the automated tooling and tests. They can periodically review the pipeline implementation and logs, and make improvements as needed. Their time and attention goes to the process and tooling, rather than inspecting each change one by one.

Guidelines for Designing Pipelines

There are a few guiding principles for designing an effective change management pipeline.

Ensure Consistency Across Stages

Environments, tooling, and processes should be consistent in the essential ways across stages.

For instance, server operating system versions and configuration should be the same across environments. This is easily done by using server templates and rolling changes to them out across environments using the pipeline.

Whenever there is a failure applying a change to a downstream system, especially production, consider whether upstream systems can be changed to more accurately emulate the conditions that led to the failure. Always be looking for opportunities to catch errors earlier in the pipeline.

Consistent environments does not mean identical environments

One objection to making testing environments consistent with production is the expense. In organizations with hundreds or thousands of servers, or very expensive hardware, it's not practical to duplicate this in each stage of the pipeline, or even in any stage of the pipeline.

However, the point isn't to have the same number or even size of servers in every environment. Here are some guidelines:

- Make sure that the essential characteristics are the same. The OS and version should always be the same. If the production environment uses a more expensive OS variant ("enterprise" editions, for example), then you either need to bite the bullet and use this in at least one earlier environment, or else make it a priority to ensure you can use on an OS that your organization can afford to use across the board.

- Replicate enough of the production characteristics so that potential issues will be caught. You don't need to run 50 servers in a load balancing pool for a test environment. But you should at least make sure you are running two servers behind a similar load balancer, and exercise it enough to uncover potential problems with state management.

- At least one environment at the early stage should replicate the complexities of production. But it isn't necessary that every single environment does. For example, the automated deployment test environment described earlier in the simple pipeline may have a load balanced pool of servers and deploy applications on to separate servers as they are in production. But even later stages like QA and UAT may be able to run all of the applications on a single server. This needs to be carefully considered to ensure you're exposing all of the potential risks due to the production environment's architecture.

When It's Too Expensive to Replicate in Test

Often, the reason that it's difficult to replicate essential production characteristics is because it involves expensive equipment. If your organization is struggling to justify buying additional devices just for testing, it's important to take a hard look at its priorities. Having an important system that can't be properly tested outside of production is unwise. Either spend the money needed for a responsible change management process, or else find solutions that the organization can afford.

Get Immediate Feedback for Every Change

Make sure the pipeline runs quickly so that you get immediate feedback on each change as it is committed. The pipeline should be the easiest way to get a quick fix through to production. If people feel the need to bypass the pipeline to make a change, it's a sign that the pipeline needs to be improved.

The pipeline should run immediately after any change is committed to its input materials. This means multiple changes will be continuously running through the pipeline as different team members make different changes.

If the pipeline takes too long for this to be practical, teams may be tempted to run the pipeline, or parts of it, on a periodic schedule (i.e., hourly, nightly, etc.). Rather than doing this, invest the effort to improve the pipeline until it's possible for the pipeline to run continuously. This is essential to ensuring fast and continuous feedback on changes.[4]

Run Automated Stages Before Manual Stages

Once you have automation that can apply changes to systems in an unattended way, it becomes cheaper and faster to run a set of automated tests against it than to have skilled humans spend time testing it. So it makes sense to run all of your automated tests first, before handing the system over to the humans.

---

4 Reducing the running time of the pipeline may require changing the architecture of the system. See "Pipelines, Architecture, and Teams: Conway's Law" on page 245 later in this chapter.

Running all of the automated test stages first makes sure that the basic problems have already been found. When a change has been handed over to humans to test, they can focus their energies on the trickier problems, without getting tripped up by trivial errors.

Get Production-Like Sooner Rather Than Later

With traditional release processes, software is only tested in the most production-like environment until just before the release is applied to production. "Preproduction" or "staging" is the final check before going live. But errors or problems found at the last minute are the most painful to fix. Fortunately, an automated change management pipeline can turn this around.

An ideal pipeline automatically applies each and every change to the most accurate test environment as it is committed. Testing at this point ensures that the change has been proven to be technically production ready before it is handed over to humans to decide if it's human-ready.

Doing this may seem counterintuitive. Leaving the comprehensive testing for the last stage makes sense when doing so is an expensive, time-consuming manual process. But when deploying changes is effortless, then comprehensively testing every change as soon as it's made aligns with the other pipeline design principles, such as running automated stages before making humans spend time testing a change, and giving immediate and full feedback on each change as it's made.

DevOops

I learned the value of managing infrastructure changes using a pipeline the hard way. I was helping a development team to automate the infrastructure they used for testing and hosting a public-facing, web-based application.

The team had a sophisticated CD pipeline that automatically deployed their application to one stage at a time, only deploying to the next stage when the previous stage passed. However, the Chef cookbooks we used to configure the servers were directly applied to all of our servers at once, across all of the testing environments.

We had decided to have Chef manage the */etc/hosts* files on the servers, so it could automatically add and update hostname mappings, instead of running a private DNS server.

You can probably see where this is going.

I made a tweak to the cookbook that built the */etc/hosts* file and pushed it to our Chef server. Unfortunately, it had a simple error that made the file completely invalid. Once my broken cookbook was applied to our servers, none of the servers were unable to resolve the hostname of the Chef server itself. I fixed my mistake and

---

pushed a new version of the cookbook to the Chef server, but none of the servers could get the updated cookbook.

Work ground to a halt for the development team, because all of their test environments were broken. Fortunately, we were not yet live, so there was no customer impact. But I had to endure the glares of my teammates while I logged into each and every server, one by one, to resolve the issue.[5]

My colleague Chris Bird described this as "DevOops"; the ability to automatically configure many machines at once gives us the ability to automatically break many machines at once.

Ever since this misadventure, I've made sure to have changes to my automated configuration automatically applied to a test environment before they're applied to any environment that other people rely on for something important.

Basic Pipeline Designs

Figure 12-1 shows the shape of a simple change management pipeline. Each change is progressively tested in automated stages and then made available for manual testing and signoff.

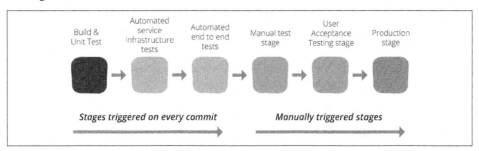

Figure 12-1. Basic change management pipeline

The following sections drill into what typically happens in different types of pipeline stages.

The Local Development Stage

Infrastructure developers check out the latest version of the definitions and other files locally, makes changes, and runs tests. They might run tests using local virtualization,

---

5 Actually, I was able to use Chef's knife tool to make the fix across our servers fairly quickly. But I was conscious of how easily this, too, could backfire.

or a cloud-based sandbox.[6] When they are satisfied with the change, they commit it to the VCS.

The Build Stage

The build stage (sometimes called the CI stage)[7] is the first stage triggered after a change is committed to the VCS. It runs on a build agent, which is a server instance managed by the CI or CD system. This agent will first check out the relevant file set from the VCS onto the local filesystem. It then carries out validation on that code, prepares it for use, and finally makes it available to be applied to other environments.

Actions that can happen in the build stage may include some of the following:

- Syntax checking and static analysis (see "Low-Level Testing" on page 204 in Chapter 11 for details on these activities).
- Compiling code, where relevant.
- Unit tests.
- Local execution tests. For software components and services, it may be appropriate to run and test it, even though it's not currently in a full deployment environment. This will normally use test doubles (as described in "Test Doubles" on page 214) rather than integrating with other systems or infrastructure elements, to keep this stage self-contained. In some cases, containerization (such as Docker) may help with this.
- Generating and publishing reports, such as code change reports, test results, generated documentation, and code coverage reports.
- Packaging code into a distributable and deployable format.

As with any stage of the pipeline, if one of these activities fails, then the stage should go red and refuse to progress the changes downstream. The results, such as test reports, should be made easily available either way, so they can be used to diagnose issues.

---

6 See Chapter 13 ("Using a Local Sandbox" on page 262) for more on how developers can work on infrastructure changes before committing.

7 The reason the build stage is called the CI stage is that it encapsulates the early approaches to continuous integration. These tended to be focused on compiling software code and creating a build artifact. Continuous delivery expanded the CI concept to deploying and testing software all the way through to production. This meant adding additional stages and linking them together in a pipeline. Many of the tools used to implement CD pipelines were originally designed for the single stage use case for CI.

The output of this stage is that whatever is being tested (e.g., a script, library, application, configuration definition, or configuration file) is now in the format that will be needed to apply it to production.

Publishing a Configuration Artifact

At the end of a successful build stage run, the configuration artifact is packaged and published. This means preparing the materials and making them available for use in later stages of the pipeline. What this involves depends on the nature of the infrastructure element. Examples include:

- Building a system or language installation package file (an RPM, *.deb*, *.gem*, etc.) and uploading it to a repository
- Uploading a set of definition files (Puppet module, Ansible playbook, Chef cookbook, etc.) to a configuration repository
- Creating a template server image (VM template, AMI, etc.) in an infrastructure platform

The classic application artifact bundles everything into a single file, but this isn't necessarily the case for infrastructure artifacts. Most server configuration tools use a set of files that are grouped and versioned as a unit, such as a Chef cookbook, but they tend not to be packed into a single distributable file. They may be uploaded to a configuration repository that understands their format and versioning. Some teams eschew this functionality and do package the files, either into a system package or general-purpose archive format, particularly when using a masterless configuration management model.

The important thing is how the artifact is treated, conceptually. A configuration artifact is an atomic, versioned collection of materials that provision and/or configure a system component. An artifact is:

Atomic
 A given set of materials is assembled, tested, and applied together as a unit.

Portable
 It can be progressed through the pipeline, and different versions can be applied to different environments or instances.

Versioned
 It can be reliably and repeatably applied to any environment, and so any given environment has an unambiguous version of the component.

Complete
> A given artifact should have everything needed to provision or configure the relevant component. It should not assume that previous versions of the component artifacts have been applied before.

Consistent
> Applying the artifact to any two component instances should have the same results.

Artifacts with a configuration master

When using a configuration master server (e.g., Chef Server, Puppet Master, or Ansible Tower) the artifacts are definition files (e.g., cookbooks, modules, or playbooks). The build stage will finish by publishing these to the master so they can be applied to servers by the server configuration tool or agent.

The master should be able to tag the definitions with a version number. It may also have a feature, such as Chef's "Environments," which can be used to assign a specific version of definition files to an environment. This feature can be used to manage the progression of the definitions through the stages of the pipeline. As each given version of the definitions passes through a pipeline stage, they can be promoted to the next stage by assigning them to the next environment in the master.

An alternative to this arrangement is to use multiple master instances. Each stage of the pipeline, or group of stages, may have its own master. Definitions are uploaded to the relevant master as they progress through the pipeline.

Artifacts with masterless configuration management

With masterless configuration management (described in "Pattern: Masterless Configuration Management" on page 139), configuration definitions are stored in a general-purpose file management system, rather than a special configuration server. This might be a file server, static web server, object store (such as AWS S3), system package repository (e.g., APT or YUM) or even a VCS.

Teams that adopt this model often package the definitions in a versioned archive (e.g., a *.tgz*, *.rpm*, or *.deb* file). The build stage of the pipeline finishes by building this package and uploading it to the central file store. In later stages, this file is downloaded to the servers being configured so they can be applied. Versioning might be inherent in the file storage (e.g., RPM files in a YUM repository), or else might simply be indicated by the filename (e.g., *appserver-config-1.3.21.tgz*).

Artifacts with an immutable server model

With immutable servers (explained in "Patterns and Practices for Immutable Servers" on page 143), the artifact is the server template image. The build stage checks a server

---

template definition file, such as a Packer template, or script out from VCS, builds the server template image, and publishes it by making it available in the infrastructure platform. With AWS, for example, this results in an AMI image.

Generally, the infrastructure platform acts as the repository for the artifact. In some cases, the template might be packaged in a file format, such as an OVF file (*https:// en.wikipedia.org/wiki/Open_Virtualization_Format*) or Vagrant *.box* file, and then uploaded to a file repository of some type. This is particularly useful to make a single server template available on multiple infrastructure platforms or instances.

Automated Testing Stages

Once the build stage has passed and the definitions have been published, they can be applied and tested in more realistic environments. The specifics will depend on what is being tested.

Automated testing may take place across multiple pipeline stages. This can be useful when different types of setup is needed for different test cases. For example, one stage might test an application server role on its own. Tests would not use a database (the database could be stubbed or mocked, as per "Test Doubles" on page 214) or anything else outside of the application server itself. A following test stage could then test the application server integrated with other infrastructure elements, including the database server.

Multiple stages should involve progressively widening scope of the infrastructure and systems being tested. This follows the test pyramid, as illustrated by Figure 12-2.

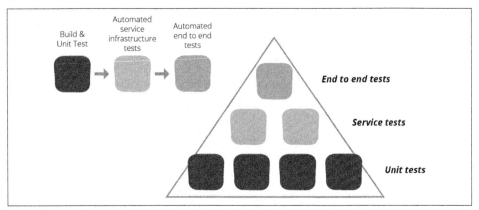

Figure 12-2. The relationship between the test pyramid and a pipeline

Progressing the testing scope this way has a few benefits. First, the wider scoped tests normally take longer to run, because there are more things to set up, and the tests tend to take longer to run. So if the earlier, faster-running tests fail, the pipeline stops and gives feedback about the error more quickly, rather than waiting for the longer tests to run first.

Second, it's easier to find the cause of a failure in the narrower-scoped tests. If a test fails in the broader test suite, there are more elements that may have contributed to the failure. If the stage that tests the application server on its own passes, you have confidence that it is being built correctly. If tests fail at the next stage, when the application server is integrated with the database and other elements, then you can guess that the problem is caused by the integration of the components, rather than the components themselves.[8]

Manual Validation Stages

Once the automated testing stages have all been run, the definitions can be made available for manual testing stages. These stages are triggered manually, typically through the UI of the CD or CI tool. But the provisioning and configuration that it triggers is executed by the same automated tooling and definitions that were used in the previous stages.

Unlike the automated testing stages, the sequence of manual stages will tend to be based on organizational process. Typically, testing for quality assurance happens in the earliest manual stages. Activities for demonstration, UAT, approvals, and the like take place in later stages. There may also be stages to deploy to externally visible environments—for example, beta testing or closed previews.

Keeping the Pipeline Moving

Don't allow work to become bottlenecked by sharing environments or stages. Often teams will try to use a single-test environment for both QA and demonstrations to stakeholders. This usually leads to QA work having to stop while the environment is carefully prepared and then frozen in the leadup to a demonstration. New changes can't be deployed for testing, possibly for days at a time, for fear that something will break the system shortly before the demo.

In these cases, it's far better to split the environments. QA work should have at least one environment, depending on how many testers are working simultaneously. Demonstrations should have their own environments. This is a huge benefit of the ability to dynamically provision consistent environments using infrastructure as code. In many cases, environments can be provisioned on demand for a demo or testing exercise and then destroyed afterward.

---

8 Of course, this assumes that all of the other components have themselves been tested, as described in the "Pattern: Fan-In Pipelines" on page 239).

Apply to Live

The final stages in a pipeline is normally the production deployment stage. This should be a trivial task, because it carries out exactly the same activities, using exactly the same tools and processes, as have been applied many times in upstream stages. Any significant risk or uncertainty at this stage should be modeled and addressed in upstream stages.

The pipeline stage to release to production may involve governance controls. For example, in some situations, legal or compliance rules require specific individuals, or multiple individuals, to authorize changes to production systems. The production stage can use authentication and authorization controls to enforce these requirements.

The capability to apply changes and deploy systems with zero downtime is essential for ensuring that changes can be made and rolled out quickly and routinely. Disruptive change processes encourage batching and infrequent releases. This in turn increases the size, complexity, and risk of releases.

It's useful to ensure that zero-downtime change processes,[9] such as blue-green deployment, phoenix deployment, and canary releases, are used and tested in at least one upstream pipeline stage, preferably an automated test stage.

Continuously Improve the Pipeline

Every problem discovered in manual testing—and in production—may be an opportunity to ask whether an automated test would catch a similar error earlier.

The Rhythm of the Pipeline

A commit will run through all of the automated stages of a pipeline, assuming it doesn't fail any of the stages. The manual stages tend to be run less often. Figure 12-3 shows a typical series of commits to a component managed by a pipeline.

---

9 Zero-downtime change processes are described in Chapter 14 ("Zero-Downtime Changes" on page 282).

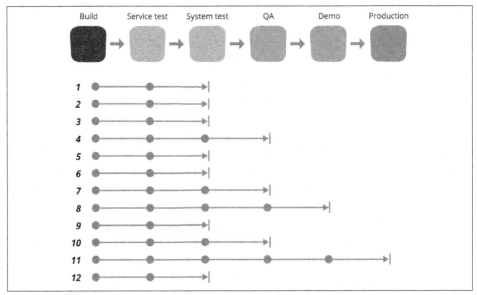

Figure 12-3. Commits reach later stages of the pipeline less often

Several commits (1, 2, and 3) run through the automated stages without being manually tested. When the tester is ready, she triggers the QA stage to apply the latest change (commit 4) to the QA environment. This version includes all of the changes from commits 1–4, so she can test everything up to this point.

In the meantime, the team commits a few more changes (5 and 6). The tester may report an issue, after which a fix is committed (7). This fix moves through the pipeline, and the tester deploys it to the QA environment. After this is tested, one more change is committed (8), tested by the tester, and then deployed to the demo environment. Again, this includes all of the previous changes.

The cycle is repeated a few more times, with commits 9 through 12 all running through the automated stages. Changes 10 and 12 are tested in the QA stage, with change 12 making it through to the demo stage, and finally to production.

This example shows that the earlier stages of the pipeline will run more often than the later stages. It also shows that not every change, even ones that pass testing and demo, are necessarily deployed immediately to production.

Practices for Using a Pipeline

The previous section describes a basic pipeline. The next section will expand this into more complex situations. However, before doing this, it's useful to consider some key practices for teams working with pipelines.

Practice: Prove Production Readiness for Every Change

Every time you commit to VCS, assume the change could be put through to production if it passes the automated checks. Don't assume you will be able to finish it off, clean it up, or make any additional edits. So don't make a change that you would be alarmed to find in production.

This can be an issue because multiple people may be making changes to the same component in the VCS during the same period. One person may commit a change that they know will need some more work before it should go to production. In the meantime, someone else may make a change that they send straight through to production, taking the first person's unfinished work with it.

The classic technique for managing this situation is to have people work on different branches, and merge each one to trunk as it's ready. However, this does not meet the criteria of keeping the codebase production ready at all times: it stores up merging and testing work to be done at some later point.

Alternative techniques for managing concurrent workstreams in a single codebase include feature hiding, feature toggles, and branch by abstraction.[10] People can use these to commit their changes to the codebase, knowing they will not be active even if they do get physically deployed to production.

Practice: Start Every Change from the Beginning of the Pipeline

Occasionally, when a change fails in a downstream stage, it's tempting to make a fix directly there, maybe even editing the files in the artifact repository. However, this is a dangerous practice, as the new edit won't have been tested in the upstream stages so may have problems that won't be caught until too late. Also, manual fixes in later environments have a habit of either becoming forgotten, or being added to a checklist of manual steps that erode the effectiveness of the automation.

Instead, the fix should be made in the source and committed to the VCS. A new run of the pipeline should start, from the beginning, to fully test the fix. The same rule applies when something breaks because of the tooling or the process that applies the change. Fix the tool or process, commit the necessary changes, and run the pipeline through from the start. If your pipeline is fast enough, this should not be painful.

---

10 These techniques are explained in Chapter 10 ("Continuous Integration (CI)" on page 183), along with the case for preferring continuous integration to feature branching.

Practice: Stop the Line on Any Failure

If a stage fails, everyone committing changes to components upstream from that stage should stop committing. Otherwise, new changes are piled onto the broken environment, making it difficult to untangle what went wrong.

So stop the line whenever there is a failure. Make sure you know who is working to fix it, and support them if they need it. If you can't come up with a fix right away, then roll back the change to get the pipeline green again.

Emergency Fixes

Emergency fixes should always be made using the pipeline. If the pipeline isn't fast or reliable enough, then improve it until it is.

In a critical outage, it might be necessary to figure out what the fix is by working directly on a production system. But once the fix is identified, it should be made in the VCS and immediately rolled out through the pipeline. If you neglect to push the fix through properly, your fix will most likely be reverted when a future change is pushed through the pipeline based on the original, unfixed source.

Scaling Pipelines to More Complex Systems

The pipeline designs described so far in this chapter have been relevant for a single component. In practice, most systems involve multiple components that may be committed and built separately, and then deployed and integrated together.

Quite often, a component, such as a service, is composed of several smaller, separately built components. For example, an application server may use an AMI server template built with Packer, Puppet manifests, a Dropwizard application (*http://www.dropwizard.io/*), and may use networking configuration specified in a Cloud-Formation template. Each of these might have its own VCS repository project and trigger its own build stage to test and publish it individually.

In some cases, elements may even be deployed and managed independently, but have runtime dependencies that may be useful to test ahead of releases to production. For example, the application may integrate with other application services managed and deployed by different teams, perhaps using services such as a message bus to communicate.

There are a number of design patterns that can be used to build pipelines for these more complex scenarios. The appropriate pattern depends on the systems and components that the pipeline manages.

Pattern: Fan-In Pipelines

The fan-in pattern is a common one, useful for building a system that is composed of multiple components. Each component starts out with its own pipeline to build and test it in isolation. Then the component pipelines are joined so that the components are tested together. A system with multiple layers of components may have multiple joins.

As an example, let's consider the kinds of environments described in Chapter 9, such as Figure 9-3, reproduced and simplified here in Figure 12-4.

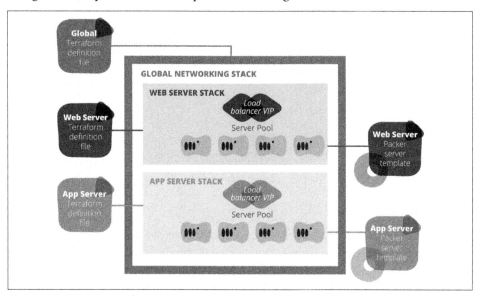

Figure 12-4. An example environment with its components

This environment is composed of several components. These include three infrastructure stacks, each defined in a Terraform definition file: one for the global infrastructure, and one each for web server and application server infrastructure.[11] There are also two different server templates, one for web servers, and one for application servers, each defined in a Packer template.

The full pipeline for the service stack is shown in Figure 12-5. It has five input materials, each in its own VCS repository:

- Packer template and scripts for the web server template
- Terraform definition for the web server infrastructure stack

---

11 The ideas behind this design are laid out in "Organizing Infrastructure" on page 158 in Chapter 9.

- Packer template and scripts for the application server template
- Terraform definition for the application server infrastructure stack
- Terraform definition for the global infrastructure stack

Each of these materials may start its own feeder branch.

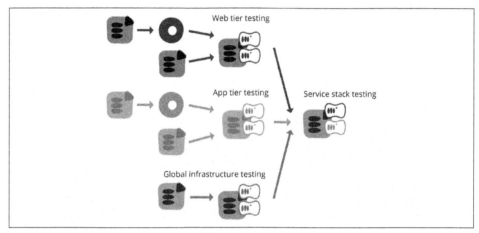

Figure 12-5. Fan-in pipeline for the full service stack

Feeder branches

A feeder branch is a pipeline section that runs some number of stages, and then joins together with other feeder branches. Figure 12-6 shows the feeder branch for the web server stack. This feeder branch itself joins two smaller feeder branches, one for the web server template, the other for the web server infrastructure.

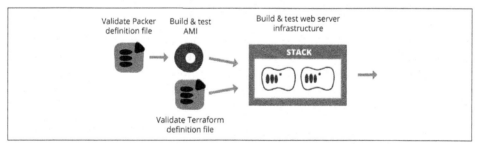

Figure 12-6. Feeder branch for the web server infrastructure component

The first branch builds the web server template from a Packer definition file, and the second validates the web server infrastructure stack using a Terraform definition file. Committing a change to either input component in VCS—the Packer definition file or the Terraform definition file—triggers the branch for that component.

A change to the Packer definition file kicks off the "Validate Packer definition file" stage. This checks out the Packer template from VCS and runs static analysis checks. If these pass, the "Build and test AMI" stage is triggered. This runs Packer on the definition file, building an AMI image.

Join stages

A join stage brings the outputs of two or more feeder branches together. When one of the feeder branches runs successfully, it triggers the join stage, which uses the new artifact from the feeder that triggered it. The join stage uses the artifact from the last successful run of each of the other branches. This means that the only one new artifact is being used and tested. If the tests in the join stage fail, it is immediately clear which input caused the failure, because only one has changed since the last time it ran.

The join stage labeled "Build and test web server infrastructure" in Figure 12-6 has two feeder branches that can trigger it. It runs the Terraform tool, using the Terraform definition from the "Validate Terraform definition file" stage to build an infrastructure stack, and using the AMI built by the "Build and test AMI" stage to create a pool of servers.

The join stage then runs automated tests to make sure that the web server stack builds and works correctly. It might use Serverspec to validate that the web server is configured correctly, and an HTTP-client testing tool to check that the web server is running and correctly serving test content.

Fan-in and the test pyramid

Figure 12-7 illustrates that a change management pipeline with fan-in pattern implements the test pyramid model.

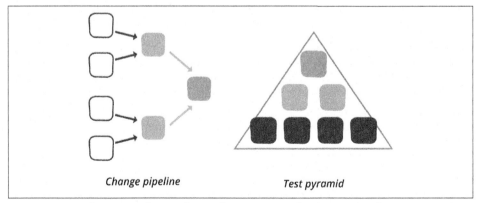

Change pipeline　　　　　　*Test pyramid*

Figure 12-7. A fan-in pipeline is the implementation of a test pyramid

The limits of fan-in pipelines

As the size of a system grows, and as the number of people working on it grows, fan-in pipelines create challenges. Join stages become bottlenecks as the number of inputs grows, with changes from feeder pipelines queuing up waiting to run. More coordination may be needed to avoid conflicts between changes to different components, which creates the need to add processes, meetings, and team roles to manage schedules and communications.

Teams should take the pressure to create manual processes and ceremonies for managing changes as a signal that the design of their system, pipeline, and/or organization is not coping with growth. Adding manual process to work around these limitations avoids addressing the real problems, and adds unnecessary overhead.

In some cases, teams can improve their designs and implementations within the fan-in model, to allow it to handle growth without limiting throughput.[12] In other cases, however, moving away from the fan-in model helps. These alternatives are, arguably, similar to the decision of whether to scale a server up by adding more hardware and optimizing the software it runs, or scale out, by distributing the system across multiple servers.

Measuring Pipeline Effectiveness: Cycle Time

As with any effort to improve a system's performance, the starting point is to measure the existing level of performance. The most effective measurement of a change management pipeline is the cycle time. Cycle time is the time between deciding on the need for a change to seeing that change in production use.

It's important that the starting point for the cycle time is early enough to reflect the full impact of the change management process. The cycle time does not start when a change is committed to trigger the pipeline. The pipeline is only one part of the change management process, and measuring it on its own is likely to suboptimize.[13]

For example, if changes often fail in the pipeline because of conflicts with changes to other components, you could enforce a policy that only one change can be committed and run through the pipeline at a time. This would allow you to tune the pipeline implementation so that it runs very quickly. But it would also create a huge backlog of changes waiting to be committed into the pipeline. From the perspective of a user needing a change, the fact that the pipeline completes within 5 minutes 99% of the

---

12 One optimization might be to allow multiple instances of a join stage to run concurrently, with different combinations of its input artifacts. I'm not aware of any CI or CD tools that naturally support this. But it sounds cool.

13 See "Track and Improve Cycle Time" on page 313 in Chapter 15 for more on cycle time.

---

time doesn't help if it takes over a week to get a change into the pipeline to begin with.

This isn't to say that measuring the end-to-end run time of the pipeline itself isn't important. However, make sure that improving the full, end-to-end cycle time of a change is the paramount goal.

Practice: Keep Pipelines Short

The longer the pipeline is, the longer it will take changes to run through. Keeping pipelines as short as possible helps to keep changes running through quickly and smoothly.

It's best to start with the most minimal pipeline, rather than starting with the more complex design that you think you might need later. Only add stages and branches to the pipeline as you discover real issues that need to be addressed. Always keep an eye out for opportunities to remove things that are no longer relevant.

Practice: Decouple Pipelines

When separate teams build different components of a system, such as microservices, joining pipeline branches for these components together with the fan-in pattern can create a bottleneck. The teams need to spend more effort on coordinating the way they handle releases, testing, and fixing. This may be fine for a small number of teams who work closely together, but the overhead grows exponentially as the number of teams grows.

Decoupling pipelines involves structuring the pipelines so that a change to each component can be released independently. The components may still have dependencies between each other, so they may need integration testing. But rather than requiring all of the components to be released to production together in a "big bang" deployment, a change to one component could go ahead to production before changes to the second component are released.

Decoupling the release of integrated components is easier said than done. Clearly, simply pushing changes through to production risks breaking things in production. There are a number of techniques and patterns for testing, releasing, and pipeline designs to help. These are discussed in following sections.

Integration Models

The design and implementation of pipelines for testing how systems and infrastructure elements integrate depends on the relationships between them, and the relationships between the teams responsible for them. There are several typical situations:

Single team

One team owns all of the elements of the system and is fully responsible for managing changes to them. In this case, a single pipeline, with fan-in as needed, is often sufficient.

Group of teams

A group of teams works together on a single system with multiple services and/or infrastructure elements. Different teams own different parts of the system, which all integrate together. In this case, a single fan-in pipeline may work up to a point, but as the size of the group and its system grows, decoupling may become necessary.

Separate teams with high coordination

Each team (which may itself be a group of teams) owns a system, which integrates with systems owned by other teams. A given system may integrate with multiple systems. Each team will have its own pipeline and manage its releases independently. But they may have a close enough relationship that one team is willing to customize its systems and releases to support another team's requirements. This is often seen with different groups within a large company and with close vendor relationships.

Separate teams with low coordination

As with the previous situation, except one of the teams is a vendor with many other customers. Their release process is designed to meet the requirements of many teams, with little or no customizations to the requirements of individual customer teams. "X as a Service" vendors, providing logging, infrastructure, web analytics, and so on, tend to use this model.

As with any model, this is a rough approximation. Most teams will have a variety of integration models, as seen in Figure 12-8.

Clearly, different approaches are needed to test and release changes across integrated components, depending on how closely the teams coordinate. As integration testing becomes a bottleneck to the cycle time for changes, it's worth considering moving toward a different model. The way to decouple components is to decouple teams. Giving individual teams more autonomy over how they build, test, and release their components empowers them to become more efficient.

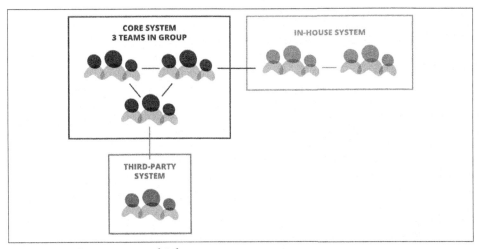

Figure 12-8. Integrating multiple systems

Pipelines, Architecture, and Teams: Conway's Law

The design of your change management pipelines is a manifestation of your system's architecture. Both of these are a manifestation of your team structure. Conway's law (*https://www.thoughtworks.com/insights/blog/demystifying-conways-law*) describes the relationship between the structure of an organization and its systems:

> Any organization that designs a system (defined more broadly here than just information systems) will inevitably produce a design whose structure is a copy of the organization's communication structure.

Organizations can take advantage of this to shape their teams, systems, and pipeline to optimize for the outcomes they want. This is sometimes called the Inverse Conway Maneuver (*https://www.thoughtworks.com/radar/techniques/inverse-conway-maneuver*). Ensure that the people needed to deliver a given change through to production are all a part of the same team. This may involve restructuring the team but may also be done by changing the system's design. It can often be achieved by changing the service model, which is the goal of self-service systems.

A key thing to remember is that designs will always evolve. Designing a new system, team structure, and pipeline is not a one-off activity. As you put designs into practice, you will discover new limitations, issues, and opportunities and will need to continually revise and adapt to meet them.

Techniques for Handling Dependencies Between Components

There are a number of techniques to ensure that a component works correctly when it integrates with another component not managed by the same pipeline. There are two sides to this problem. Given two integrated components, one provides a service, and the other consumes it. The provider component needs to test that it is providing the service correctly for its consumers. And the consumer needs to test that it is consuming the provider service correctly.

For example, one team may manage a monitoring service, which is used by multiple application teams. The monitoring team is the provider, and the application teams are the consumers. Other examples of provider teams include:

- A shared infrastructure team, which defines and manages networking constructs used by multiple teams

- An infrastructure platform team, which provides a virtualization, cloud, or automated hardware provisioning toolset with an API used by other teams

- A database service team, which manages an API-driven service used by application teams to provision, configure, and support database instances

Pattern: Library Dependency

One way that one component can provide a capability to another is to work like a library. The consumer pulls a version of the provider and incorporates it into its own artifact, usually in the build stage of a pipeline. For example, a team may maintain an Ansible playbook for installing and configuring the nginx web server. Other teams consume this, applying the cookbook to their own web server instances.

The important characteristic is that the library component is versioned, and the consumer can choose which version to use. If a newer version of the library is released, the consumer may opt to immediately pull it in, and then run tests on it. However, it has the option to "pin" to an older version of the library.

This gives the consumer team the flexibility to release changes even if they haven't yet incorporated new, incompatible changes to their provider library. But it creates the risk that important changes, such as security patches, aren't integrated in a timely way. This is a major source of security vulnerability in IT systems.

For the provider, this pattern gives freedom to release new changes without having to wait for all consumer teams to update their components. But it can result in having many different versions of the component in production, which increases the time and hassle of support. In Figure 12-9, one team provides an Ansible playbook for installing and configuring the nginx web server. Another team owns an application microservice and uses the playbook to install nginx on their application server.

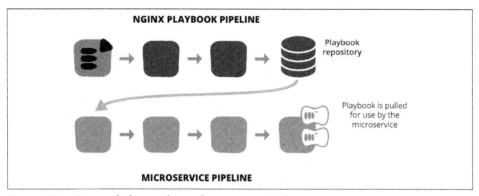

Figure 12-9. Decoupled provider and consumer pipelines

This pattern is commonly used to share standard server templates across teams. One team might create a standard Linux VM template image for the organization. This would have the standard build of a Linux distribution, with common configuration and packages for things like shared authentication, network configuration, monitoring, and security hardening. Other teams can then pull the latest version of this image to build their servers or perhaps use them as a base to build their own layered template (as in "Pattern: Layered Template" on page 129 in Chapter 7).

Repository as an Artifact

Another way to promote sets of package versions between pipeline stages is on the repository side, using the "repository as an artifact" pattern.[14] A team using this approach sets up a separate package repository mirror for each environment. The upstream stage updates packages from public repositories and triggers tests. As each pipeline stage passes its tests, the packages are copied to the next stage's repository mirror. This ensures the consistency of the full set of dependencies.

Repository as an artifact can be implemented with systems like Spacewalk channels, or more simply with things like reposync (*http://linux.die.net/man/1/reposync*) or even rsync.

---

14 I learned about this pattern from my colleague Inny So (*https://twitter.com/mini_inny*).

Pattern: Self-Provisioned Service Instance

The library pattern can be adapted for full-blown services. A well-known example of this is AWS's Relational Database Service, or RDS (*https://aws.amazon.com/rds/*), offered by AWS. A team can provision complete working database instances for itself, which it can use in a pipeline for a component that uses a database.

As a provider, Amazon releases new database versions, while still making older versions available as "previous generation DB instances" (*https://aws.amazon.com/rds/previous-generation/*). This has the same effect as the library pattern, in that the provider can release new versions without waiting for consumer teams to upgrade their own components.

Being a service rather than a library, the provider is able to transparently release minor updates to the service. Amazon can apply security patches to its RDS offering, and new instances created by consumer teams will automatically use the updated version.

The key is for the provider to keep close track of the interface contract, to make sure the service behaves as expected after updates have been applied. Interface contracts are discussed in more detail in "Practice: Test the Provider with Contract Tests" on page 254. An update that changes expected behavior should be offered as a new version of the service, which can be explicitly selected by consumer teams.

This pattern is often useful for infrastructure and platform services such as monitoring, databases, and dashboards. Consumer teams can have their pipelines automatically spin up a service instance to test against, and then tear it down again after the testing stage is finished.

Providing Pre-Release Library Builds

Teams providing libraries often find it useful to make pre-release builds available for consumer teams to test against. Betas, snapshots, and early releases give consumers the opportunity to develop and test the use of upcoming features. This gives the provider feedback on their changes, and allows the consumers to be prepare before new features are released.

Pre-release builds should be generated by a pipeline stage. This could be an inline stage that produces a pre-release build for every build that passes a certain stage, as in Figure 12-10. Or it could be a fork, where a person selects and publishes a pre-release build, as in Figure 12-11.

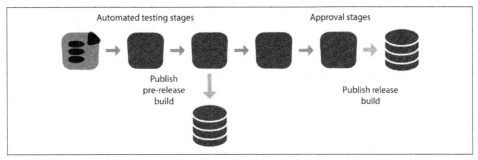

Figure 12-10. Publishing pre-release builds with an inline stage

In Figure 12-10, every build that reaches the pre-release stage is published. The build published as a full release at the end of the pipeline will also have been a pre-release build. On the other hand, the build published as a full release build from the forked pipeline in Figure 12-11 will not necessarily have been previously selected to publish as a pre-release build.

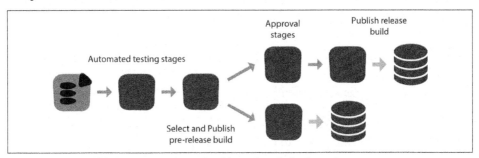

Figure 12-11. Publishing pre-release builds with a forked pipeline

Providing Test Instances of a Service to Consumers

The provider of a hosted service needs to provide support for consumers to develop and test their integration with the service. This is useful to consumers for a number of purposes:

- To learn how to correctly integrate to the service
- To test that integration still works after changes to the consumer system
- To test that the consumer system still works after changes to the provider
- To test and develop against new provider functionality before it is released
- To reproduce production issues for troubleshooting
- To run demonstrations of the consumer system without affecting production data

An effective way for a provider to support these is to provide self-provisioned service instances. If consumers can create and configure instances on-demand, then they can easily handle their own testing and demonstration needs.

For example, a database service team in a larger organization could make it possible for other teams to spin up and manage their own instances of the database server. Consumer teams can use this capability to experiment with new configuration options, without polluting their production database.

Providers can supplement test instances by making it possible for consumers to provision pre-release builds of their service. This is the same idea as a pre-release library, but offered as a hosted service.

Data and configuration management is a challenge with test instances of a service. It's important that consumer teams are able to automatically load appropriate data and configuration to the service instance. This could be artificially constructed test data, to enable automated tests. Or it could be a snapshot of production data, useful to reproduce production issues or demonstrate functionality. Service provider teams may need to develop APIs, tooling, or other mechanisms to help consumer teams do this easily.

For services that can't be self-provisioned, running test instances is more challenging. Configuration and data in a long-lived test instance can become stale over time and easily drifts so that it becomes inconsistent with production. This makes testing less accurate. Multitenancy test systems are even more likely to become messy. Teams in this situation would do well to move their systems toward single-tenancy and to provide self-provisioning capabilities to their consumers.

Using Test Instances of a Service as a Consumer

A team that consumes a service provided by another team can include stages in their pipeline that deploy and test integration with a test instance of the provider.

For example, if an application team is using monitoring from a central monitoring service team, they can have a test stage that is monitored by a test instance of the monitoring server. They can use this to test changes to the monitoring configuration. They can also have automated monitoring tests, artificially causing failures to their own application to prove that the correct monitoring alerts fire. This can catch issues where a change to the application makes existing monitoring checks invalid.

Normally, automated testing against a test instance of a provider will run near the end of the automated stages of the pipeline, after testing with the provider mocked out.[15] This is illustrated in Figure 12-12.

---

15 As described in "Techniques to Isolate Components for Testing" on page 213 in Chapter 11.

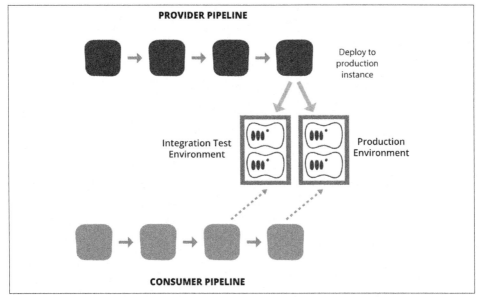

Figure 12-12. Automatically testing against provider instances

If the provider also deploys pre-release builds of its service to a test instance, then the consumer team can use this as well. Having a pipeline stage that integrates with a pre-release build helps to uncover potential issues with upcoming releases of the provider. This works well in conjunction with version tolerance (described later), to ensure that the consumer component will work easily with either the new or old version of the provider. This frees the consumer team from worrying about the provider's release schedule.

As mentioned earlier, managing data in test instances can be challenging. Long-running test instances can become polluted with old test data. This complicates automated tests and can result in test systems that don't represent the production instances very well.

Automated test suites should set up the test data they need when they run. It may be possible to load snapshots of production data. However, automated tests should not make assumptions about data that they have not explicitly constructed; otherwise they can't be guaranteed to run consistently.

In some cases, it's possible to run tests against production instances of a third-party system. This is obviously fine when the consumer doesn't alter data in the other system. For example, when you have an external service that provides lookups, such as DNS, there isn't much call to have a special test server to integrate with.

Testing while integrating with a production system can also work when the data from the consumer test can be easily segregated. For a monitoring service, for example, the test instances of the consumer can be tagged as a separate environment, which is configured as noncritical. This keeps the production system monitoring data clearly segregated from the test system data.

Practices for Managing Interfaces Between Components

A cornerstone of independently deployable components is loose coupling. Ideally, changing one part of the system won't have any impact on other parts of the system. The way in which one component integrates with another is the interface.

An interface could be a formal API. A server provisioning script may use a monitoring server's REST interface to add and remove checks for servers. It could be less formal, such as the arguments accepted by a command-line tool that is executed in a Bash script. Or it could be a matter of filesystem locations where a script or tool can expect to find executables, libraries, or configuration files.

One of the most important jobs of a pipeline is to make sure that when a change is made to one (or both!) side of these interfaces, everything still works correctly. If the pipelines are decoupled so that the pieces on each side of the interface are released on their own, there is a risk that problems with the integration between these interfaces will only be discovered in production.

Clearly this would be bad. But there are a number of techniques to catch integration errors with independent pipelines.

Practice: Ensure Backward Compatibility of Interfaces

Providers should work hard to avoid making changes that break existing interfaces. Once a release is published and in use, new releases should not change the interfaces used by consumers.

It's normally easy to add new functionality without breaking interfaces. A command-line tool can add a new argument without changing the behavior of existing arguments.

When improvements are made to the way those existing arguments work, the results should be the same as before. This can be tricky with bug fixes. Ideally, fixing incorrect behavior should only make consumers happy, but often what people build on top of something buggy may rely on the incorrect behavior. The provider needs to make a call on this. In some cases, vendors have actually maintained incorrect behavior to avoid breaking their users' systems.

If there is a need to make drastic changes to an existing interface, it's often better to create a new interface, leaving the old one in place. The old interface can be deprecated, with warnings to users that they should move to using the new version. This gives consumers time to develop and test their use of the new interface before they switch, which in turn gives the provider the flexibility to release and iterate on the new functionality without having to wait for all of their consumers to switch.

For example, a team may install a new version of a library or command-line tool on a different filesystem path. User might change environment variables or paths in their scripts in order to use the new version when they're ready.

Practice: Decouple Deploying from Releasing

Many organizations that operate very large-scale systems find that testing changes in pre-release environments has low value. The number, complexity, and versions of components running in production may be large and constantly changing. This makes it difficult to reproduce production conditions in a meaningful way.

The difficulty is not only cost, but time, effort, and opportunity cost. In order for testing in a pre-release environment to be even moderately viable for catching issues, the pace of change needs to be kept slow. Throttling the pace of IT change can be dangerous for a business that relies on it to remain competitive.

So a common technique is to deploy changes into production without necessarily releasing them to end users. New versions of components are put into the production environment and integrated with other components in ways that won't impact normal operations. This allows them to be tested in true production conditions, before the switch is flipped to put them into active use. They can even be put into use in a drip-feed fashion, measuring their performance and impact before rolling them out to the full user base.

Techniques for doing this include those used to hide unfinished changes in the codebase, such as feature toggles, as well as zero-downtime replacement patterns.[16]

Practice: Use Version Tolerance

The flipside of maintaining backward compatibility for providers is for consumers to ensure version tolerance. A consumer team should ensure that a single build of their system can easily work with different versions of a provider that they integrate with, if it's a likely situation.

It can be nice to handle this version detecting and switching dynamically, detecting the version and using options and parameters accordingly. A shell script can check to see which version of an executable is available on the system, and adapt its behavior accordingly. A provisioning script can change the version of the monitoring server's REST API it assumes after querying the API version.

---

16 See "Zero-Downtime Changes" on page 282 in Chapter 14, as well as "Managing Major Infrastructure Changes" on page 192 in Chapter 10.

But in some cases, it's useful to control which version of the provider is used. For example, a consumer team may want to continue using the previous version of an API in production until the latest version has stabilized.

Some teams will resort to building different versions of their consumer system or component to integrate with different versions of the provider. But this risks diverging the codebase, which degrades the effectiveness of continuous integration.

Another option is to use a feature toggle to explicitly set the version of the upstream provider interface to use in different environments.

Practice: Provide Test Doubles

Teams responsible for a system that integrates with a service provided by another team sometimes find that the provider instance causes issues with testing. This is especially common with test instances, which may be slow, unreliable, or poorly supported. This can be frustrating, because it makes it difficult for the team to get feedback on changes to their own system.

Test doubles[17] offer a way to work around these situations. Early pipeline stages can provision a system, integrating with a mock service that emulates the provider service. The mock service is a dummy that allows the consumer system to run and be tested. These stages validate the consumer system's own functionality, so test failures indicate a problem with the team's own code, not the provider service.

Later stages of the pipeline, such as ones at the end of the automated sequence of stages, can deploy and integrate with the provider service instance, and run tests that ensure the integration is correct.

Providers might consider making stubs or other types of doubles for their systems available for consumers to use in their own testing. Some infrastructure platform API libraries (e.g., *fog.io*) include mocks so that developers writing scripts to use an infrastructure provider's API can test their code without provisioning real infrastructure.

Practice: Test the Provider with Contract Tests

Contract tests are automated tests that check whether a provider interface behaves as consumers expect. This is a much smaller set of tests than full functional tests, purely focused on the API that the service has committed to provide to its consumers.

By running contract tests in their own pipeline, the provider team will be alerted if they accidentally make a change that breaks the contract.

---

17 See "Test Doubles" on page 214 in Chapter 11.

Writing these tests help a provider to think through and clearly define what consumers can expect from their interface. This is an example of how test-driven development (TDD) helps to improve design. The tests themselves can also become documentation for consumers to see how to use the system.

Practice: Test with a Reference Consumer

A variation of contract testing is for a provider team to maintain a simple example of a consumer application. For example, the team that manages the infrastructure platform could write an example Terraform definition file for an application stack. Whenever they make a change to the platform, their pipeline uses this definition to provision an instance of the reference application stack and run some automated tests to make sure everything still works as expected.

This reference consumer can also be made available to consumer teams as an example. Examples of this kind work best when they are actively used and continuously tested. This ensures they are kept up to date and relevant to the latest version of the provider.

Practice: Smoke Test the Provider Interface

In some cases, it may help teams building and running consumer systems to automatically validate the interfaces of components and systems provided by other teams. The value of this tends to be higher as the two teams involved are less well connected. The consumer team can check that new versions of the provider meet their own assumptions for how they behave.

When the provider is a hosted service, the consumer may not have visibility of when changes are made to it and so may want to run these tests more frequently. For example, they might do this whenever they deploy a change to their own system. Consumer teams might even consider running these tests from the monitoring server so they can receive alerts when the provider changes in a way that will break their own system.

Practice: Run Consumer-Driven Contract (CDC) Tests

A variation on these previous practices is for a provider to run tests provided by consumer teams. These tests are written to formalize the expectations the consumer has for the provider's interface. The provider runs the tests in a stage of its own pipeline, and fails any build that fails to pass these tests.

A failure of a CDC test tells the provider they need to investigate the nature of the failed expectation. In some cases, the provider will realize they have made an error, so they can correct it. In others, they may see that the consumer's expectations are incorrect, so they can let them know to change their own code.

Or the issue may not be as straightforward, in which case the failed test drives the provider to have a conversation with the consumer team to work out the best solution.

Conclusion

Implementing change management pipelines for infrastructure transforms the way IT systems are managed. When done well, people spend less time and energy on individual changes—planning, designing, scheduling, implementing, testing, validating, and fixing them. Instead, the focus shifts to the processes and tooling that make and test changes.

This transformation helps the team to focus on improving their workflow. Their goal becomes being able to quickly and reliably make changes to adapt services to the needs and opportunities of the organization. But it's also a major change in the way that people work on their infrastructure. The next chapter takes a look at team workflow with infrastructure as code.

## CHAPTER 13

Workflow for the Infrastructure Team

Managing infrastructure as code is a radically different way of working for most IT operations people. This chapter aims to explain how an IT operations team gets their work done in this kind of environment, with some guidance for how to make it work well.

The big shift is away from working directly on servers and infrastructures, to working on them indirectly. An infrastructure engineer can no longer just log onto a server to make a change. Instead, they make changes to the tools and definitions, and then allow the change management pipeline to roll the changes out to the server.

This can be frustrating at first. It feels like a slower, more complicated way to do something simple. But putting the right tooling and workflows into place means that people spend less time on routine, repetitive tasks. Instead, they focus their energies on handling exceptions and problems, and on making improvements and changes that will make exceptions and problems less common.

A good infrastructure-as-code workflow makes it easy to work indirectly on servers this way. But it can be challenging to get the workflow right and keep it that way. If the tooling and processes aren't easy, then team members will often find they need to jump onto a server or configuration UI and make a quick change outside the automation tools. It might be necessary to do this in the early days of moving to infrastructure as code, but it should be a priority to address whatever shortcomings make this necessary.

The main characteristics of a good automation workflow are speed and reliability. It must be possible to get a change through to systems fast enough that it's a valid way to handle emergencies. The person making a change must be confident that it will work as expected and know whether it will create any new problems.

Automate Anything That Moves

The most important habit of an effective infrastructure coder is automating tasks whenever possible. You might carry out a task by hand the first time, in order to understand how it works. But doing the same task multiple times is boring.

The Virtue of Laziness

Larry Wall describes laziness as the first of the three great virtues of a programmer. He defines it as "The quality that makes you go to great effort to reduce overall energy expenditure. It makes you write labor-saving programs that other people will find useful, and document what you wrote so you don't have to answer so many questions about it."[1]

Be on the lookout for user requests, issues, or tasks that crop up again and again, and find ways to avoid needing to do them. There is a hierarchy of techniques, starting with the most preferred:

1. Redesign or reconfigure things so the task isn't necessary at all.

2. Implement automation that handles the task transparently, without anyone needing to pay attention.

3. Implement a self-service tool so that the task can be done quickly, by someone who doesn't need to know the details, preferably the user or person who needs it done.

4. Write documentation so that users can easily carry out the task on their own.

Obviously, documentation or a self-service tool needs to be appropriate for the user. Very few marketing managers want to log into a Linux server to run a shell script to run a report, but most would be be OK with a browser-based dashboard.

The essential goal is to remove the system administrator from the flow for getting a task done. The role of the system administrator is to build the automation, prevent and handle problems, and make improvements. Using the assembly line example, you don't want workers to be handling each part as it passes through the line; instead, you want them working on the robotic machinery that handles the parts. The assembly line should keep running even when you turn your attention to some other task.

Let's consider different ways that a system administrator in an IT operations team might make a configuration change on their web servers. Imagine that the sysadmin

---

1 Read about the three virtues on the c2 wiki (*http://c2.com/cgi/wiki?LazinessImpatienceHubris*), or in the book *Programming Perl* by Larry Wall, Tom Christiansen, and Randal Schwarz (O'Reilly).

discovers a web server configuration setting that will make the servers more secure, and decides to apply it.

Make the Change Manually

The fastest and simplest way to make the configuration change would be to log onto the web servers and edit the configuration file.[2] This will be tedious if the team has very many web servers. Worse, the change won't be visible to other people on the team. Someone might even notice the change, assume it was a mistake, and undo it. Or another person might set up a new web server without using the improved configuration, leading to inconsistently configured servers.

Even if the other team members do know about the change, they may not know how to implement it when they set up a new server. For example, they may not realize that the change needs a new web server module to be installed. They will realize their mistake when the web server fails to start, but it wastes their time. They might then resolve the issue in a different way than the first person did, which again leads to inconsistency.

Ad Hoc Automation

If the team has very many web servers, the sysadmin will probably write a script to make the change, to avoid the tedium of making the same change manually on one server at a time.

So the sysadmin writes a script that runs across all of the web servers and makes the change to the configuration file on each one. The script could simply copy a new web server configuration file into place. Or if the configuration files vary between servers, the script might instead do a search and replace. This would only change the relevant lines of the file, or maybe just append new lines to the file. The script can also install the module and reload the server process, maybe even running a simple smoke test to let the sysadmin know if it fails for some reason.

Teams often adopt remote command execution tools[3] to make it easier to write and run scripts across many servers.

This is an improvement over making changes manually. Other members of the team can see how the change was applied, and might be able to use the script again on other web servers.

---

2 Using vi, obviously.

3 See "Tools for Running Commands on Servers" on page 66 in Chapter 4

But there are a few problems with this approach. One is that there is no assurance that the configuration change will be applied to new web servers. Other team members might remember to run it, or they might copy the configuration from an existing server, but there's no guarantee.

And there's a high likelihood that other changes could be made to the web server configuration that break the way the script works. Nobody is likely to go back and fix the script until they try to run it later on and find it's broken. The temptation will be not to bother trying to fix and reuse the script, but probably to write a new one.

Running a variety of scripts on an ad hoc basis yields unpredictable results and inconsistent infrastructure, as shown in Figure 13-1. This is the root of the automation fear spiral.[4]

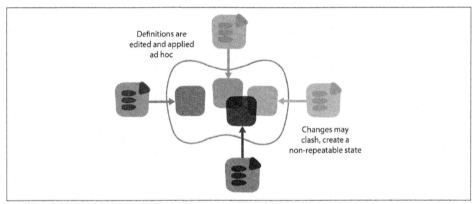

Figure 13-1. Ad hoc automation scripts have unpredictable results

Autonomic Automation

In order to get the assurance that the right configuration will be applied even without someone having to think about it, the team could create a script, or a collection of scripts, that will be run every time a new web server is created. Ideally, they'd run these scripts periodically to ensure configuration stays the way they'd like. This gives them continuous configuration synchronization (as described in Chapter 4).

The aim is to have infrastructure management systems that work autonomically. In physiology, autonomic functions happen without conscious effort (e.g., breathing or heart rate). You might be able to override some of these (e.g., by holding your breath). But you don't normally need to think about doing it.

---

4 The automation fear spiral was introduced in "Automation Fear" on page 9 in Chapter 1.

Autonomic automation is the secret to making infrastructure as code work reliably. When the team finds a new web server configuration option that improves security, they embed that into their automation tooling. They know that it will be applied to all relevant servers, current and future, without anyone having to think about it again.

The team also knows that the automation is continuously reapplied. So if any change is made that will break the automation, it will be discovered immediately and can be fixed right away. The infrastructure is always kept consistent, and the automation is always workable.

Configuration tools like Chef or Puppet are designed to work autonomically, with their declarative syntax and idempotent operation.[5] But it isn't the tool that makes infrastructure autonomic. System administrators have been writing scripts to carry out tasks autonomically for decades.

On the flip side, there are IT operations teams who use tools like Ansible, Puppet, and Chef for ad hoc automation. They write a configuration definition when they want to make a change, but only run the tool to apply it as a one-off. This is common for teams who aren't experienced with infrastructure as code, as it's a way of using old habits and working practices with new tools. But it doesn't help to shift the team's workload onto the tools. Running the automation tool by hand, ad hoc, makes it less likely it will just work. So routine tasks still need the close involvement of a human.

Tools Versus Automation

In *The Practice of Cloud System Administration* (*http://amzn.to/ 22xJczg*) (Addison-Wesley), Limoncelli, Chalup, and Hogan talk about tool building versus automation. Tool building is writing a script or tools to make a manual task easier. Automation is eliminating the need for a human to carry out the task. They make the comparison to an auto factory worker using a high-powered paint sprayer to paint car doors, versus having an unattended robotic painting system.

Autonomic Automation Workflow

With infrastructure as code, when engineers need to make a change, they start by checking out the relevant files out from VCS. They might do this on a local workstation or else in a home area on a remote machine. The files are typically configuration definitions, scripts, configuration files, and various other things.

In a simple workflow, the engineer makes the change to their local files and then commits the modified files back to the VCS. The commit triggers the change man-

---

5 As described in "Choosing Tools for Infrastructure as Code" on page 42 in Chapter 3.

agement pipeline, as described in the previous chapter. Depending on how the team has designed their pipeline, the change might be automatically applied to the target environments if the pipelines stages pass. Or the pipeline could have one or more approval stages, where a person reviews the results of tests before pushing them out to production infrastructure.

This process can take a while. The time it takes for the change to roll out to all the servers may be over an hour if, for example, there is an hourly schedule for configuration agents to run on servers to pull and apply the latest configuration. Even finding out whether the change works correctly on test servers may take a matter of minutes.

This can be a very slow loop: edit the file, commit, wait, see a red build, read the logs, edit the file, repeat. A person who is accustomed to just logging onto a server to edit the file and see whether it works may be forgiven for deciding pushing changes through a pipeline is a ridiculous way to work. Fortunately, there are better ways, such as using a local sandbox to work on changes.

Using a Local Sandbox

A sandbox is an environment where a team member can try out changes before committing them into the pipeline. It may be run on a local workstation, using virtualization, or could be run on the virtualization platform. Both of these options are explained in more detail later in this chapter.

Ideally, team members can reproduce the key elements of their infrastructure in a sandbox and run automated tests against them. This gives them confidence that they've got the change right before committing it. Figure 13-2 shows how this fits into the flow of a pipeline. Checking changes before committing reduces failures and red builds in the pipeline, which improves the overall productivity of the team.

The tooling for testing pre-commit changes needs to be easy to set up and maintain or else people will avoid using it. This is yet another of those practices where good habits lead to a virtuous cycle. Use it often, fix problems immediately, and remove anything that makes it awkward to use. Letting things slip discourages people from using the toolset, which will cause it to become out of date and even less pleasant to use.

One of the key principles for making a sandbox environment work is consistency. The sandbox needs to represent the real infrastructure well enough that everyone is confident changes that work in one place will work in the other.

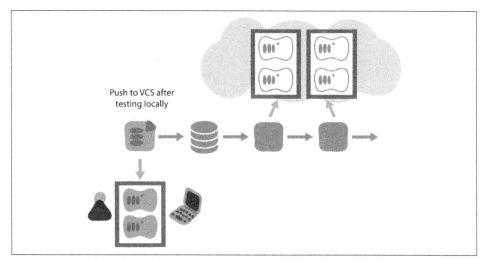

Figure 13-2. Testing in local sandbox before committing to the pipeline

The most reliable way to achieve this is to use the same tools and configuration across sandbox and real infrastructure wherever possible. The same operating system builds, server configuration tools and definitions, and even network configuration where relevant, should be used across the board.

This should happen naturally; the entire purpose of a local sandbox is to develop and test infrastructure configuration. Normally, team members will routinely destroy their sandbox when they aren't using it, rebuilding it from scratch when they sit down to do some work. This keeps the sandbox up to date and proves the automation works correctly.

Using Local Virtualization for a Sandbox

Developing and testing server configuration definitions locally requires running virtual machines locally. There are a number of virtualization products designed for running VMs on desktop and laptop systems, including Oracle's VirtualBox, Parallels, VMware Workstation, VMware Fusion, and Microsoft's Hyper-V. People running Linux can also use hypervisors like Xen and KVM.

Ideally, people should be able to start local VMs from the same server templates that are used for starting servers in the real infrastructure. Chapter 7 described using the Packer tool to build server templates. Packer can use a single definition file to generate template images for multiple virtualization platforms, including local virtualization systems.

Infrastructure teams who generate server images automatically using a pipeline often generate locally usable images at the same time that they generate images for the infrastructure. This ensures that people always have the latest, consistently built image available for developing and testing.

Vagrant (*https://www.vagrantup.com/*)[6] is an invaluable tool for managing local sandboxes. Vagrant is essentially an infrastructure definition tool like those described in Chapter 3, but designed for use with local virtualization. Vagrant gives you an IaaS cloud on your desktop.

Vagrant uses a definition file to define compute (one or more VMs), networking, and storage for an environment that can be created and run with a local virtualization tool. Because the definition is in an externalized file, as with any infrastructure defined as code, a Vagrant environment is reproducible. The entire environment can be torn down, and then rebuilt with a single command.[7]

A team can create a Vagrant definition file for its local sandbox environment and commit it to their VCS. This definition can then be used by any member of the team to easily spin up their own instance of the sandbox to develop and test in. New team members can get started quickly. Improvements can be made to the definition file and shared with the whole team. Anyone can reproduce an issue seen by their colleagues.

Vagrant has hooks for server configuration tools including Ansible, Chef, and Puppet, which makes it easy to provision machines the same way they are provisioned in the real infrastructure, and to test changes to them. It's possible to tweak the Vagrant setup in various ways—for example, to test only certain parts of the provisioning process to simplify and speed up testing.

Example 13-1 shows a Vagrant file that a team uses to test the configuration of their Jenkins CI system. It downloads a server template from an internal web server, presumably one built the same was as server templates for production. It then defines two virtual machine instances, one for a Jenkins server, and one for a Jenkins agent. Each of these virtual machines is configured by applying Ansible playbooks. These playbooks, *jenkins-server.yml* and *jenkins-agent.yml*, are the same ones used to configure the production Jenkins servers and agents.

Example 13-1. Sample Vagrantfile

```
Vagrant.configure('2') do |config|

  # Use a standard base image to build new machines
  config.vm.box = "centos-6.5"
  config.vm.box_url =
```

---

6 Not coincidentally, Vagrant is made by HashiCorp, the same company that makes Packer.

7 That single command is `vagrant destroy -f ; vagrant up`. I admit this is cheating slightly.

```
        'http://repo.local/images/vagrant/centos65-x86_64-20141002140211.box'

    # Define the Jenkins server
    config.vm.define :jenkins_server do |server|
      server.vm.hostname = 'jenkins_server'

      # Set the IP address so the agent can find it
      server.vm.network :private_network, ip: '192.1.1.101'

      # I can use http://localhost:8080 to access the server
      server.vm.network "forwarded_port", guest: 80, host: 8080

      # Run Ansible, using the "jenkins_server" role
      server.vm.provision "ansible" do |ansible|
        ansible.playbook = "jenkins-server.yml"
        ansible.sudo = true
        ansible.groups = {
          "jenkins_server" => ["jenkins_server"]
        }
      end
    end

    # Define the Jenkins agent
    config.vm.define :jenkins_agent do |agent|
      agent.vm.hostname = 'agent'
      agent.vm.network :private_network, ip: '192.1.1.102'

      # Run Ansible, using the "jenkins_agent" role
      agent.vm.provision "ansible" do |ansible|
        ansible.playbook = "jenkins-agent.yml"
        ansible.sudo = true
        ansible.groups = {
          "agent" => ["jenkins_agent"]
        }
      end
    end

end
```

Example Workflow with Local Testing

Your workflow to make a change using a local sandbox with the Vagrant definition in
Example 13-1 might look something like this:

1. Check out the latest versions of the *Vagrantfile*, Ansible playbooks, and test
   scripts from VCS.

2. Build the local VMs (`vagrant up`).

3. Run the automated test scripts to make sure everything works.

4. Write an automated test for the change you plan to make.

5. Edit the Ansible playbooks to implement the change.

6. Apply the change to the local VMs (`vagrant provision`).

7. Run the tests to see if they work. Repeat steps 4 through 7 until happy.

8. Update the files from VCS again, to merge any changes that other people have made since you checked out in step 1.

9. Destroy and rebuild the local VMs (`vagrant destroy -f ; vagrant up`) and run the tests again to make sure everything still works after the merge.

10. Commit your changes to VCS.

11. Verify that the changes pass successfully through the pipeline's automated stages.

12. Once the changes reach production, verify that everything works the way you wanted.

In practice, people experienced with this workflow like to make the smallest change they can get away with and run it through this workflow. When you get into a good rhythm, you might commit a change at least once an hour.

Personally, I occasionally fall out of this rhythm and make a very large set of changes locally before I commit them. I inevitably suffer when I find that I've built up uncommitted local changes. Other people have usually made changes that affect what I've done, forcing me to rework things. The longer my changes have built up—a day, several days—the worse it is.

Keeping the whole change/commit cycle short needs some habits around how to structure the changes so they don't break production even when the whole task isn't finished. Feature toggles and similar techniques mentioned in Chapter 12 ("Practice: Prove Production Readiness for Every Change" on page 237) can help.

The advantage of working this way is your changes are constantly integrated and tested with everything everyone else is doing. Other people can see what you're doing and easily pick up the task for you if you are interrupted by other priorities.

Using the Virtualization Platform for Sandboxes

In some cases, local infrastructure development environments are either not feasible, or they can't meaningfully represent the real infrastructure platform. For example, a team's infrastructure might make extensive use of services provided by a cloud platform, to the point where duplicating or mocking these on local VMs is too much work.

In this situation, members of the team can run sandbox environments on the main infrastructure platform. Rather than using something like Vagrant to run infrastructure locally, a team member spins up their own copy of the relevant infrastructure in the cloud. Figure 13-3 illustrates the flow. The team member works on infrastructure

---

definitions locally and applies them to a hosted sandbox environment, using the same tools, scripts, and definitions used to manage testing and production environments. Once they are happy with the changes, they commit their changes to the VCS, which triggers the pipeline to roll the changes out.

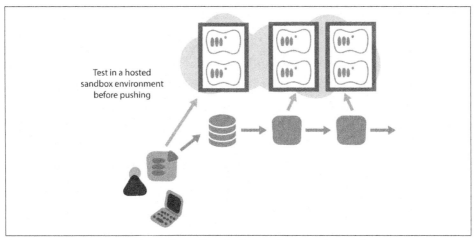

Figure 13-3. Testing in a hosted sandbox before pushing to the pipeline

Codebase Organization Patterns

One of the challenges for teams adopting infrastructure as code is finding a good way to organize their codebase of definitions, scripts, and configuration files. A good structure allows multiple team members to easily work on different tasks without tripping each other up. For larger teams, codebase organization is even more important to allow teams to work independently, without needing complex processes, tooling, and roles to coordinate changes across them.

"Organizing Infrastructure" on page 158 discussed ways of organizing infrastructure to keep things loosely coupled. As mentioned in "Pipelines, Architecture, and Teams: Conway's Law" on page 245, there is a direct relationship between the system architecture, team structure, and the design of the change management pipeline. When these three elements are well aligned, the proof is in the workflow: people and teams are able to easily get their jobs done with few coordination issues. When they aren't aligned, it shows up in the workflow.

There are three main patterns used for organizing larger codebases: branching, one trunk per component, and single trunk.[8]

Antipattern: Branch-Based Codebases

Branches can be useful for short-lived, tactical purposes. However, it works poorly as a method of organizing work across multiple teams. This point has been belabored in this book ("Continuous Integration (CI)" on page 183) and elsewhere, but it's controversial because it's so commonly accepted.

Rather than reiterating these arguments here, I'll make a single suggestion for teams that do use branching. Measure the cycle time and analyze the value stream for a single change, as discussed in more detail later in this chapter. Consider how much of the cycle time is spent in activities due to merging and post-merging testing activities.

Moving to either of the trunk-based approaches discussed in this chapter should completely eliminate the need for these activities. If your team uses short-lived branches, and spends little or no time merging and testing after merges, then there is not much to be gained by switching. But most teams that use branches routinely spend days or weeks massaging the codebase after merges before they're able to put them into production.

Merge Monkeys

"Monkey" roles are often found on teams to take care of routine tasks that don't directly add value to the team. Many software development teams used to have a "build monkey" who made sure the software compiled properly. Better automation practices have made this particular role obsolete.[9] But it's still common to assign team members to clean up the messes that unoptimized engineering practices produce.

I once saw a team of a few dozen developers which had two developers assigned full-time to merging code branches in the VCS repository. This should have been a clear sign that they had too many people working on a poorly organized codebase. Restructuring the code would have freed these people to do more valuable work.

---

8 It's informative to see how other organizations manage their workflows. Jon Cowie has presented "Workflow Design: Extracting Signal From the Noise - ChefConf 2015" (*https://www.youtube.com/watch?v=lsup JuAkfwQ*), and the folks at Chef have created an RFC documenting several workflows (*https://github.com/ chef/chef-rfc/blob/master/rfc019-chef-workflows.md*).

9 Although many teams still have similar roles. To avoid appearing unfashionable, they often misapply the term "DevOps" as a title for the person who maintains the automated build and CI tooling.

Pattern: One Trunk per Component

Keeping the code for each component or service in its own VCS repository project is arguably the most common approach for teams working with a microservices-style architecture. This allows people to check out the component locally and work on it independently of work being done on other components.

The challenge with this pattern is when a change involves modifying parts of more than one component. It isn't difficult to check out all of the affected components so you can work on them and test them locally. But when you commit the changes, the components may not progress evenly through the pipeline. One of the changed components may reach a downstream stage before the other, failing tests because it is being integrated with an older version of the other component.

This can be managed by making the components version tolerant ("Practice: Use Version Tolerance" on page 253), but does add complexity.

Pattern: Single Trunk

An alternative to giving each component its own VCS project is to keep all of the source together in a single project. This forces the entire codebase to be consistent for a given commit. It also simplifies the problem of keeping different components working together; developers can't commit changes without ensuring that everything they have changed works and passes their tests.

The challenge with this approach is that it requires a different approach to tooling for building and CI, especially at scale. It should be easy to run only the tests that apply to code that has been changed, rather than being forced to run the full test suite for all of the components. Similarly, only the pipeline stages for modified components should be run after the change is committed.

This approach, sometimes called scaled trunk-based development (*http://paulhamm ant.com/2013/05/06/googles-scaled-trunk-based-development/*), is used by Google among others. Very few publicly available tools are designed to support this way of working. Google has created custom tooling to manage their codebase like this.

Workflow Effectiveness

Every team wants to work more effectively. It is important for teams to have an awareness of what effectiveness means for them. Is it being able to respond to business needs quickly? Is it to ensure high levels of availability? The team and its stakeholders should discuss and agree on the high-level values for the team before moving on to decide on metrics.[10]

Expediting Changes

An ineffective workflow, or an overloaded team, becomes a particular problem when a production issue needs to be correctly quickly. Many teams consider creating a separate process to expedite emergency changes.

The Best Process for Emergency Fixes Is the Normal Process

If your organization finds itself considering a special, separate process for expediting emergency changes, this is a sign that the normal process has issues. Rather than creating a separate process, the organization should look at improving the normal process.

An emergency change process can speed things up in two different ways. One is to leave out unimportant steps. The other is to leave out important steps.

If you are able to identify steps that can be safely removed for an emergency process, chances are they can be safely removed from your normal process as well. In lean process theory, these steps are called waste.

And an emergency situation is the worst time to leave steps out of a process when those steps truly add value—for example, activities that help to catch errors. These are high-pressure situations, when humans are most likely to make a mistake. And mistakes at these times tend to compound the original problem, often turning a small outage into a disaster.

Rather than designing an emergency change process by starting with a "proper" process and removing steps, consider designing the normal process by starting with the bare minimum of steps that you would need in an emergency process.

The largest part of most change processes, and the part that tends to get cut in emergencies, is up-front reviews of planned changes. The practices described throughout this book should reduce the need for these. Automating the process for applying changes with testing and monitoring reduces the chance of an error slipping through to production. They also make it much quicker to detect and fix errors that do slip through.

---

10 The section "Measuring Effectiveness" on page 311 in Chapter 15 touches on some common metrics for measuring the effectiveness of a team's workflow, and techniques for measuring and improving them.

Code Reviews

There is still a need for human involvement in quality control of individual changes. Some development teams use pair programming to ensure that two people are involved in making any change, acting like a continuous code review. Although this may seem wasteful, it's far more effective than having someone review code after it's written. Code reviews done after a delay may be skimped or skipped. Even when done thoroughly, feedback from a code review requires someone to go back and re-implement a change. All too often, code reviewing becomes a wasteful activity that doesn't lead to improvements actually being made to code. Pair programming is more rigorous, with input from two people leading to better design and improvements made in real time. This is obviously in addition to benefits of knowledge sharing, learning, and shared code ownership.

Changes made through source control and automated application can also be reviewed afterward. This makes it possible to monitor the quality of work and systems design, without having to put changes through a process bottleneck. Many teams, especially distributed teams, automatically send emails with each change made to a mailing list. Peers and leaders can review changes and give feedback, sparking team discussions that help to shape common styles and practices.

Fitting Governance into the Workflow

For many organizations, especially larger ones and those subject to detailed legal regulations, governance is a major concern. "Governance" refers to the processes that ensure that work is carried out according to relevant policies, to ensure efficiency and legal compliance.

Governance is sometimes a sticking point for organizations adopting technology and methodologies that enable frequent, rapid changes with short turnaround times. There is often a concern that changes made too quickly will bypass proper governance, creating risk of operational problems, security breaches, or even criminal violations. On the other side, there can be a perception that governance processes are wasteful and unnecessary.

Infrastructure as code seeks to manage risks more effectively, and also to enable fast delivery, through automation. Instead of implementing systems manually based on detailed specification documents, teams generate systems automatically based on configuration definition files. Rather than throttling work through gates, which are limited by the scarce time of specialist reviewers, work can be rapidly and repeatedly validated by automated tests.[11]

---

11 See Chapter 11 for more on automating operational quality tests, in particular, the section "Testing Operational Quality" on page 211.

Manual gates add considerable time to the process of making a change, as shown in Figure 13-4. Often, the time spent actually reviewing the change is much less than the delays waiting for people to become available, writing documentation, filling in request forms, and other overhead from the process itself.

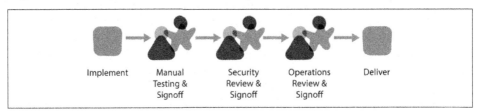

Implement   Manual   Security   Operations   Deliver
           Testing &   Review &   Review &
           Signoff   Signoff   Signoff

Figure 13-4. Workflow with manual gates

The adage "too many cooks spoil the broth" applies here. Dividing the responsibility for a change across many people not only makes it difficult to coordinate, it also reduces awareness of the big picture. Specialists focus on the narrow part of the system they are responsible for, and lack awareness of the impact their work has on other parts of the system.

Automated validation can dramatically reduce delays and help to scale the number of projects and changes that specialists can manage. These specialists, who include technical specialists and those with governance responsibilities, can invest their time and energy in ensuring the automated validation works well, rather than spending their time reviewing each individual change. They can regularly audit the automation and validation scripts, as well as samples of change history and the resulting systems, to ensure that changes are being correctly handled. Figure 13-5 removes the manual work from the main workflow.

This approach to governance of change management has several benefits:

- Changes are made consistently and reliably, rather than depending on individuals to follow documented processes they may find tedious and inconvenient.

- Changes are logged, which improves the auditability of what was done, by whom, how, and why.

- Specialists spend less time on routine inspections and reviews, which allows them to spend more time raising the level of the governance tooling, and coaching other teams on their areas.

- Teams making changes are responsible for making them correctly, and so gain a deeper understanding of the theory and practice of operational concerns such as security.

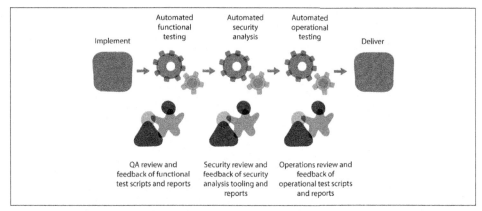

Figure 13-5. Workflow with automated compliance testing

An issue discovered by a manual governance gate late in the process is likely to be either ignored, or papered over with a shoddy workaround. Automated, continuous validation catches issues much sooner, when there is still time to make a meaningful correction. This enables people to take a more evolutionary, iterative approach to designing solutions based on proving implementations, rather than forcing compliance to speculative up-front designs. The outcomes are not only delivered more quickly, but with higher standards of quality.

Conclusion

When a team adopts infrastructure as code, its members should find themselves spending less time carrying out routine activities, and more time improving the system itself. The workflow for making changes will tend to be more indirect, but a well-designed process and toolset should give fast feedback and be able to apply changes quickly. It's important that the routine process for making changes is fast and effective enough that it can handle emergency fixes reliably and thoroughly enough to satisfy requirements for quality and compliance.

The next chapter delves more deeply into questions of operational quality. How can dynamic infrastructure and infrastructure as code be leveraged to ensure continuous service in the face of disruption?

Continuity with Dynamic Infrastructure

The previous chapters in this part of the book have focused on how to make changing infrastructure configuration easy while also maintaining high levels of quality, through testing, using an automated change pipeline, and effective workflows. This chapter is concerned with the operational quality of production infrastructure.

I use the term "continuity" as a catchall for operational quality. The goal of continuity is for services to be continuously available to users without interruption. Services should perform quickly and correctly. Data should be available and correct. Malicious people should not be able to compromise the service in any way. If something goes wrong, it should be quickly detected and recovered, with little or no impact to users.

The traditional approach to continuity is to limit and control change. Any change creates the risk of breaking something.[1] So processes and systems focus on minimizing the number of changes and thoroughly evaluating each change before it is made.

Dynamic infrastructure disrupts this approach, in pretty much every sense of the word. Systems are constantly being changed. Resources may be added, removed, resized, and reconfigured throughout the day. Early morning maintenance windows aren't compatible with the need to automatically scale a server pool to adjust to hourly traffic patterns. Continuous change feels like a recipe for continuous outages.

The modern organization's imperative for quick turnaround of IT changes only adds to the sense of chaos and anarchy. Agile software projects, Lean MVPs (minimum

---

1 According to the Visible Ops Handbook (*http://www.amazon.com/Visible-Ops-Handbook-Implementing-Practical-ebook/dp/B002BWQBEE*), 80% of unplanned outages are caused by changes made by staff.

viable products), and cross-functional product teams[2] mean more people are making more changes, more often, with less time spent analyzing their impact.

The goal of infrastructure of code is to flip the speed-versus-stability dynamic on its head. Rather than fighting the tide of pervasive change, organizations can take advantage of the ease of making changes to continuously improve operational continuity. Rather than degenerating into post-apocalyptic chaos, the system can be made more reliable than ever before.

This chapter explains how to use dynamic platforms and the principles of infrastructure as code to achieve high levels of operational quality. The aspects of continuity discussed in this chapter include:

Service continuity
　　Keeping services available to end users in the face of problems and changes

Data continuity
　　Keeping data available and consistent on infrastructure that isn't

Disaster recovery
　　Coping well when the worst happens

Security
　　Keeping bad actors at bay

Service Continuity

System components fail. Software crashes. Resources become exhausted. Even when there are no unplanned issues like these, people make changes. They upgrade systems and software. They add, remove, or reallocate resources. They deploy new applications and integrate them with existing ones. They deploy updates. They optimize configurations.

The goal of service continuity is to ensure that users don't notice any of this, except for the pleasant discovery of new features and faster responsiveness.

Continuity is often discussed in terms of uptime or availability. Sometimes, however, these are defined in ways that don't take the full picture into account.

True Availability

Many IT service providers use *availability* as a key performance metric or SLA. This is a percentage, often expressed as a number of nines: "five nines availability" means that the system is available 99.999% of the time.

---

2 I'll talk more about cross-functional teams in the next chapter.

But it's common practice for providers to caveat this tough-sounding SLA with a qualifier about "unplanned" outages. That is, if they deliberately take the system off-line for planned maintenance or upgrades, it doesn't count against their availability, as long as they let users know ahead of time.

Availability excluding planned downtime has value as a metric. It helps teams to measure how well they're doing to manage unexpected failures. But it doesn't measure how well the team is doing at minimizing the impact of planned changes. In some situations, this may be acceptable; it may be that the system's users only use it at certain times, such as during business hours.

True availability is the percentage of time the system is available and fully usable, without exclusions. By tracking this number, a team raises its awareness of planned changes. They can work to improve their processes, tooling, and system designs to reduce the types of changes that require taking the system offline for users.

The Hidden Impact of Out-of-Hours Maintenance

At one organization I worked in, we measured the availability of a system that was mostly used by people during working hours from 8 AM to 6 PM every day. This was convenient for us, because we had a monthly batch operation that took most of a night to complete.

However, the time to run the batch job grew as the size of our user base grew. When it became too long to run overnight, we were forced to invest in changes to the software so the job could be split over multiple evenings. This was great for our metrics: we were able to continue hitting our SLA targets, even as the job grew to take a full week to complete on a nightly basis.

But this had a hidden cost. The overnight batch jobs required significant out-of-hours work for our operations staff to set up, and then to break it off and bring the systems back online in the morning. So our staff ended up working after hours and early mornings for an entire week out of every month.

There were a number of solutions proposed to enable the batch work to run without downtime, and without manual work. But these solutions required spending on software development work, which didn't seem necessary to management. The existing solution achieved the business target metrics, and the out-of-hours work was "free." The funds to implement the zero-downtime, automated processing solution were only approved after three-quarters of the operations staff resigned.

Using Dynamic Server Pools for Recovery

Many dynamic infrastructure platforms have the capability to dynamically manage a pool of servers. Amazon's Auto Scaling groups is a well-known example of this. The pool is defined by declaring a server template to use for creating new instances, and rules that specify when to automatically add and remove instances from the pool. In Example 14-1, the pool is declared as MyPool, and the details of how to launch a new server instance are declared in MyPoolLaunch.

Example 14-1. AWS CloudFormation definition for an Auto Scaling group

```
"MyPool" :{
    "Type" : "AWS::AutoScaling::AutoScalingGroup",
    "Properties" : {
        "AvailabilityZones" : [ "eu-west-1a", "eu-west-1b", "eu-west-1c" ],
        "LaunchConfigurationName" : "MyPoolLaunch",
        "MaxSize" : "10",
        "MinSize" : "2"
    }
},

"MyPoolLaunch" : {
    "Type" : "AWS::AutoScaling::LaunchConfiguration",
    "Properties" : {
        "ImageId" : "ami-47a23a30",
        "InstanceType" : "m1.small"
    }
}
```

In addition to handling changes in workload, dynamic pools can automatically replace failed servers. The platform uses health checks to detect when a server is no longer working correctly, at which point it can provision a new instance and destroy the old one. Even servers running software not intended for clustering can take advantage of this, by setting the pool with a minimum and maximum size of "1". The platform will then ensure there is always a single working instance of the server.

Using dynamic server pools effectively usually requires customizing the health check. The default health check is likely to be based on response to a ping of the server. But this will not detect when the application running on the server has a problem. So it may be desirable to have a check of a particular network endpoint on the server, or even a specific result string or response code.

A pitfall of using dynamic pools to automatically replace failed servers is that it can mask a problem. If an application has a bug that causes it to crash frequently, it may take a while for people to notice. So it is important to implement metrics and alerting on the pool's activity. The supporting team should be made aware when a server instance fails, even if it's replaced without interrupting service. The team should be sent critical alerts when the frequency of server failures exceeds a threshold.

Not all applications are designed to run on dynamic infrastructure, so may not gracefully handle having servers automatically replaced. The next section discusses this in more detail.

Software Design for Dynamic Infrastructure

Traditionally, software has been written with the assumption that the infrastructure it runs on is static. Installing a new instance of the software, even in a cluster, is not a routine event, and probably requires some manual work. Removing an instance of the software from a cluster can be disruptive.

Software that has been designed and implemented with the assumption that servers and other infrastructure elements are routinely added and removed is sometimes referred to as "cloud native." Cloud-native software handles constantly changing and shifting infrastructure seamlessly.

12-Factor Applications

The team at Heroku published a list of guidelines for applications to work well in the context of a dynamic infrastructure, called the 12-factor application (*http://12factor.net/*).

Some of the items on the 12-factor application list are implementation-specific. For example, there are alternatives to using environment variables for configuration. However, they each point to an important consideration that an application must take into account in order to play nicely in a dynamic infrastructure.

I. *Codebase*
    One codebase tracked in revision control, many deploys.

II. *Dependencies*
    Explicitly declare and isolate dependencies.

III. *Config*
    Store config in the environment.

IV. *Backing services*
    Treat backing services as attached resources.

V. *Build, release, run*
    Strictly separate build and run stages.

VI. *Processes*
    Execute the app as one or more stateless processes.

VII. *Port binding*
    Export services via port binding.

VIII. Concurrency
   Scale out via the process model.

IX. Disposability
   Maximize robustness with fast startup and graceful shutdown.

X. Dev/prod parity
   Keep development, staging, and production as similar as possible.

XI. Logs
   Treat logs as event streams.

XII. Admin processes
   Run admin/management tasks as one-off processes.

The phrase lift and shift describes installing software that was written for static infrastructure (i.e., most software designed with legacy, pre-cloud assumptions) onto dynamic infrastructure. Although the software ends up running on a dynamic infrastructure platform, the infrastructure must be managed statically to avoid breaking anything. These applications are unlikely to be able to take advantage of advanced infrastructure capabilities such as automatic scaling and recovery, or the creation of ad hoc instances.

Some characteristics of non-cloud-native software that require "lift and shift" migrations:

- Stateful sessions
- Storing data on the local filesystem
- Slow-running startup routines
- Static configuration of infrastructure parameters

For example, it's unfortunately common for applications to need configuration files that set the IP addresses of infrastructure elements such as databases. If the number or location of one of these elements changes, updating the configuration file may involve rebooting the application so that it picks up the changes.

Lift and shift is often necessary when there are components of a system or service that will take considerable time and expense to replace with cloud-native software. As of this writing, most established enterprise software vendors release products for on-premise installation (i.e., as opposed to SaaS offerings) that are not designed as cloud-native. But this is legacy, because the products were developed before dynamic infrastructure become mainstream. These vendors are changing their strategy to provide hosted SaaS solutions, rewriting their software to be cloud-native, or else are holding out until they are superseded by competitors that do make the move.

Building on Unreliable Infrastructure

At cloud-scale, you can be sure hardware will fail. This is true even with hardware engineered for high reliability. At a scale of tens of thousands, or hundreds of thousands of servers, even 99.999% reliability means you will have failures. So you're forced to design your systems to tolerate hardware failure.

The economics of this scale have led companies operating large-scale infrastructures, including Google, Facebook, and Amazon, to build their infrastructure using cheap commodity hardware. Paying top price for more reliable hardware doesn't make sense when they need to build resilience into your systems and software in any case. They know their systems will cope with the inevitable failures, so it is more cost effective to simply replace the hardware when it fails.

Sam Johnston described the shift (*http://samj.net/2012/03/08/simplifying-cloud-reliability/*) from unreliable software (with low tolerance for instability in its infrastructure) running on reliable hardware to reliable software running on unreliable hardware.

Compartmentalizing for Continuity

The architectural principle of preferring small, loosely coupled pieces can help with continuity. For example, there is a trend toward breaking single, monolithic monitoring server processes into multiple services.[3] The smaller services handle aspects of monitoring, one polling infrastructure elements to determine state, another storing state information, and other processes that handle sending out alerts, providing a status dashboard, and graphing dashboards.

One benefit is that a failure of one component can leave at least some capabilities in service. For example, a dashboard failing doesn't stop alerts being sent out. It is often easier to scale smaller individual services out for redundancy than it is with a large monolithic service. And of course it's easier to fix, update, and upgrade smaller services, with less impact to the overall service.

It's also often preferable to split a given type of tool into multiple instances. For example, some organizations aspire to have a single instance of their configuration management server, CI system, etc., which all teams in the organization will share.

---

3 The open source Prometheus (*http://prometheus.io/*) monitoring system is based on a microservices architecture.

But this creates unnecessary challenges to continuity. A single team can potentially cause problems for other teams using the same instance.

If instances of the tool can be provisioned automatically, then it's trivial to give each team its own instance. This also helps with upgrades and maintenance, as it's not necessary to find a single time slot which all of the user teams will accept to take the service down (assuming zero-downtime replacement is not an option, of course).

Zero-Downtime Changes

Many changes require taking elements of the infrastructure offline, or completely replacing them. Examples include upgrading an OS kernel, reconfiguring a network, or deploying a new version of application software. However, it's often possible to carry out these changes without interrupting service.

Making the service available around the clock, and avoiding the need for out-of-hours work by staff are obvious benefits of zero-downtime changes. But a powerful benefit that's often overlooked is reducing a major barrier to continuous improvement.

Out-of-hours changes are fraught with risk, and tend to become bottlenecks. This ends up delaying changes at best, discouraging them at worst. This in turn encourages a "good enough" culture, where minor problems and "known issues" are tolerated. But being able to apply fixes and improvements at any time makes high quality routine.

Many of the patterns in this section are based on zero-downtime application deployment patterns. But they can be adapted to managing changes to infrastructure elements, including networking, load balancing, and even storage devices.

The basic idea of zero-downtime deployment is obviously to change an infrastructure element without interrupting service. All of the patterns described here involve deploying the new version of the element while the previous version is still in use. The change can be tested before the new element is actually used. Once it is tested and considered ready, usage is switched over to the new element. The previous element can be kept running for a period, to offer a quick rollback if something goes wrong with the new one.

Pattern: Blue-Green Replacement

Blue-green replacement is the most straightforward pattern to replace an infrastructure element without downtime. This is the blue-green deployment pattern for software[4] applied to infrastructure. It requires running two instances of the affected infrastructure, keeping one of them live at any point in time. Changes and upgrades are made to the offline instance, which can be thoroughly tested before switching usage over to it. Once the switch is made, the updated instance can be monitored for a time, with the first instance kept ready to fail back if something turns out to be wrong with the change. Once the change is proven, the old instance can be used to prepare the next change. This sequence is illustrated in Figure 14-1.

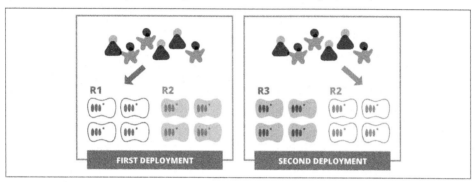

Figure 14-1. Blue-green replacement

There are several challenges with blue-green deployments. They do require more intelligent routing, as discussed in "Routing Traffic for Zero-Downtime Replacements" on page 286. The time needed to switch over between instances can become unmanageable with larger systems. And handling data can be quite complicated for zero-downtime. All of these challenges are discussed later in this chapter.

Pattern: Phoenix Replacement

Phoenix replacement is the natural progression from blue-green using dynamic infrastructure. Rather than keeping an idle instance around between changes, a new instance can be created each time a change is needed. As with blue-green, the change is tested on the new instance before putting it into use. The previous instance can be kept up for a short time, until the new instance has been proven in use. But then the previous instance is destroyed. Figure 14-2 shows this process.

The phoenix approach makes more efficient use of infrastructure resources. It also regularly exercises the process for provisioning infrastructure, which has side benefits. Problems with the provisioning process are made visible quickly, presumably in a

---

4 The blue-green deployment pattern for software was described in Farley and Humble's *Continuous Delivery* book (*http://www.amazon.com/Continuous-Delivery-Deployment-Automation-Addison-Wesley/dp/0321601912*), and is documented in an article on Martin Fowler's bliki (*http://martinfowler.com/bliki/Blue GreenDeployment.html*).

test environment. And when infrastructure is routinely provisioned and reprovisioned for changes, doing it in an emergency is less fraught than if it's an unusual activity.

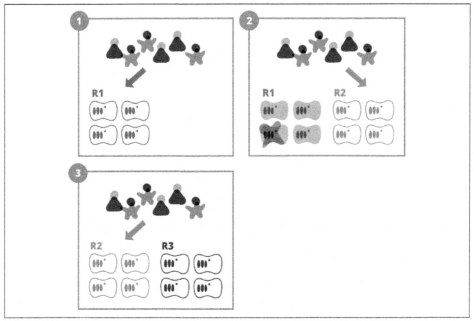

Figure 14-2. Phoenix replacement

Phoenix replacement is the foundation for continuous disaster recovery, as described later in this chapter. It's also the basis for the phoenix server pattern and immutable infrastructure.[5] These extend the phoenix replacement pattern to become the only method for changing the configuration of a server.

Practice: Reduce the Scope of Replacement

Applying blue-green and phoenix replacement patterns becomes impractical for large sections of infrastructure. If making a change using these patterns becomes unwieldy, the system design should be evolved to break it into smaller, independently deployable pieces. This aligns with the architectural theme of small, loosely coupled pieces that runs throughout this book. Figure 14-3 shows how a single server within a set of servers is replaced using the blue-green approach.

---

5 See "Pattern: Phoenix Servers" on page 137 and "Immutable Servers" on page 135 in Chapter 8.

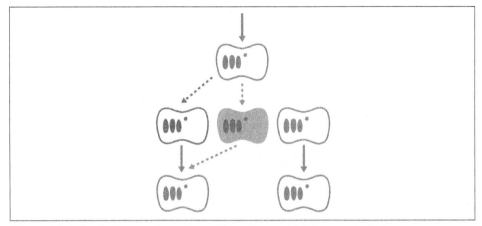

Figure 14-3. Replacing a sub-section of the system with blue-green deployment

One organization I worked with implemented blue-green using a second data center that had originally been provisioned for DR. Their application was a set of interrelated services, which they would deploy to whichever data center was currently not live. Once the new release was fully tested, they would switch over. This worked well for a while, and they were able to release daily if they chose.

But over time it became a heavy process. Data needed to be synchronized between the two data centers for a new release, and before long this was taking an hour or more. It was becoming difficult to manage even a weekly release. This was an especially annoying limitation for smaller changes.

So the team decided to break the release process down by service. It took some work to ensure that each service could be deployed on its own, but it radically improved their ability to make changes quickly and more often.[6]

Pattern: Canary Replacement

Most of the replacement patterns described become difficult or impossible with larger-scale systems with a large number of identical elements. When a team has hundreds of instances of a single element, it may be too expensive to maintain enough resources to duplicate the production instance. Organizations like Google and Facebook typically use the canary release pattern (*http://martinfowler.com/bliki/ CanaryRelease.html*) for this reason.

---

6 The advice in Chapter 12 on scaling pipelines ("Scaling Pipelines to More Complex Systems" on page 238) is particularly relevant.

The canary pattern involves deploying the new version of an element alongside the old one, and then routing some portion of usage to the new elements. For example, with version A of an application running on 20 servers, version B may be deployed to two servers. A subset of traffic, perhaps flagged by IP address or by randomly setting a cookie, is sent to the servers for version B. The behavior, performance, and resource usage of the new element can be monitored to validate that it's ready for wider use. Figure 14-4 shows the canary pattern.

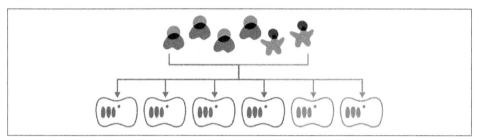

Figure 14-4. Canary replacement

The rest of the instances can then be incrementally replaced, until either a problem is discovered that triggers a rollback, or else until the release is complete.

Dark Launching

Unlike the other patterns described in this section, dark launching (*http://agiletest ing.blogspot.co.uk/2009/07/dark-launching-and-other-lessons-from.html*) doesn't involve having multiple versions of an element deployed at the same time. Instead, a new version of an element is deployed and put into use, but with the new feature hidden from human users.

This is particularly useful for testing new features at scale. Test script can exercise the feature on the production deployment before it is ready for users to see. The team needs to pay close attention to monitoring, so they can shut the test down if it seems to have a negative impact for users.

This approach is often the only way to gauge the performance and operational impact in very large-scale systems.

Routing Traffic for Zero-Downtime Replacements

The descriptions of these patterns make it sound simple to replace infrastructure elements without downtime. But in practice, they add complexity for all but the simplest cases. The complexity is often worth it in order to keep services running without interruption in an environment that is continuously changing, but it's important to understand how to implement it.

Zero-downtime change patterns involve fine-grained control to switch usage between system components. The mechanism for doing this will depend on the type of component. Web-based applications and services (i.e., those using the HTTP and/or HTTPS protocols) are an extremely common case. A standard HTTP/S load balancer can often be used to enable zero-downtime deployments.

A simple way to implement this is to exclude the newly provisioned elements from the load balancer until they've been tested and made ready. This is shown in Figure 14-5. They might not be included in the load balancer pool, or could be included but configured in a way that causes them to fail the load balancer's health check.

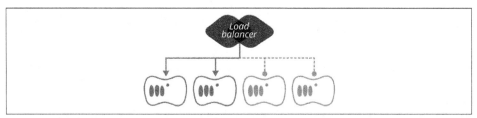

Figure 14-5. The load balancer can exclude new servers from the pool

This is unlikely to create a smooth transition once the new servers are added, and the old ones removed.

Another option is to have two load balancer pools, one for the new set of servers and one for the old, as shown in Figure 14-6.

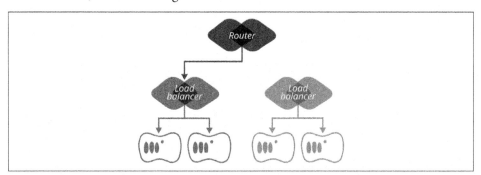

Figure 14-6. Routing traffic to two load balancer pools

A router in front directs traffic to the correct load balancer pool. This allows the testers to access the new set of servers using the second pool's URL, before it is made available to the public. The router switches traffic to the new pool once it's ready.

This can be extended for the canary pattern with some additional functionality on the router. Users can be conditionally routed to one pool or the other, as illustrated in Figure 14-7.

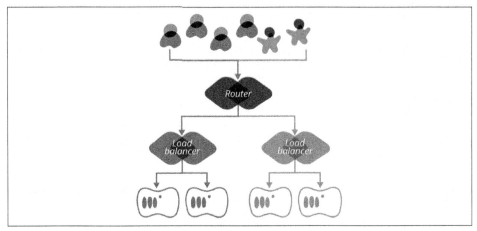

Figure 14-7. Routing for canary changes

Different approaches can be used to route traffic. Users can be selected randomly, based on IP address, geographical region, or by explicitly opting-in (this is often done for user interface changes). Cookies can be set to ensure that, once selected, a user is consistently directed to the same pool of servers.

Most organizations that implement this type of approach end up writing customized routing. This gives them control to manage how users are selected, and to adjust the balance of users between pools as the rollout progresses. Connection draining is also useful, to ensure that all of the sessions using the old pool have completed before the pool is completely removed from service.

Zero-Downtime Changes with Data

Data creates a particular challenge for zero-downtime change strategies. All of the patterns described involve running multiple versions of a component simultaneously, with the option to roll back and keep the first version of the element if there is a problem with the new one. However, if the components use read/write data storage, this can be a problem.

The problem comes when the new version of the component involves a change to data formats so that it's not possible to have both versions share the same data storage without issues.

This isn't an issue when the data is read-only, because it can simply be copied, so that the new version of the component uses its own copy of the data. If the data format isn't actually affected by the component versions, then it's even easier, because the component versions can still share the same data. This is usually the case with web servers hosting static web content.

Beyond these cases, it's normally necessary for the component or application to be written in a way that enables zero-downtime deployment in spite of the data. For example, the component can be written to have a read-only mode that is activated during upgrades. Or it can use a transaction log, so that changes written to one instance of the data store can be replayed on the new instance after the upgrade is complete.

An effective way to approach data for zero-downtime deployments is to decouple data format changes from software releases. This requires the software to be written so that it can work with two different data formats, the original version and the new version. It is first deployed and validated with the data in the original format. The data is then migrated as a background task while the software is running. The software is able to cope with whichever data format a given record is in. Once the data migration is complete, compatibility with the old data format should be removed from the next release of the software, to keep the code clean.[7]

Data Continuity

Data persistence is a particular challenge with dynamic infrastructure. Zero-downtime changes and cloud-native applications sound simple when you assume everything is stateless. But real-world systems need data to be continuously available and consistent. How can this be supported in an environment where every element of the infrastructure is disposable?

There are many techniques that can be applied to this problem. A few include:

- Replicating data redundantly
- Regenerating data
- Delegating data persistence
- Backing up to persistent storage

These are not new[8] or unique to dynamic infrastructure. But it's worth touching on how they may be applied in these situations.

---

7 More information about this can be found in the book *Refactoring Databases* (*http://databaserefactoring.com/*) (Addison-Wesley).

8 There are many great references for managing data continuity in a distributed environment. Limoncelli, Chalup, and Hogan cover this in Chapter 2 of *The Practice of Cloud System Administration* (*http://www.amazon.com/The-Practice-Cloud-System-Administration/dp/032194318X*).

Replicating Data Redundantly

A common approach to persisting data is to ensure it is replicated across multiple instances, with redundancy. For example, a database cluster can duplicate data across multiple nodes, or use a parity scheme, to ensure that it can be recovered if a node is lost. This can provide data continuity with a certain level of tolerance, but if too many nodes are lost at once, the data can't be rebuilt. So this approach is typically useful as a first line of defense, but is not a complete solution.

Tools Versus Automation

Clusters can actually be more fragile in an automated environment, where a "DevOops" error (see "DevOops" on page 228) can quickly tear across all of the servers in a cluster. A layered strategy for protecting data mitigates against this.

Redundant data is particularly useful for replacing infrastructure. Servers in a database cluster can be upgraded or replaced sequentially, waiting for data to be replicated onto each new node before moving onto the next.

Multiregion infrastructure platforms offer the possibility to easily replicate data across geographical areas. It may also be useful to partition database clusters and manage different parts of the clusters separately. An upgrade may be applied to one section of the cluster and tested before it is rolled out to the others.

Regenerating Data

Chapter 6 described the different things that go onto a server, including software, configuration, and data (see "Types of Things on a Server" on page 105). Software and configuration are managed through configuration management mechanisms, so they can be built and rebuilt whenever needed. However, in some cases, things that people think of as data can actually be treated like configuration.

Many systems use content that is created and curated in a separate system and then loaded into a runtime system. The system that generates the data and is ultimately responsible for it is the System of Record (*https://en.wikipedia.org/wiki/ System_of_record*). If the system you are managing is not the system of record, you may not need to invest as much in protecting the data. Instead, you may be able to retrieve or regenerate the data.

Examples include geographical mapping data, publications and documents, catalogs, medical guidelines, and reference data. In this situation, the runtime system may not need to treat the data with the same care as it otherwise would.

Delegating Data Persistence

It's often possible to delegate the storage of data to a dedicated service, perhaps one run by another group. The classic example is a managed database service such as AWS's relational database service (RDS). Your own systems can write their data to the other service, and so don't need to worry about persistence, assuming you can trust the people managing the other service to do it well.

In one sense, this is cheating, passing the buck on the problem of data continuity. But in another sense, this is a reasonable way to separate concerns. Even if your own team needs to build and run the data persistence service, having it as a decoupled concern simplifies the design of other parts of the system.

Other variations of this are using a storage area network (SAN) in a data center, or even a distributed filesystem such as NFS or GlusterFS.

Backing Up to Persistent Storage

Most of the preceding approaches refer to handling runtime data. This is not enough to protect against data corruption. Any mechanism that efficiently replicates data across distributed storage will replicate corrupted data just as happily as good data. A data availability strategy needs to address how to preserve and restore previous versions of data.

This is another topic that is relevant beyond the use of dynamic infrastructure or automation. However, there are a few recommendations to be made that are specific to dynamic platforms.

Be sure to understand where your data is stored. A cloud platform creates the illusion that everything is stored in some magical other dimension. But if your persistent storage is actually sitting in the same rack as your compute servers, a single accident can destroy everything. Be sure your data is archived in different physical locations.

Consider archiving data with a different vendor than your infrastructure platform. This can often be done easily and securely, streaming data backups to a third-party service over an encrypted connection.

Practice: Continuously proving backups

Make sure your backups are routinely retrieved and used so that it will become naturally obvious if they aren't being stored correctly and completely. For example, you could regularly rebuild a test environment by restoring backup data. Most experienced system administrators can share stories of running backups for years before discovering, at the worst possible time, that they weren't actually backing up the data properly. Continuously proving that your backups are valid prevents this kind of unpleasant discovery.

Disaster Recovery

Organizations have a disaster recovery (DR) plan to restore service when there is a failure.[9] Because a disaster is (hopefully!) an exceptional event, most IT organizations' DR plans involve unusual processes and systems, which are only rarely exercised.

Extra infrastructure is provisioned and kept available. Extra servers, network connections and devices, and even extra data centers are set up in different locations. If something bad happens, service will be migrated to this extra infrastructure, routing will be changed, and fingers will be crossed.

The finger crossing is important because the process to handle a disaster is rarely carried out, so its reliability is uncertain. Tests and exercises can be conducted to improve confidence. But it's not possible to test a complicated, exception-based DR process every time configuration changes. So it's a given that the recovery of the infrastructure's current configuration has almost never been accurately tested.

And many organizations lack the resources, particularly staff time, to invest in doing this as often as they'd like. So in practice, most IT organizations accept a certain level of risk that a disaster will not be handled flawlessly. People expect a disaster to be painful and messy. So IT organizations hope that everyone will cut them some slack —or simply hope that a disaster won't happen.

But some IT organizations appear to cope with potentially disastrous situations with ease. A major outage at a widely used hosting provider like AWS is followed by a list of high-profile companies whose services were disrupted, and a few examples of those who survived without their users ever noticing.

The key characteristic of those IT operations that handle outages smoothly, without investing in military-grade bomb-proofing, is that their mechanisms for handling disasters are the same mechanisms they use for routine operations. They practice what could be called continuous disaster recovery.

Prevention Versus Recovery

Iron-age IT organizations usually optimize for mean time between failures (MTBF), whereas cloud-age organizations optimize for mean time to recover (MTTR). This isn't to say that either approach ignores the other metric: organizations that strive to avoid failures still want to be able to recover quickly, and those aiming for rapid recoveries still take measures to reduce their occurrences.

---

9 See Wikipedia's definition of disaster recovery (*https://en.wikipedia.org/wiki/Disaster_recovery*).

The trick is not to ignore one of these metrics in favor of the other. Arguably, traditional approaches have sacrificed recovery time in hopes of eliminating all errors. Making changes overly difficult may prevent some failures, but at the cost of making it difficult to fix errors when they do occur.

However, embracing the goal of making it easy to rapidly recover from errors, by making it easy to make changes, does not need to come at the cost of higher rates of failure.

Continuous Disaster Recovery

An interesting thing about a dynamic infrastructure platform is that it looks a lot like unreliable infrastructure. Servers routinely disappear and are replaced. This happens when resources are automatically scaled up and down, and may even happen as a byproduct of the mechanism for making routine changes, deploying software, and running tests.

So the techniques for managing dynamic infrastructure can also be used to ensure continuity when things fail.

Effectively handling continuity looks like a natural extension of day-to-day operations. Recovering from a server failure is a trivial event: the server is automatically rebuilt, using the same process that is used to scale up a cluster, or to roll out a new server template. Larger-scale failures, such as a data center losing its network connection, can be handled by automatically provisioning an environment in a different data center. Again, this should be the same process used to build a test environment, something that probably happens several times a week, if not several times a day.

This doesn't happen without effort. You should make sure you have everything you need to provision services available to other data centers. You need monitoring to let people know when something goes wrong, and potentially to trigger recoveries.

The best way to ensure that your infrastructure can handle large-scale issues such as a data center outage is to actually run services from multiple data centers. This is far more reliable than simply having an additional data center ready on cold standby, because all data centers are proven to be up to date and fully operational.

There are a few caveats to this approach. Enough infrastructure must be provisioned, or the capacity to provision it made available, to cope with the full load when another part of the infrastructure disappears. Spreading traffic between three data centers is fine to continuously provide that all three are operational. But if, when one data center has a failure, the total traffic is more than the remaining two can handle, then services will fail. Keep in mind that, in the event of a large-scale failure of a popular hosting provider, your team may not be the only one scrambling to ramp up capacity in other data centers. So consider ways to ensure you can get the capacity you need in a pinch.

Also, it's important to prove that redundant elements can actually work when their peers are offline. Unintended dependencies between elements of an infrastructure often creep in and only become apparent when they fail. Regular exercises that involve taking parts of the system offline help to surface these dependencies. Automating these exercises is the best way to ensure they take place frequently.

Netflix and the Simian Army

Netflix famously uses an automated tool called Chaos Monkey to prove its infrastructure's resilience to individual server failures. Chaos Monkey semi-randomly destroys server instances, automatically. Staff have no notice of when this happens, so any weaknesses introduced to their infrastructure are quickly identified.

This is routine.

Chaos Monkey is only one element of Netflix's Simian Army (*http://tech blog.netflix.com/2011/07/netflix-simian-army.html*). Another is the Chaos Gorilla, which removes an entire data center (Amazon Web Services available zone) from play to prove that the rest of the infrastructure can carry on uninterrupted. Latency Monkey introduces artificial delays into client-server communication to see whether upstream servers handle service degradation correctly.

Due to their aggressive, continuous validation of their DR process, Netflix routinely survives failures of Amazon's cloud infrastructure without interruption.

The DR Plan: Planning for Disaster

If your entire infrastructure was wiped out, what would you need to rebuild it? For each vendor, imagine their service disappeared, along with everything you keep on it. Could your scripts, tools, backups, and other systems be used to rebuild it and repopulate it quickly from a blank slate? How much time would it take? How much data would be lost?

What if the vendor disappeared completely? Do you have what you need to start fresh with another vendor? Are there vendors that provide a compatible service, or would you need rewrite things to a new API? What could you do in the meantime?

Consider the infrastructure and services you manage yourself. Can you rebuild all of it from scratch? How long would it take? What knowledge would it take? Ideally, your scripts and tooling could reprovision servers, networking, and the like without needing someone to remember and think through the right way to do key steps, and without needing to refer to documentation that may well be out of date or incomplete.

Your data should be backed up somewhere separate from where it's used, in a way that's easily and reliably accessible.

Having configuration definitions and scripts that can rebuild your entire infrastructure and services from scratch is essential. However, think about where those are stored, and what would happen if that disappeared. What if you lose your VCS? If you use a VCS provided by a vendor, what happens if they go out of business or are hacked? Your VCS should be regularly backed up to a completely different location, so you can extract it and bring up a new VCS in an emergency.

Practice: Prefer Rebuilding Things over Cold Standby

Rather than keeping extra infrastructure configured and on cold standby for active/passive recovery strategies, being able to quickly rebuild failed elements may be more effective and even more reliable. This relies on the ability to rebuild quickly, and assumes that the time to detect a failure and complete the rebuild is acceptable for the service involved.

A common implementation of this for servers is using automatic scaling functionality, as described earlier in this chapter. With an auto-scaling pool of servers, when one server fails, the platform should detect the missing server and automatically build a replacement.

This can be leveraged to provide automated DR for singleton servers that can't easily be clustered. Example 14-2 shows an excerpt from an AWS CloudFormation definition for a GoCD server. This sets an autoscaling group with a minimum and maximum size of 1. If the server fails health checks, a new one will be automatically created. It also uses an Elastic Load Balancer (ELB) to ensure that traffic is always routed to the current server instance.

Example 14-2. AWS CloudFormation snippet for a single-server autoscaling group

```
"GoCDServerPool" :{
    "Type" : "AWS::AutoScaling::AutoScalingGroup",
    "Properties" : {
        "LaunchConfigurationName" : "GoCDServerLaunch",
        "LoadBalancerNames" : [ "GoCDLoadBalancer" ],
        "MaxSize" : "1",
        "MinSize" : "1"
    }
}
```

Use of this pattern works well when most of the provisioning process is done in the server template,[10] as it means new server instances will be created quickly.

Continuous Monitoring through the Pipeline

Monitoring[11] is clearly essential to continuity strategies. Monitoring can even be configured to trigger automated recovery routines, replacing elements of the infrastructure that are found to be faulty or failing.

As with any core function of infrastructure, it's important to ensure that monitoring is continuously validated. Some organizations only monitor production infrastructure, but there are huge benefits from applying the same monitoring to all environments in development and test.

Running monitoring against development and test environments gives the opportunity to validate the correctness of the monitoring itself. Changes to application code or infrastructure might change the relevance of a particular monitoring check. For example, a monitoring check that tests whether an application is up could fail because of a change to networking routing, or a change to the part of the UI that the monitoring system tests.

So it can be useful to incorporate tests of the monitoring system itself into change management pipelines, perhaps automatically bringing the application down and polling the monitoring system to see that it has correctly flagged the application's status.

Using a monitoring tool with externalized configuration allows changes to the monitoring itself to be automatically validated before being rolled out to production monitoring systems. For example, when defining a new subnet, you might add a monitoring check to prove that resources in the subnet are reachable. The definitions for both the subnet and the monitoring check should be committed to VCS, along with a few automated tests, such as Serverspec checks.

The VCS commit triggers the change pipeline. At least one of the automated stages of the pipeline will cause the subnet to be provisioned in a test environment, and the monitoring check to be added to the monitoring server instance for that environment. One of the Serverspec tests will validate that the monitoring check appears and lists the subnet as accessible. Another test alters the subnet configuration so that it no longer works correctly, and then validates that the monitoring check for the subnet detects the problem.

---

10 See "Provisioning in the Template" on page 119 in Chapter 6.

11 Monitoring tooling is discussed in "Alerting: Tell Me When Something Is Wrong" on page 87 in Chapter 5.

Fully monitoring development and test systems also helps development and infrastructure teams. When automated testing fails in an environment, monitoring can be valuable in debugging the issue. This is especially helpful finding issues in the interplay between applications and infrastructure, such as problems with resource usage (e.g., memory, disk, and CPU).

Monitoring and testing

Monitoring and automated testing have a lot in common. Both make assertions about the state of an infrastructure and its services, and both alert the team that there is a problem when an assertion fails. Combining or at least integrating these concerns can be very effective. Consider reusing automated tests to validate whether systems are working correctly in production. Some caveats, however:

- Many automated tests have side effects, and/or need special setup, which may be destructive in production.
- Many tests aren't relevant for production monitoring. Monitoring checks for problems that can happen because of changes in operational state. Testing validates whether a change to code is harmful. Once the code is changed and applied to production, rerunning a functional test may be pointless.
- Reusing code between tests and monitoring is only useful if it makes life easier. In many cases, trying to bend and twist a testing tool so it can be used for production monitoring may be more effort than simply using two different tools.

Monitoring and antifragility

As mentioned in Chapter 1, the key to an antifragile infrastructure is making sure that the default response to incidents is improvement. When something goes wrong, the priority is not simply to fix it, but to improve the ability of the system to cope with similar incidents in the future.

A team typically handles an incident by first making a quick fix, so that service can resume. They then work out the changes needed to fix the underlying cause, to prevent the issue from happening again. Tweaking monitoring to alert when the issue happens again is often an afterthought, something nice to have but easily neglected.

A team striving for antifragility will make monitoring, and even automated testing, the second step, after the quick fix and before implementing the long term fix.

This may be counterintuitive. Some system administrators have told me it's a waste of time to implement automated checks for an issue that has already been fixed, because by definition it won't happen again. But in reality, fixes don't always work, may not resolve related issues, and can even be reversed by well-meaning team members who weren't involved in the previous incident.

Monitoring-driven development

So the workflow for fixing production issues could be:

1. Restore service to end users.

2. Create a monitoring check that detects the issue, and an automated test to replicate the issue and prove the check works.

3. Create the fix for the issue.

4. Commit all of these—fix, test, and monitoring check—to VCS and see that they progress through the pipeline to production.

This is test-driven development (TDD) for infrastructure.

Security

Security must be woven into the design and implementation of any IT system. Infrastructure as code, by building and proving systems repeatably, reliably, and transparently, can be used as a platform to ensure systems are well protected. However, the automation used to provision and manage systems, and the programmable infrastructure platforms it it built on, can itself create new openings for attackers to exploit.

Automatically Papering over Compromises

Some of the patterns and practices discussed in Chapter 8 might seem useful for automatically countering security breaches, but they aren't reliable defenses.

Continuous synchronization[12] might reverse changes made by attackers—assuming they don't make changes in areas not managed by the configuration tool.[13] Frequently destroying and rebuilding servers[14] is more likely to reverse unauthorized changes. But if someone is able to gain access to a server once, they can do it again after the server is rebuilt.

So while these practices might inconvenience an attacker, they can't be relied on to stop them. Worse, they might actually help the attacker to cover their tracks, by removing the evidence. Automated configuration doesn't replace the need for strong defenses and intrusion detection.

---

12 Described in "Patterns and Practices for Continuous Deployment" on page 138.

13 Recall "The Unconfigured Country" on page 141.

14 Refer back to "Pattern: Phoenix Servers" on page 137.

Reliable Updates as a Defense

Modern software systems of any size or complexity inevitably contain security vulnerabilities. The Common Vulnerabilities and Exposures system (CVE) (*https://cve.mitre.org/*) is a catalog of known vulnerabilities, which is used by vulnerability databases and security tools. Resources like this ought to help IT operations teams keep their systems more secure.

However, even well-publicized vulnerabilities such as the Heartbleed bug (*http://heartbleed.com/*) remain unpatched on production systems for years after being discovered and published.[15] This is a natural result when systems are difficult to update, and suffering from configuration drift.

So one of the biggest payoffs of an effective infrastructure-as-code regime is the ability to roll out patches easily, keeping systems consistently configured with the latest updates.

Provenance of Packages

Another common risk is installing outside software into a system that has had vulnerabilities deliberately added by attackers. The modern IT landscape is built on a vibrant ecosystem of shared code, both open source and commercial. But people with bad intentions can and do hide backdoors and Trojans in this code.

Whom to Trust?

While you may not blindly trust code downloaded from a random user on GitHub, you might be tempted to assume that you can trust code—and hardware—from a "reputable" vendor. Sadly, this is not the case. As I write this, the blogs and IT news outlets are in a tizzy over the discovery of a long-standing "malicious back door" in hardware firewall products made by a major corporation.[16]

This is only the latest such incident, at the end of 2015. There have been similar revelations for other vendors, and more will certainly come. The truth is that, code reviews, testing, and security analysis that goes on behind closed doors can't be fully trusted. Anyone who has seen inside the sausage factory[17] knows that shortcuts, expediency, commercial pressures, and laziness are common.

---

15 *https://www.venafi.com/assets/pdf/wp/Hearts-Continue-to-Bleed-Research-Report.pdf*

16 *https://www.schneier.com/blog/archives/2015/12/back_door_in_ju.html*

17 John Godfrey Saxe (*https://en.wikiquote.org/wiki/John_Godfrey_Saxe*) said, "Laws, like sausages, cease to inspire respect in proportion as we know how they are made." Software and IT systems should be added to this list, especially those built and run in large commercial organizations.

Teams should be sure they understand the provenance of all of the software they use (i.e., where it comes from) and have a realistic view of how well they can trust it. "Where things come from" on page 106 in Chapter 6 lists typical sources of software on a server, but there are many other sources of software used in an infrastructure. Examples include configuration definitions (e.g., cookbooks, playbooks, manifests, etc.) from community sources, Container images (e.g., Docker images), and snippets of scripts found on websites.

The measures a team takes to manage externally sourced software will vary based on needs. Some teams only use software from sources that have been rigorously vetted, or even insist that all source code must be audited. But this limits the ability of the team to take advantage of third-party products.

Methods of establishing trust in third-party software

Vendor code review
> Commercial vendors should be motivated and qualified to ensure their code is thoroughly inspected for vulnerabilities. But again, experience has shown that this is not always true.

Public code review
> Open source code is visible for many experienced people to review. "Given enough eyeballs, all bugs are shallow," according to Linus's Law (*https://en.wiki pedia.org/wiki/Linus%27s_Law*) stated by Eric Raymond. However, experience has proven that there is no guarantee that qualified people will actually take the time to review any given bit of open source code. The Heartbleed bug existed for two years in open source software that was used at the core of many security tools.

Direct code review
> Arguably the most effective method of ensuring that the code you use is secure is to review the code yourself. In practice, this is limited by your skill at security analysis of code, as well as your available time to do it.

Contracted code review
> You can contract a qualified third party to review code on your behalf, which can help ensure the right skills. Some vendors offer to review and certify open source packages. While this may be a reasonable compromise, you are limited by the capacity of the vendor to review the packages you want to use in the timescales you need them. This is part of the service offered by many Linux distribution vendors, but it's common for teams to install newer packages, not yet included in a distribution, rather than wait for new releases.

Penetration testing

Having a qualified third party review not only your code, but also your implementation, configuration, and how you use software, can be a valuable check.

Legal and/or contractual protection

One measure an organization can take is to ensure that there is a vendor who takes legal responsibility for all software used. This may require direct contractual relationships. This can mitigate at least some of the commercial risk of a vulnerability by passing it on to the vendor. But it does not mitigate the reputational risk, as users and customers do expect you to take ultimate responsibility for what you provide to them.

This is the basic trade-off. Teams balance their flexibility to select useful third-party software against their level of confidence in the security of that software. However, it's possible to mitigate this trade-off by ensuring the ability to quickly correct.

In other words, as with other aspects of continuity, a team can decide to optimize for recovery rather than assume perfect prevention. Again, this doesn't mean neglecting prevention, but it allows more leeway in selecting software if the team knows it can quickly roll out patches and fixes as vulnerabilities become known.

Automated Hardening

An obvious way to leverage infrastructure as code to improve security is to automate server and network hardening. "Hardening" refers to configuring a system to make it more secure than it would be out of the box. Typical activities include:

- Configuring security policies (e.g., firewall rules, SSH key use, password policies, sudoers files, etc.).

- Removing all but the most essential user accounts, services, software packages, and so on.

- Auditing user accounts, system settings, and checking installed software against known vulnerabilities.

There are many references available with specific suggestions for hardening servers.[18]

Teams should ensure their configuration definitions for servers, networks, and other infrastructure elements harden their systems sufficiently. There are frameworks and

---

18 A few security hardening references include "Proactively Hardening Systems Against Intrusion: Configuration Hardening" (*http://www.tripwire.com/state-of-security/security-data-protection/automation-action-proactively-hardening-systems-intrusion/*) on the Tripwire website, "25 Hardening Security Tips for Linux Servers" (*http://www.tecmint.com/linux-server-hardening-security-tips/*), and "20 Linux Server Hardening Security Tips" (*http://www.cyberciti.biz/tips/linux-security.html*).

scripts that can be applied, such as those found at *https://github.com/dev-sec*. It is essential that the members of the team review and understand the changes made by externally created hardening scripts before applying them to their own infrastructure. External resources can be a useful starting point, but the people who own a given system have a deeper understanding of the characteristics and needs of their system.

Hardening rules should be applied to server templates, to ensure the baseline for new servers has been locked down appropriately. But hardening should also be applied at the end of the provisioning process, to ensure that configuration changes and packages installed during the process have not inappropriately weakened the server's security. Continuous synchronization can ensure that hardening rules are kept in place during the life of the server.

Automating Security Validation in the Pipeline

The use of a change management pipeline to test changes before applying them to important systems creates the opportunity to validate security. Automated tests can check that security policies have been properly applied, and that they work well in practice.

There are a number of security scanning and penetration testing tools that can be executed as part of the change pipeline.[19] As with other types of tools, it's useful to select tools that are designed to run unattended, and which can be configured and scripted through externalized files managed in VCS.

As with availability monitoring, there is—or should be—overlap between tools run to validate changes in the pipeline and those run in production to detect intrusions. Automated tests can prove that configuration of intrusion detection tools are correctly configured.

The Change Pipeline as a Vulnerability

An automated change management pipeline is a powerful tool to manage the validation and authorization of changes. But it also creates an attractive vector for attack. An attacker who compromises any of the components of a change pipeline—including the VCS, the CI/CD orchestration tool, or artifact repositories—can potentially exploit it to make unauthorized changes.

Considering how central these tools are to an automated infrastructure, they should be among the most rigorously controlled systems in the estate. Strategies for securing systems should include the pipeline used to configure those systems into their scope. For example, if access to a system is segregated to a subgroup within the organiza-

---

19 Some example tools were listed in "Testing Operational Quality" on page 211 in Chapter 11.

tion, only that subgroup should have access to the relevant files and configuration of the change pipeline.

As of early 2016, many of the tools commonly used to implement pipelines are not well designed to secure and segregate access between groups that share it. VCS and artifact repositories tend to have reasonable controls to lock down access across projects and folders.

But the current generation of CI and CD orchestration tools tend to be trivial to exploit to gain access across projects hosted on the same instance. On one popular CI tool, it's possible for you to configure a job to use encrypted secrets, such as database access credentials. However, commonly used plug-ins allow other users to run a job that reads and decrypts your credentials.

Organizations that require secure segregation across teams are potentially better off running multiple instances of their CI/CD tool. Each team is given a dedicated instance, so there is no need to expect the tool to protect secrets internally.

Managing Security Risks with Cloud Accounts

The automated infrastructure platform is another key vector for attackers. If someone can gain access to the credentials used to manage infrastructure resources they can do considerable damage.[20] Fortunately, there are a number of practices that can mitigate risks when using cloud services. These are particularly important when using public clouds, but should not be neglected even inside your own data center.

Practice: Use segregated cloud accounts

Rather than running the entire infrastructure in a single account, accessible with a single set of credentials, the infrastructure should be segregated into accounts with their own credentials. The goal is to limit the damage that can be done by an attacker who gains access to a set of credentials. Exercises such as threat modeling (*http://bit.ly/1TQ0Qy3*)[21] are useful to design the segregation of the system to defend against different types of attacks and compromises.

---

20 The end of Code Spaces, a source code hosting company, is a cautionary tale for cloud hosting. Attackers gained access to the company's AWS credentials, demanded a ransom, and then destroyed the company's data. Cloud Spaces used AWS in common ways that made it difficult for them to defend themselves. Specifically, they had everything hosted under a single account, including their backups. For more information, see "Murder in the Amazon Cloud" (*http://bit.ly/25AR0pj*) and "Catastrophe in the Cloud: What the AWS Hacks Mean for Cloud Providers" (*http://bit.ly/1t1f0kj*).

21 Also see Adam Shostack's Threat Modeling: Designing for Security (*http://www.amazon.com/dp/B00IG71FAS*).

Logging and alerting out

Detecting intrusions and other problems is an important element of a defense strategy. Attackers will attempt to cover their tracks by erasing or overwriting logs, and by disabling logging and alerting. Defensive designs should involve ensuring that the evidence of a system being compromised is handled by a separate system, with completely separate access credentials.

For example, logs should be streamed to a separate log aggregation service, which is configured to alert on suspicious activity. A separate system should handle monitoring, again alerting when there is evidence that the client system may have been compromised.

This then requires an attacker to compromise more than one system in order to cover their tracks. While this is possible, it should be a more difficult barrier. However, for this to be effective, it should not be possible to exploit the monitoring or log aggregation service to gain access to the protected system. A monitoring server that has unattended SSH access to systems it monitors (e.g., in order to run scripts to check status) gives an attacker a single point for attacking the system while also covering their tracks.

Use strong authentication and manage credentials well

Cloud providers and platform vendors are increasingly offering more options for managing authentication. Teams should take full advantage of these. More rigorous authentication mechanisms may be intimidating or just seem like too much work, but the habits of using them become easier with time.

Examples of good practices for authentication and credentials include:

- Use multifactor authentication (MFA).
- Set up delegated roles and authentication for each person, application, service, and so on.
- Don't share credentials; each team member should have their own credentials.
- Use truly strong, unique passwords,[22] using a good password manager such as 1Password or Lastpass.
- Don't store credentials in a VCS, artifact repository, file server, etc., even if they are obfuscated.

---

22 See xkcd's "Password Strength" comic (*https://xkcd.com/936/*) for an illustration of why mixing case, symbols, and numbers into a password doesn't make it particularly strong.

The use of credentials by automated processes and applications is particularly tricky. A password that is available to an unattended application or script is also available to an attacker who gains sufficient access to the system that it runs on.

Credentials can be stored in an encrypted secrets repository such as HashiCorp Vault, Ansible-Vault, Chef encrypted databags, or similar solutions. However, an unattended application or script will still need to be authorized to retrieve those secrets from the repository, which can again be exploited by an attacker.

There are a few techniques to reduce the vulnerability created by authorization of unattended processes:

- Control access to the system where it runs.
- Ensure authorization is only usable from controlled locations/instances.
- Limit the lifespan of credentials.
- Limit the number of uses for a given credential.
- Log access to/use of credentials, generating alerts for unusual usage.
- Only give credentials read-only access unless absolutely required.

Be able to rebuild

The ability to effortlessly rebuild any part of an infrastructure is a powerful defense. If an attacker gains the credentials for an infrastructure hosting account, the ideal is to be able to completely rebuild everything in a new account, load data from backups, and then reroute traffic to it so that the original account becomes expendable.

This is the essence of Disaster Recovery, and as discussed earlier in the chapter, this will ideally make use of mechanisms that are exercised as a routine part of operations. But DR should be designed to be effective in the face of bad actors who gain unauthorized access to parts of the system. This involves ensuring that all of the materials needed to rebuild any part of the system, and to put it into service, are segregated.

Having the source control, definition files, data backups, and so on all accessible with a single set of credentials is unsafe. Ideally, each of these should be managed in separate services and accounts. Access should be minimized between these accounts.

For example, a system that provisions infrastructure probably doesn't need write access to the VCS where configuration definitions are managed. If it does have write access, an attacker who compromises the provisioning system can destroy or compromise the definition files, preventing the team from easily recovering and rebuilding their infrastructure.

But if the provisioning system only has read access to the VCS, then the team can shut it down, and use the definitions to build a new one and resume operations.

Conclusion

The practices and techniques described in this chapter focus on keeping systems stable in the face of failures and attacks. This is the essence of "robustness." But a more ambitious goal is antifragility. Rather than simply recovering from problems, you should aim to continuously strengthen and improve the reliability and effectiveness of your systems.

The next and final chapter of this book gives guidance for adopting infrastructure as code in the organization. This provides the foundation for moving from keeping systems running, to continuously improving the effectiveness of service.

## CHAPTER 15

Organizing for Infrastructure as Code

This book is primarily focused on the technical implementation of infrastructure as code with dynamic infrastructure. This final chapter takes a look at implementing it from an organizational point of view.

The premise of infrastructure as code is that cloud and dynamic infrastructure creates opportunities to use completely new practices and techniques when working with infrastructure. Using the old ways of working, such as configuring servers by hand, wastes the benefits of the new technology.

In the same way, using cloud practices with old operational models for IT service wastes the benefits of the new technology and working practices.

Teams can deliver and run software-based services far more effectively using cloud-age technologies and practices. But they can only do this if the organization as a whole understands how to make it work and ensures that its structure and processes are designed for it.

Infrastructure as code, in combination with cloud services, can help organizations to easily respond to changing needs with reliable, high-quality services. The organizational principles that enable this include:

- A continuous approach to the design, implementation, and improvement of services
- Empowering teams to continuously deliver and improve their services
- Ensuring high levels of quality and compliance while delivering rapidly and continuously

There is no guaranteed formula for success. But the recommendations in this chapter are based on patterns seen in organizations that make particularly effective use of emerging infrastructure technologies and practices. Common themes are having a culture, structure, policies, and processes that encourage flexibility, decentralized decision making, and continuous improvement.

Evolutionary Architecture

Every IT organization is unhappy with its current architecture. It has grown organically into a spaghetti-shaped mess, burdened with technical debt. Of course, there is a plan to transform to a new world, a beautiful, cleanly designed platform. It will be based on the most up-to-date architectural patterns and principles and will use the latest technologies.

Unfortunately, the road to the new world is filled with obstacles. There isn't enough time, commercial pressures divert focus, and services running on the old platforms still need support. It doesn't help that the shiny new technologies turn out to have unexpected limitations. Or that it's only after getting the new system built that you truly understand how you should have built it. At the end of the transformation, you have a new spaghetti-shaped mess, burdened with technical debt. The new mess is inevitably intertwined with leftover pieces of the previous generation mess, simply adding a new layer of legacy.

Organizations usually end up in a messy end-state because they take a static view of architecture, rather than an evolutionary view.[1]

The traditional approach to software and system design emphasizes the need for a design to be complete and correct. Once implementation has started, any changes indicate a flaw in the design. Evolutionary and iterative approaches, on the other hand, start by understanding the direction, and then designing and implementing the smallest thing that can be used to progress and learn. Changes are welcomed, because they show that the team has learned something.

The foundation of evolutionary design and implementation is the ability to make changes continuously, easily, safely, and cheaply. Teams who embrace this approach know that they won't achieve a perfect "final" design. Anyway, the right design is continually changing. So they become comfortable, and proficient, with continuous change.

---

1 See "Evolutionary Architecture and Emergent Design: Investigating Architecture and Design" (*http://www.ibm.com/developerworks/library/j-eaed1/*) for more information on evolutionary architecture.

The Road to the Cloud

An online commerce company decided that migrating from a data center to a public cloud provider could help them manage variations in demand. Their volumes had fairly large variations on daily, weekly, and annual patterns, so could potentially save money by scaling down during slower periods.

We started by identifying one part of the service that could benefit from this capability, and that seemed the most amenable to quickly implementing and testing on the new cloud platform. We spent a few weeks experimenting with running it on the new cloud platform and choosing some tools. Then we put the new part of the service live, integrating it with the rest of the platform still running in the data center.

This helped us to learn how to work with the new cloud provider to meet the needs of our service. For example, we settled on transaction rates, as reported by our application, as the best metric to trigger scaling up and down. But we also found that the lag to create new instances when there was a sudden surge in traffic, such as those caused by television commercials, was too slow. We found that running a capacity buffer—two additional instances—gave the automated scaling enough time to respond.

We also found an initial set of automation tools and approaches that we were happy with as a team. We completely ripped out and replaced our original infrastructure definition tool. We also scrapped the server configuration tool we had started out with in favor of an immutable server approach, to speed up the automated scaling process.

We were under no illusions that these technologies and practices were the "final" ones. As the team migrated more services onto the cloud, we found that some needed different approaches. In some cases, such as when a new service needed better monitoring than the simple tool we had installed, we moved the services already running on the cloud over to it as well. In other cases, as when a new service needed a customized database, we kept the existing services on the cloud provider's DBaaS (Database as a Service).

The organization has no "end state" platform. They still have some services running in their old data center, although 80% of their estate is now in the public cloud. They might end up migrating the remaining services to the cloud in the future, but only when they have a proven need to do so.

Learning under Fire

A spike (*https://www.mountaingoatsoftware.com/blog/spikes*) is a timeboxed experiment, intended to answer some particular question, such as which metric to use to trigger automated scaling. It might be appropriate to carry out a spike in a lab environment. But spikes should be used in a very limited way. The best learning environment is one that involves real user loads.

Use zero-downtime replacement patterns (such as those discussed in "Zero-Downtime Changes" on page 282) to carry out tests with real production traffic, while keeping the control to shut down experiments that go wrong. Have monitoring and measurement in place so you have visibility of the impact of what you're doing. This should include commercial metrics such as transactions, so you are aware quickly if your experiment is causing serious harm.

In some cases, A/B testing (*https://en.wikipedia.org/wiki/A/B_testing*) can be useful for infrastructure testing. This involves putting two different implementations live, and measuring the results to see which is more effective.

Start with a Trailblazer Pipeline

Many teams approach automation with a big bang, "boil the ocean" project. However, these have a number of risks that can lead to failure. One risk is that the sheer size may require too much work before anyone sees anything useful come out of the project. Another risk is that by the time something does emerge, it has already become so large and complex that it's difficult to reshape and tweak it as the team gains experience from using it in anger.

A third risk comes from implementing changes "breadth-first." For example, the work might be done in stages: first implement configuration definitions for everything, then move on to implement automated tests, then move on to build a change pipeline. The issue with this is that this limits the opportunity to incorporate learning that happens between these stages.

The trailblazer pipeline[2] is a more evolutionary approach to implementing infrastructure automation. It takes a "depth-first" approach, building a simple, end-to-end change management pipeline. The team starts building a trailblazer pipeline by choosing a single, simple change. For example, one team started by writing a Puppet manifest to set the *motd*[3] on their Linux servers.

The team's trailblazer pipeline had the basic, end-to-end stages. They set up a Git repository using Atlassian Stash, which they were already using for scripts and other things, and a Jenkins CI server. The initial stages of their pipeline were:

1. CI stage, triggered on commit to the Stash repository, for some basic validation of the manifest

---

2 Another term for a trailblazer pipeline is a tracer bullet (*http://kief.com/tracer-bullet.html*) pipeline.

3 *motd* is the message of the day, seen when users log into a shell.

---

2. Test stage, which applied the manifest to a test server

3. Prod stage, which applied the manifest to several severs used by the infrastructure team, including DNS servers and file servers

They chose a few tools for testing, including puppet-lint for the CI stage, and Serverspec to run against the test server to prove that the *motd* file is in place.

This was a very crude start, and deliberately so. The change being managed was trivial. The testing was not thorough. The team hadn't put in all of the tools they would eventually need. The were using some tools that they didn't expect to carry on with. None of this mattered, because they could evolve from this base with confidence.

The team moved on to more complex changes—for example, managing the system account that the team members used to log into the Linux servers. They wrote a Puppet manifest to create an account and add their public SSH keys to the authorized keys file. Then they expanded the testing to prove that SSH access to the account still worked. If someone committed a malformed change when adding or removing an SSH key, then it would be caught in the test stage, before being applied to more important systems.

Measuring Effectiveness

It's important for teams to understand and agree on what outcomes they're trying to achieve. They can then continuously assess how well they are doing so that they can decide what improvements to make next.

Agree on Desired Outcomes First

The goals for IT services, including infrastructure, should be driven by the users and other stakeholders. All too often, IT teams start initiatives with little if any input from these people.

Bringing stakeholders, users, and IT staff together to discuss current problems and needs often raises surprising issues. Gaining agreement, across the board, on what these are is an essential first step before moving on to considering initiatives such as cloud or automation.

Workshops such as futurespectives, elevator pitch, and product in a box can help groups to raise and discuss issues. These kinds of sessions should build a common understanding of the problems that the organization needs to address, potential approaches to them, and ways of measuring progress and making improvements over time.

User Experience Design for Infrastructure

Projects to build customer-facing software typically kick off with a great deal of activity to understand what users need, and how to meet those needs. Infrastructure and other IT projects would be far more successful if they took the same approach.

It might seem odd to create user personas for a private PaaS initiative. But without taking the time to consider who the potential users are, and to talk to them about what they need, you are simply guessing. Spending piles of your organizations' money on initiatives based on guessing what might be useful is simply not responsible.

Two books to consider include:

- *Agile Experience Design* (*http://www.amazon.com/Agile-Experience-Design-Designers-Continuous/dp/0321804813*) by Lindsay Ratcliffe and Marc McNeill (New Riders)
- *User Story Mapping* (*http://bit.ly/user-story-mapping*) by Jeff Patton (O'Reilly)

Choose Metrics that Help the Team

Teams should choose measurements that are useful to them, based on their goals and situation. There are many potential pitfalls with metrics. There is a natural temptation to over-focus on specific metrics, forgetting that they are only a proxy for performance. Metrics become especially damaging when they are used for incentives.[4] Metrics are best used by the team to help itself, and should be continually reviewed to decide whether they are still providing value.

Some common metrics used by infrastructure teams include:

Cycle time
> The time taken from a need being identified to fulfilling it. This is a measure of the efficiency and speed of change management. Cycle time is discussed in more detail later in this chapter.

Mean time to recover (MTTR)
> The time taken from an availability problem (which includes critically degraded performance or functionality) being identified to a resolution, even where it's a workaround. This is a measure of the efficiency and speed of problem resolution.

---

4 See "Why Incentive Plans Cannot Work" (*https://hbr.org/1993/09/why-incentive-plans-cannot-work*) in the *Harvard Business Review*.

Mean time between failures (MTBF)
The time between critical availability issues. This is a measure of the stability of the system, and the quality of the change management process. Although it's a valuable metric, over-optimizing for MTBF is a common cause of poor performance on other metrics.

Availability
The percentage of time that the system is available, usually excluding time the system is offline for planned maintenance. This is another measurement of system stability. It is often used as an SLA in service contracts.

True availability
The percentage of time that the system is available, not excluding planned maintenance.[5]

Track and Improve Cycle Time

Cycle time measures the time taken to implement changes. The time is measured starting from when a need has been identified, and ending when the change is in use and delivering value. The intention is to understand how quickly the organization responds to changing needs.

Value stream mapping is an exercise used to to analyze the cycle time for changes, breaking down activities to understand how much of the cycle time is spent on different activities, which may be optimized, and waste, which may be removed.[6]

For example, it may take a member of the infrastructure team 5 to 10 minutes to provision a new server using a cloud or virtualization platform. But when the full cycle is analyzed, starting from when a user requests a new server and ending when she is able to use it, the total time might vary from a minimum of 6 days up to 18 days. This includes activities such as filling in the request form with a business case; considering the request in a change advisory board (CAB) meeting; and testing the server after it has been provisioned but before it is turned over.

Figure 15-1 shows an example of a value stream map for an infrastructure change. The map shows the time that a task spends waiting, such as waiting 1–5 days for the next CAB meeting.

---

5 True availability was discussed in Chapter 14 ("True Availability" on page 276).

6 A good reference for carrying out value stream mapping exercises is *Value Stream Mapping: How to Visualize Work and Align Leadership for Organizational Transformation* (http://www.amazon.com/Value-Stream-Mapping-Organizational-Transformation-ebook/dp/B00EHIEJLM) by Karen Martin (McGraw-Hill).

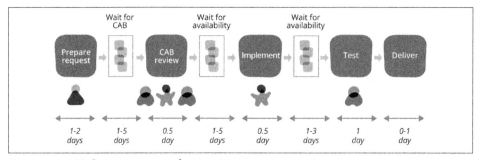

Figure 15-1. Value stream map for provisioning a server

This example value stream is not very efficient for normal changes. But it's a simpler process than what happens at many larger organizations. In real-world scenarios, a new server might need multiple separate requests for different teams to carry out tasks such as adding user accounts, installing middleware, and network configuration. This is why many large organizations spend large amounts of money to buy and install private cloud and automation software, and still find that it takes weeks or months to provision a single server.

Some teams make a point of regularly reviewing cycles times and discussing ways to improve them. Other teams stop to do this kind of analysis when the cycle time becomes a problem, maybe as an outcome of a post-mortem or retrospective (both explained later in this chapter).

It's important not to include everything in the cycle time, even nontechnical activities and those not under the control of the team that owns the process. For example, you need to see whether delays are caused by the difficulty of getting time from busy people who need to review and approve changes, or because of a lack of testers. This is critical information and it needs to be made visible, even if the organization decides it's not something that can reasonably be cut or reduced.

If a change takes between 8 and 36 hours to make it to production, and the automated activities only account for 35–45 minutes of this, there is no value in spending time and money to speed up the automation.

Another key point for analyzing a value stream is that it measures the time for a single change. The cycle time is not the time to deliver a project, but rather the time it takes for a single change, which may be delivered as part of a project. It's not uncommon to see that less than 5% of the cycle time for a particular change is spent actually working on that change. There may only be a few days of work involved in specifying, developing, and testing a specific change. But weeks and months are spent waiting while other requirements in the same project is being done.

This observation—that the amount of time a change spends waiting while work is done on other changes in a project—leads to a preference for a process that emphasizes flow over batching. Once an activity is completed on a piece of work, such as analyzing a requirement, then it will ideally be immediately passed along to the next phase of work. This is a major change in mindset, which is the basis for lean thinking.

Lean

Cycle time is a core concept of lean theory. Lean is a set of principles and ideas for continuously improving work processes. It emerged from manufacturing processes, particularly Toyota's "Toyota Production System" (TPS), and has been used widely for process improvement. Lean focusing on ways of getting rid of wasteful activities by making work visible, by encouraging people who do the work to take ownership of how it's done, and by eliminating wasteful activities.

Tom and Mary Poppendieck have written several excellent books on Lean software development, such as *Implementing Lean Software Development: From Concept to Cash* (*http://www.amazon.com/Implementing-Lean-Software-Development-Addison-Wesley-ebook/dp/B00HNB3VQE*) (Addison-Wesley).

The term "lean" has become somewhat overloaded. Eric Ries has adapted the term for product development, describing the idea of building the most minimal implementation of a product in order to measure customer interest in his book *The Lean Startup* (*http://www.amazon.com/Lean-Startup-Entrepreneurs-Continuous-Innovation-ebook/dp/B004J4XGN6*) (Crown Business). My (current and former) colleagues Joanne Molesky, Jez Humble, and Barry O'Reilly, have written about how larger organizations can adopt lean product development approaches in their book *Lean Enterprise* (*http://bit.ly/lean-enterprise-book*) (O'Reilly).

Quite often, cycle times that run to hours or days are caused by coordinating and orchestrating changes between different system elements in larger teams. The most likely avenue to radically cutting these times involves restructuring system architecture, team structures, and processes in order to decouple changes to parts of the system.

Use Kanban to Make Work Visible

A kanban board is a powerful tool to make the value stream visible. This is a variation of an agile story wall, set up to mirror the value stream map for work. As a person completes a work item, they pull a new item from the previous column of the board into their own column to show that they're working on it.

Bottlenecks become quickly visible, as items pile up in a particular column. In the example kanban board shown in Figure 15-2, work is piling up in the testing column. There could be several reasons for this. Testers may be starting too many tasks before having finished others, in which case the team should drill into the reasons why this is happening. Are testing activities becoming blocked for some reason, such as lack of testing environments? Is it too common for tasks to come into testing with issues that need rework? Or are tasks piling up after being tested, waiting for a deployment to live?

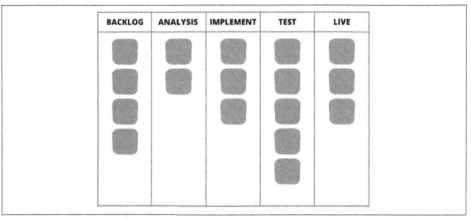

Figure 15-2. A kanban board

Kanban in Operations

There are a number of good resources for understanding Kanban, and how it can be applied to operations work:

- *Kanban: Successful Evolutionary Change for Your Technology Business* (*http://www.amazon.com/Kanban-David-J-Anderson-ebook/dp/B0057H2M70*) by David J. Anderson (Blue Hole Press)
- "Kanban vs Scrum vs Agile" (*http://www.agileweboperations.com/scrum-vs-kanban*) by Matthias Marschall
- "Reflections on the use of Kanban in an IT Operations team" (*http://iancarroll.com/2013/02/06/reflections-on-the-use-of-kanban-in-an-it-operations-team/*) by Ian Carroll

Retrospectives and Post-Mortems

Retrospectives and blameless post-mortems are important practices to support continuous improvement.

A retrospective is a session that can be held regularly, or after major events like the completion of a project. Everyone involved in the process gathers together to discuss what is working well, and what is not working well, and then decide on changes that could be made to processes and systems in order to get better outcomes. Doing this regularly should result in streamlining processes, getting rid of wasteful or harmful activities.

Post-mortems are typically conducted after an incident or some sort of major problem. The goal is to understand the root causes of the issue, and decide on actions to reduce the change of similar issues happening. The goal should not be to decide whose fault the issue was, but rather to identify changes that should be made to processes, systems, and ways of working to make future issues less likely, and to make them easier to detect and fix.

More on Retrospectives and Blameless Post-Mortems

Two good references on retrospectives include *Agile Retrospectives: Making Good Teams Great* (*http://www.amazon.com/Agile-Retrospectives-Making-Teams-Great/dp/0977616649*) by Esther Derby and Diana Larsen (Pragmatic) and *The Retrospective Handbook: A Guide for Agile Teams* (*https://leanpub.com/the-retrospective-handbook*) by Patrick Kua (Leanpub).

John Allspaw wrote a seminal article on blameless post-mortems (*https://codeascraft.com/2012/05/22/blameless-postmortems/*), explaining the importance of focusing on improving systems and processes rather than assigning blame to individuals.

Organize to Empower Users

The most powerful way to manage large-scale infrastructure for multiple users is to delegate control and responsibility to those users. A key principle of lean process theory is to "move the work to the workers." That is, the people closest to the sharp end have the most knowledge about the problems they need to solve. So, give them what they need to shape their tools and working process.

Unfortunately, the norm in most organizations is to structure teams and working processes in ways that disempower teams.

Pitfalls of the Divided Function Model

Traditional service models divide people into functional teams. The work of designing, implementing, and supporting services is divided between these teams.

There are several reasons why this seems like a good idea. Teams of functional experts can become "centers of excellence," which are very good at their specialism. Work can be divided into tidy, well-defined chunks, and parceled out to functional teams who don't need to understand the context for their work.

However, the result of this model is inevitably to fragment the knowledge and accountability for the service. It adds significant overhead to coordinate the work across the teams. And the team that owns the service lacks deep understanding of how it works.

Dividing the implementation and support of services across functions tends to create a number of problems.

Pitfall: Design fragmentation

Designs and specifications must be centrally created and apportioned to the various teams to implement. Often, the people in these teams have little visibility, and not enough time to understand the big picture. More often than not, integration between the functional parts doesn't work as well as planned, needing testing, arbitration to resolve conflicts between the teams, and unplanned rework at the last minute.

Core Competency

In the past decade or so, many organizations have decided to outsource technical work as "non-core" and cut down their in-house technical staff. Nearly every one of these I've encountered has, over time, replaced these people with project managers, business analysts, architects, and QAs. These people are needed to have any hope of managing the work done by the outsourced technical group.

These groups are at constant war with their suppliers. They never seem happy with the services they are able to offer to their own customers, the time it takes to deliver improvements and fix issues, or the costs involved.

It's hard to avoid the conclusion that technology is more important to these businesses than they want to believe. Discarding technical capability in exchange for project management capacity seems to do more harm than good.

Pitfall: Scheduling rigidity

When implementation is split across multiple teams, each of which is involved in implementing multiple projects, then scheduling becomes critical. Project plans and resource scheduling create rigid, inflexible schedules. There is no tolerance for things going wrong, much less for improving on the original designs as the team learn more. This results in cascades of slippages.

Pitfall: Long cycle times

Cycle times can be cut dramatically by reducing the number of teams involved in carrying out a piece of work. Each handover between teams adds overhead, as seen in Figure 15-3. There is communication overhead, often in the form of documentation and meetings. There is overhead of the receiving team asking questions and needing changes before the handover can be complete. And there is overhead of idle time, waiting for busy teams to become available to pick up the work.

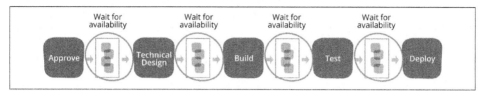

Figure 15-3. Value stream with handovers between teams

Adopt a Self-Service Model

Infrastructure users can be empowered through a self-service model. Rather than asking a team that provides infrastructure to define, provision, and configure infrastructure for them, the user team can do this on their own. The provider team can make sure that the user teams have the tools they need to do this effectively. They can also support user teams, by offering advice, assistance, and implementation reviews.

For example, an application team may be able to write their Terraform file to define the environment for their application, and then configure a pipeline to test the file and use it to provision and manage test and production environments. The application team's environment definition might integrate with shared infrastructure resources, such as monitoring services and network structures.

A networking team might help the application team by explaining how to configure this integration. A security team could make sure that the team knows which security tests run in the pipeline. They might periodically review the configuration of the infrastructure, pipeline, and tests, along with the test results, to ensure that changes are being handled responsibly.

The crucial point is that the application team has the control, and the responsibility. They don't wait for other teams to configure networking or perform security audits for each change. They can experiment with different options, see what works best for them, and seek help when they get stuck.

The result of this model is to streamline the value stream. A single set of people can take the work through design, build, test, and deployment. Because the same people are involved, there is little to no handover. Work doesn't wait for people to become available between steps.

The team that owns the application knows the most about it, so is able to make the best decisions about changes to it. If they make a mistake, they will be the first to discover it, and are able to quickly make the needed adjustments.

Take Full Responsibility: You Build It, You Run It

Traditional IT models divide implementation and support into separate teams, some-times referred to as "build" and "run," or "development" and "support." Figure 15-4 depicts this division, showing separation between build and run teams for applications, as well as build and run teams for infrastructure.

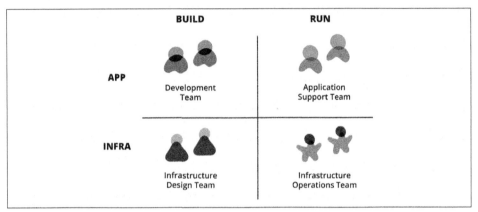

Figure 15-4. The classic development/operations divide

Responsibilities become even more divided than shown here in larger organizations. More horizontal layers are added for operating systems, middleware, and so on. Vertical silos are added for design/architecture, release management or transition, and even separate teams to deploy and manage different types of testing.

The result of this is to isolate the people building a from any problems they create. It leaves the people who run the system with little ability to make meaningful improvements as they discover problems. Because the most valuable learning opportunities come from how a system is used in production, this dev/ops divide limits continuous improvement.

A valuable strategy to empower teams is to give them end-to-end responsibility. This is most effectively done through the principle of "you build it, you run it" popularized by Amazon and Netflix, among others. The application team takes responsibility for supporting their application in production, rather than just handing it over to a separate support team.

This usually means the application team takes on-call duties for the application. When there is an incident, the on-call application team member investigates. Because he has ownership of the application and infrastructure configuration, he is able to investigate and fix problems at those levels. If the problem is with the core infrastructure or platform elements managed by another team, the application person sends the incident to a member of those teams.

Organizing into Cross-Functional Teams

Cross-functional teams put all of the people responsible for building and running an aspect of a system together. This may include testers, project managers, analysts, and a commercial or product owner, as well as different types of engineers. These teams should be small; Amazon uses the term "two-pizza teams," meaning the team is small enough that two pizzas is enough to feed everyone.

The advantage of this approach is that people are dedicated to a single, focused service or small set of services, avoiding the need to multitask between projects. Teams formed of a consistent set of people work far more effectively than those whose membership changes from day to day.

In some smaller organizations, a cross-functional team may own the entire stack, from application to servers to metal. In larger organizations, this can be more difficult. It may be sensible to have teams own different, interdependent services, including infrastructure services, as seen in Figure 15-5. The key principles to ensure efficient value streams is to retain end-to-end ownership—you build it, you run it—and to ensure that teams are fully empowered to deliver what they need without waiting on gates and request queues.[7]

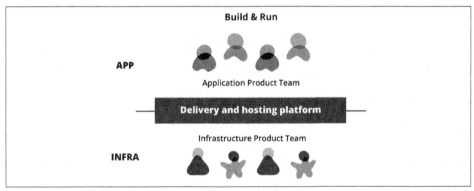

Figure 15-5. An example of you build it, you run it

---

7 The *Harvard Business Review* has published an article (*https://hbr.org/2015/06/75-of-cross-functional-teams-are-dysfunctional*) explaining why many cross-functional teams are dysfunctional, which offers insight into how to make them work well.

> ## Tribes: Keeping Up Functional Expertise with Cross-Functional Teams
>
> Organizations that go all-in on cross-functional teams risk losing functional exper-
> tise, and losing the benefits of sharing tools. Not every team can have people with
> deep skills in databases, Linux, networking, etc. And different teams may select wildly
> different tools and practices for dealing with common concerns.
>
> A common approach to counter this is cross-team communities, or tribes. Spotify
> popularized the concept of "tribes" in technical organizations thanks to a series of
> videos and blog posts they have shared on their engineering culture. The first video in
> the series (*https://labs.spotify.com/2014/03/27/spotify-engineering-culture-part-1/*) is a
> good place to start.

Governance through Continuous Change Management

Empowering cross-functional teams to build and run services and applications can
conflict with traditional approaches to governance. The traditional, iron-age philosophy is to rely on manual approvals and inspections every time a change is made to
production systems. This encourages batching changes and making them less frequently.

However, the techniques described throughout this book enable a different, and more
powerful approach to change management. Continuous change management takes
advantage of automated processes to ensure that each change is validated early, and
corrected immediately. This doesn't require humans to manually inspect each
change, but instead builds compliance checking and auditing into the pipeline tooling.

Well-implemented automation can make compliance and legal audits painless and
stress-free. Taking an evolutionary approach to implementing the change management process means that consultants can dip in, and provide feedback that is itera-
tively built into the pipeline. Comments from auditors can be easily and rapidly
incorporated into the pipeline, sometimes before the auditor has even left the building.

There are several elements of an effective change management process using infrastructure as code. These include providing building blocks to teams, providing readiness with the pipeline, sharing ownership of quality, reviewing and auditing the
pipeline, and optimizing the time to detect and correct.

Provide Solid Building Blocks

Infrastructure service teams can provide building blocks for other teams to use, and can make sure those blocks are solid and compliant. For example, they may provide server templates with a hardened OS, and with security and monitoring tools pre-installed. They can make sure that the tooling that provisions servers and configures infrastructure does the right things, such as wiring new servers into monitoring and security services.

It's important that providing these capabilities doesn't tie the hands of application teams. Quite often, other teams will need to have variations to the pieces provided by the infrastructure team. There should be a quick, reliable process for trying out these variations. Ideally, application teams should be able to make and try out variations on their own, by editing definition files and applying them to test environments. Once they have worked out what they need, their variations can be validated, either through automated validation or technical reviews, if not both.

Primitives, Not Frameworks

Amazon CTO Werner Vogels shared a list of lessons Amazon has learned in building AWS (*http://www.allthingsdistributed.com/ 2016/03/10-lessons-from-10-years-of-aws.html*). This list is excellent advice for anyone planning or building an IT platform.

Vogels' third point is "primitives, not frameworks." That is, rather than attempting to build a single, one-size-fits-all platform, build multiple, individual components. Users can pick and choose the elements to fit their needs, avoiding the constraints of those that don't fit their use case. This aligns with the Unix philosophy of "do one thing and do it well."[8] This design philosophy has paid off very well for AWS.

Prove Operational Readiness in the Pipeline

Even when an application team builds their infrastructure using properly prepared building blocks, there is still a need to check that the resulting solution passes muster before putting it into an environment where it can have an operational impact. This is where the change management pipeline comes into play.

Operational and infrastructure teams should work with application teams to make sure that their pipelines effectively validate operational readiness. Each change to an

---

8 The Unix philosophy is described in the c2 wiki post "Unix Design Philosophy" (*http://c2.com/cgi/wiki?Uni xDesignPhilosophy*). It is also discussed in the book *The UNIX Philosophy* (*http://www.amazon.com/UNIX-Philosophy-Mike-Gancarz-ebook/dp/B002OL2G4Gp*) by Mike Gancarz (Digital Press).

application or its infrastructure should be automatically tested for compliance before being pushed to an important environment. For example, automated penetration testing and security scans can be run against test instances of servers created by an application team. These can prove that no unexpected network ports are opened, no unauthorized processes are running, and that only authorized user accounts have been created.

Sharing Ownership of Operational Quality

Operational staff should seek to remove themselves from being gatekeepers so that they aren't spending all of their time reviewing designs and implementations. People such as security and compliance staff can instead spend their time educating and coaching users. People across the organization should not see these concerns as the sole responsibility of specialists. Instead, everyone needs to understand security, performance, compliance, stability, and so on.

Specialists should spend time with other teams, helping them to take ownership of those areas. Teach them the principles and practices of the topic. Help set up tooling that empowers them to check and improve operational quality. All engineers should be able to write and run performance and penetration tests against the system.

Review and Audit Automated Processes

Automated operational and compliance testing is not bulletproof. Bugs and gaps leave room for issues to slip through. Changes may be made to configurations and systems without relevant changes to the tests, leaving new failure scenarios unchecked. And in some cases, people may deliberately evade automated tests.[9]

Experts have a role in reviewing the processes and outcomes of operational testing. They shouldn't need to play this role by acting as gatekeepers for every change. But they can periodically review the pipelines and test automation, looking for gaps and problems. They can review logs and test reports to help assess how well the process is working. People who do this across multiple teams can share knowledge and techniques across those teams, helping to raise the level of the process across the organization, or multiple organizations.

---

9 As I was writing this book, Volkswagen made the news for deliberately programming their cars to behave differently when being tested for compliance to emission standards. Although it's disappointing that they got away with it for several years, the cheating was implemented in code, so the evidence of the cheating is explicit and undeniable now that it has been uncovered. This is a lesson for anyone who tries to code around automated compliance tests in a software change pipeline.

Optimize for Time to Detect and Fix Problems

As mentioned in the conclusion of Chapter 1, your team should aim to be very good at catching problems and making fixes quickly. Too many teams believe it's possible to prevent mistakes from ever happening, if they can only invest enough time and energy. But while this book strongly encourages a culture of quality and effective continuous testing processes, it's important to get the cost/benefit balance right. The benefit of a fast time to market may outweigh a risk that has a fairly low cost, especially when the risk can be detected and corrected very quickly.

Conclusion: It's Never Finished

Building an automated infrastructure is not a job that is ever complete. Sometimes an organization's leaders look to automation as a way to eliminate work, hoping that IT capabilities can be built and will then run indefinitely with minimal ongoing investment. But this isn't the case, at least not with current IT systems.

Ideally, IT systems would be like a consumer automobile. You buy a new car off the assembly line, and periodically pay to keep it fueled and maintained, occasionally replacing parts as they wear out or fail. You don't need to keep the engineers who designed and assembled the car on staff.

In practice, modern IT systems are more like a Formula One race car. Each one is custom-built, even if they use standard parts and follow common patterns. It takes continuous work to keep it running well, patched and secure. And the needs that IT systems must satisfy are constantly changing, as the way technology is used by consumers and businesses is constantly changing. This in turn means that an organization's IT systems must constantly change.

So the organizations most successful in using IT don't make the mistake of seeing it as a one-off cost that can be paid and then ignored. They see it as a core capability that helps them to adapt to continuously changing requirements.

This book set out to help people find ways to use the new generation of infrastructure technology—cloud, virtualization, and automation—to fundamentally change the way work is done. Adopting the principles and practices described here can help operations teams to stop spending their time handling streams of routine requests, and instead spend their time continuously improving systems that help other people to take ownership of the infrastructure they need to do their own work.

What we've covered in this book is not enough. It's simply not feasible to hit every aspect of every topic, and especially not down into the details of technical implementation with specific tools. And things are moving too quickly to capture.

So it's important to keep abreast of what's happening in the industry. Aside from books, infrastructure practitioners can keep up with blogs, talks, podcasts, and various other channels of information.

It's an exciting time to be part of this industry, and I hope this book has helped!

Index

About the Author

Kief Morris started his first bulletin board system (BBS) in Florida in the early 1990s, later enrolling in a MSc program in computer science at the University of Tennessee because it seemed like the easiest way to get a real Internet connection. Joining the CS department's system administration team gave him exposure to managing hundreds of machines running a variety of Unix flavors. When the dot-com bubble began to inflate, Kief moved to London, and he's stayed in Europe ever since. Most of the companies he worked for were post-startups, building and scaling. The titles he's been given or given himself include Deputy Technical Director, R&D Manager, Hosting Manager, Technical Lead, Technical Architect, Consultant, and Practice Lead. Across these roles, he has managed servers and other infrastructure using shell scripts, Perl, CFEngine, Puppet, Chef, and Ansible. He has automatically provisioned hardware with FAI and Cobbler, and managed servers on VMware, AWS, RackSpace Cloud, and OpenStack. Kief became a ThoughtWorks consultant in 2010, where he helps clients with ambitious missions take advantage of cloud and infrastructure automation through Lean, Agile, and DevOps ways of working.

Colophon

The animal on the cover of *Infrastructure as Code* is Rüppell's vulture (*Gyps rueppellii*), native to the Sahel region of Africa (a geographic zone that serves as a transition between the Sahara Desert and the savanna). It is named in honor of a 19th-century German explorer and zoologist, Eduard Rüppell.

It is a large bird (with a wingspan of 7–8 feet and weighing 14–20 pounds) with mottled brown feathers and a yellowish-white neck and head. Like all vultures, this species is carnivorous and feeds almost exclusively on carrion. They use their sharp talons and beaks to rip meat from carcasses, and have backward-facing spines on their tongue to thoroughly scrape bones clean. While normally silent, these are very social birds who will voice a loud squealing call at colony nesting sites or when fighting over food.

The Rüppell's vulture is monogamous and mates for life, which can be 40–50 years long. Breeding pairs build their nests near cliffs, out of sticks lined with grass and leaves (and often use it for multiple years). Only one egg is laid each year—by the time the next breeding season begins, the chick is just becoming independent. This vulture does not fly very fast (about 22 mph), but will venture up to 90 miles from the nest in search of food.

Rüppell's vultures are the highest-flying birds on record; there is evidence of them flying 37,000 feet above sea level, as high as commercial aircraft. They have a special hemoglobin in their blood that allows them to absorb oxygen more efficiently at high altitudes.

This species is considered endangered and populations have been in decline. Though loss of habitat is one factor, the most serious threat is poisoning. The vulture is not even the intended target: farmers often poison livestock carcasses to retaliate against predators like lions and hyenas. As vultures identify a meal by sight and gather around it in flocks, hundreds of birds can be killed each time.

Many of the animals on O'Reilly covers are endangered; all of them are important to the world. To learn more about how you can help, go to *animals.oreilly.com*.

The cover image is from Cassell's *Natural History*. The cover fonts are URW Typewriter and Guardian Sans. The text font is Adobe Minion Pro; the heading font is Adobe Myriad Condensed; and the code font is Dalton Maag's Ubuntu Mono.

Get even more for your money.

Join the O'Reilly Community, and register the O'Reilly books you own. It's free, and you'll get:

- $4.99 ebook upgrade offer
- 40% upgrade offer on O'Reilly print books
- Membership discounts on books and events
- Free lifetime updates to ebooks and videos
- Multiple ebook formats, DRM FREE
- Participation in the O'Reilly community
- Newsletters
- Account management
- 100% Satisfaction Guarantee

Signing up is easy:

1. Go to: oreilly.com/go/register
2. Create an O'Reilly login.
3. Provide your address.
4. Register your books.

Note: English-language books only

To order books online:
oreilly.com/store

For questions about products or an order:
orders@oreilly.com

To sign up to get topic-specific email announcements and/or news about upcoming books, conferences, special offers, and new technologies:
elists@oreilly.com

For technical questions about book content:
booktech@oreilly.com

To submit new book proposals to our editors:
proposals@oreilly.com

O'Reilly books are available in multiple DRM-free ebook formats. For more information:
oreilly.com/ebooks

O'REILLY®

CPSIA information can be obtained
at www.ICGtesting.com
Printed in the USA
BVOW11s0019110616

451625BV00003B/3/P